Swords at Sunset

Last Stand of North America's Grail Knights

Michael Bradley
with
Joëlle Lauriol

Foreword by
John Robert Colombo

Library and Archives Canada Cataloguing in Publication

Bradley, Michael, 1944-
   Swords at sunset: last stand of North America's grail knights /
Michael Bradley with Joelle Lauriol.

Includes bibliographical references and index.

ISBN 0-9736477-4-4

   1. North America--Discovery and exploration. 2. Templars. 3. Grail.
I. Lauriol, Joelle, 1962- II. Title.

E103.B73 2005   970.01'1   C2005-
905992-3

Swords at Sunset: Last Stand of North America's Grail Knights

Published Oct. 30, 2005, by Manor House Publishing Inc.
452 Cottingham Crescent, Ancaster, Ontario, L9G 3V6
www.manor-house.biz   905-648-2193

Cover illustration by Michael Bradley and Joëlle Lauriol
Cover design/realization: Bradley/Lauriol/M. B. Davie/R. Kosydar
Graphics-generated sunset background courtesy of Steve Stone

Printed in Canada by Webcom Limited/First edition.
The publisher gratefully acknowledges the financial support of the Book
Publishing Industry Development Program (BPIDP), Department of
Canadian Heritage, the Ontario Arts Council and the Canada Council for
the Arts.

Prologue:

"Kyot, the master of high renown, found, in confused pagan writing, the legend which reaches back to the prime source of all legends."
   - From *Parzival* by Wolfram von Eschenbach.

And now, after more than twenty years of following the trail of the Grail, we can dimly discern this prime source of all legends as being gossamer memories of "Atlantis."

The lost Atlantic islands, whether legendary "Atlantis" itself or truly geographical Lyonesse, perished in a tectonic catastrophe that also ended the last Ice Age. This geophysical cataclysm began our own chapters of Western history.

The ancestors of about half the population of our present Western world were refugees from the Atlantic Coast of Europe.

They were able to preserve very little of what they had once known of "Atlantis" that had so suddenly perished.

But they did cherish a few memories of their culture, scraps of their unique alphabetic writing system, wisps of their previous technology, hints of their former sexual values and they created much artwork depicting their emotional orientation to life.

These recollections animated their myths, their legends and their religion.

This religion out of the Atlantic West, with its all-but-lost secrets for creating a fulfilling way of human life on earth, gradually came to be known as the Holy Grail.

This book is for my companion, friend and wife, Joëlle Lauriol.

And it is for all those who would pray for peace in the world.

But I have a plea of my own for you:

Try your best to avoid supplicating that Caucasian God who has become most familiar to Jews, Christians and Moslems.

It is probably true that every war of the Western world for the past 2,000 years, at least, has been fought in "His" name.

And all protagonists have usually claimed this God was on their side.

This jealous God has ever deceived you with lies and distortions of the human condition that were intended solely to ensure human psychological dependence upon "Him."

"His" chauvinistic injunctions were, of course, really born only in the psychosexually troubled minds of those who conceived "Him."

Must you submerge your purely human intelligence, compassion and respect for life in the childlike belief that there is a parental Divinity that can guide you?

But if you feel compelled to do so, then pray instead to the ancient Great Goddess and her Good Shepherd consort.

They have always reflected more truly the psyche of the vast majority of humankind.

If your prayers are directed to them, there may be a chance for peace in the world and for the environmental survival of our earth.

- Michael Bradley

Contents

Other works by the same author

Nonfiction
The Cronos Complex I
The Iceman Inheritance
Chosen People from the Caucasus
Dawn Voyage: The Black African Discovery of America
Holy Grail Across the Atlantic
The Columbus Conspiracy
Grail Knights of North America
More Than a Myth
Crisis of Clarity

Fiction
Imprint
The Mantouche Factor
The Quebec War of Independence
The Magdalene Mandala

Acknowledgements

*S*words *at Sunset* ends a trilogy of books about the Holy Grail in North America that began with the 1981-1983 investigation of a ruined castle in mid-peninsular Nova Scotia. This book naturally follows *Holy Grail Across the Atlantic* (Hounslow Press, Toronto, 1988) and *Grail Knights of North America* (Dundurn Press, Toronto, 1998).

In some ways, *Swords at Sunset* is also a follow-up on yet another book, *The Columbus Conspiracy* (Hounslow Press, Toronto, 1991) that presented some of the same evidence and arguments. As the final sequel of a trilogy, *Swords at Sunset* offers an explanation for the destruction of two settlements of Grail-believing religious refugees that were established in the Great Lakes Basin.

One settlement was in the Green Mountains foothills on the border of Vermont and Quebec on the shore of Lake Memphremagog. In its medieval European heyday, this settlement was apparently called "Alma" and it was an agricultural centre and metal-mining emporium.

The other major Grail Refugee colony in the Great Lakes Basin was located on the Niagara Escarpment above Niagara Falls in order to promote navigation into the far west by the Upper Great Lakes. It was seemingly called "Zarahemla" during the fifteenth century. The communities of Alma and Zarahemla apparently flourished as recognizable "European" settlements in the North American wilderness from about AD 1425 until about AD 1571.

But there was, doubtless, much native mixture in both settlements from their beginning and this influence must have increased as time passed. If we have interpreted the slim clues that remain at all correctly, Alma was massacred by, and assimilated within, the Mohawk Iroquois between the years AD 1571 and about AD 1607. Zarahemla fell to the Seneca and Cayuga Iroquois in AD 1571 and its last European survivor perished as a hunted fugitive in the upper New York State wilderness in the year AD 1587.

But, inevitably, over the twenty years of writing and researching the trilogy itself with *The Columbus Conspiracy* as a kind of book-length sidebar, much more was learned about the "Holy Grail" than I ever suspected back in 1981. What was it exactly? Why had it inspired so much desperate conflict in the Western world?

I have offered my answers, primarily in Chapters 3 and 7 of *Swords at Sunset*, although they were hinted as early as 1988 in *Holy Grail*

Across the Atlantic (page 14). These answers will not please everyone, and they will inevitably infuriate some people.

My understanding of the Holy Grail gradually came to be that it was a legend of Neolithic-megalithic times that persisted into the medieval period, particularly in southern France but also throughout the Mediterranean's islands and coasts. This "Great Legend" incorporated memories of an ancient "Old European Civilisation" and of a kind of European and Ancient Egyptian "Christianity before Christianity." And this Great Legend sometimes also conveyed whispers of the way things had been on Atlantis, including the apparent existence of alphabetic writing at least 9000 years old.

This oldest expression of reverence for the Great Goddess and Her world-saving Messiah husband and son had nothing whatever to do with the New Testament and the Judeo-Christian tradition. In fact, this oldest form of Christianity was older than Judaism by thousands of years.

It also had nothing to do with monotheism because, by its very definition, it incorporated reverence for the Great Fertility Goddess (our "Mary") and Her continually resurrected husband-as-son (our "Jesus") who grew up to permit the ongoing regeneration of both the biological and spiritual worlds through Her. Before the Judeo-Christian creation of the New Testament, *that* was our continual and *only* "Salvation". Perhaps it still is.

Literally hundreds of people have helped me over the past twenty-two years of investigating the Holy Grail. I have thanked many of them in the previous books, *Holy Grail Across the Atlantic* and *Grail Knights of North America*.

But I have also thanked many people by name in the pages of *Swords at Sunset* as their contributions occurred in unravelling what amounts to a historical detective story. Some who are not mentioned in the book, and to whom I am grateful, include: Rae Thurston, Vice-President of Production Services film equipment rental company, a constant source of encouragement from the beginning. Michael B. Davie and Manor House Publishing Inc. had the courage to publish this book after Dundurn Press dropped it from its publishing program, deeming it too controversial. The well-known Canadian writer and researcher, John Robert Colombo, never lost his empathy with my work, although I know that he has sometimes lost his patience.

Very special thanks are due to Marty Myers, owner of "Catfish Calhoun Sportswear" in St. Catharines, Ontario. Myers's involvement began when Don Fraser of *The Standard* newspaper of St. Catharines published a full page article on April 28, 2001 about my quest for medieval artefacts in the Niagara Region. The article quoted me asking residents and the newspaper's readers for any information about "strange" artefacts that anyone might know about.

Marty Myers saw the article and was fascinated with the idea of Grail Refugees having settled the St. Catharines area before the known and accepted colonials. He immediately called me in Toronto and offered any and every assistance to assess and photograph any artefacts that might be reported for the book the article said that I was researching.

I'm not sure that I was prepared for Marty Myers's level of enthusiasm and energy, the same commitment and drive that have made "Catfish Calhoun's" such a local success. Marty tracked down several artefacts that were reported because of the newspaper article and sent high-quality digital scans of them almost faster than we could handle them. Of these images contributed to this book by Marty Myers, the late medieval religious medallion owned by Dennis Farkas of Wainfleet, Ontario is illustrated and discussed in the text.

More recently, as sheer age combined with financial expenses associated with Grail-related research culminated in health problems that endangered my ability to complete this work, I encountered new friends who helped me to carry on with it. Richard Guest of Toronto and David Hughes of Hantsport, Nova Scotia provided invaluable assistance.

I am also indebted to Dave Hughes for working with my wife Joëlle Lauriol to produce the military style maps I thought were appropriate to chronicle the heyday of Zarahemla about AD 1537 and the Fall of Zarahemla in AD 1571.

The defeat of the Grail Refugees' Zarahemla on the Niagara Escarpment led to the final battle of Hill Cumorah where the eleventh generation (if our chronology is correct) of Henry Sinclair's Nova Scotia colonists of 1398 were massacred. At any rate, that is how I interpret the existing artefacts and documents, and the maps prepared by David Hughes and Joëlle Lauriol show the progressive acts in the final drama.

Phil Davies of Yorkshire, England has shown unflagging interest over three years. Ted Thomas of Campbellton, New Brunswick proved assiduous in archiving the various versions and "re-versions" of *Swords at Sunset* as it came off the computer. This was in case our own old Toshiba gave up its tired ghost at a critical moment.

Hamdi Beqa, an Albanian immigrant into Canada, and owner of Beqa Variety on Queen Street West, shared his surprising research that the Albanian language may be the closest living survivor to the pre-Greek "Pelasgian" language of Old Europe.

This research, though presently "unpublished" (except in Albanian!) gave further support, in addition to the one hundred archaeological sites mentioned in the text of *Swords at Sunset*, that there had been an "Old Civilisation" in Europe which was primarily maritime in nature. In this, although he did not know it, Hamdi Beqa is in good company with Dr. Marija Gimbutas. Hamdi Beqa also helped us with our research in much more mundane ways.

When it became clear that I needed to be near the St. Joseph's Health Centre at extremely short notice on occasion, The Queens Hotel on Queen St. offered accommodation that was just three blocks from the hospital. The antics of some of Parkdale's more colourful denizens was also more than compensated by the hotel's convenient access to major TTC routes and to the Lakeshore Blvd. leading to Niagara.

Finally, I would like to thank my wife, Joëlle Lauriol, who answered an advertisement for a "Companion of the Grail" on April 19, 1997. She has seldom faltered, although our trail of the Grail proved more arduous than she could have ever imagined at the time. Her constancy through many hardships helped me keep a fifty-year-old promise.

The Ku Klux Klan burned our home in Jackson, Mississippi in August 1954, scattering our family into the night in terror and confusion. Klansmen caught and bullwhipped me. Somehow, after this agony was over, I managed to drag myself in the flickering darkness up into the boughs of an apple tree. I hid from the Klan until morning in its late summer foliage. I remember it was August. I sat among apple boughs throughout that terrible night in pain, and also in frantic fear for what had happened to my mother, father and sister. I vowed to explain to the world why there was such a high level of aggression or "hatred" in the Western world and why this hatred had so often been justified by religion.

Keeping that promise made in an apple tree long ago became a driving, dedicated lifelong obligation. It resulted in most of my books. But the unremitting pressure of that self-imposed task gradually undermined my health, especially during the years I shared with Joëlle.

In recent years, when things became critical on more than one occasion in more than one Emergency Room, Joëlle would hold my hand and remind me that I had *almost* kept the 1954 promise that I had made in a Jackson, Mississippi apple tree.

"Just a little longer, Michael," she would whisper above the hiss of oxygen. And so *Swords at Sunset* was done.

Foreword
by John Robert Colombo

My favourite book when I was a youngster was *Ripley's Believe It or Not*. I did not have many books but that one I did have and I loved it. I remember spending hours turning its paperback pages and marvelling at the outrageous statements made by Robert L. Ripley, the Manhattan-based journalist and cartoonist. He was dubbed "the modern Marco Polo" because he visited country after country in search of incredible artefacts for his collections (stuff like shrunken heads now displayed in his BION museums) and for his daily and weekly newspaper columns in hundreds of newspapers around the world. Today Ripley is less popular in print than he was in the days of my youth, but more popular on television, and there are those "odditoriums" (more than 46 of them in 10 countries).

The audacity of Ripley was such that he once drew a cartoon that featured Charles Lindbergh piloting the "Spirit of St. Louis." It was captioned, "Lindbergh was the sixty-seventh man to make a non-stop flight over the Atlantic." Thousands of readers thought they had caught him in error. "Surely Lindbergh was the *first* pilot to make such a daring flight!" "No," replied Ripley, delighted with the response. "Lindbergh was the sixty-seventh. But he was the first to make that flight *solo*."

On another occasion Ripley wrote, "If all the Chinese in the world were to march – four abreast – past a given point they would never finish passing, though they marched forever and ever." He illustrated this statement with a memorable pencil sketch of an endless stream of Chinese wearing coolie hats and marching four abreast seemingly around the globe. He proved the Chinese would never stop marching by taking the most recent census figures for China that he could find. These happened to be for the years 1402 and 1403, and he read into them a population gain of nineteen per cent per annum. In computing China's birth and death rates, he ignored, strangely, war, famine, flood and pestilence. At U.S. Army marching regulations – three miles an hour, fifteen miles a day – it would take the six hundred million Chinese (China's population at the time) twenty-two years and 302 days to pass a given point. This would be ample time for a whole new generation of Chinese to be born and begin again the long, unending march. Ingenious!

Robert L. Ripley was my hero for three reasons. He was a lively journalist, he was a stylish cartoonist, and he was a popular artist who could see what others could not. He saw Lindbergh in a new light, and the same applies to the notion of the size of the Chinese population. I saw Ripley in a new light, too: as an artist of the outrageous.

In much the same way do I see Michael Bradley. I did not ask if Ripley was right or wrong. I was astonished at what he said. Similarly, one does not ask if Bradley is right or wrong. This is not the question to ask. If you want to ask questions about him or about his work, the ones you should be asking are the following: Could he *possibly* be right? If he is *possibly right*, why are his ideas so *irritating*?

I contributed the foreword to an earlier book of his titled *Holy Grail Across the Atlantic.* It was published in 1988 and was deemed to be quite controversial at the time (though it seems less so in light of all the books on the Grail legend that have appeared since then). I was not asked to write a foreword to its 1998 successor, *Grail Knights of North America*; it did not need a foreword.

But I agreed to contribute one to the third volume in this series, *Swords at Sunset*; I think it requires one or benefits from one, if only to suggest to the unwary reader that there are different ways to approach a book like this one, different ways to interpret the author's argument and intention, than to regard them as expressions of some "gospel truth."

I find *Swords at Sunset* to be an astonishing work of speculative non-fiction. I think it is wrong in some particulars, possibly right in a number of ways, but always suggestive of broader perspectives and horizons. The picture of civilization and human nature painted in its pages is a panorama of crime and aggression, creativity and caring, conspiracy and compassion. So let me tell you what I like and dislike about this book.

I really enjoy some of the author's insights and statements. They are worthy of Ripley, and I quote them without comment because they illustrate major themes of the book:

- "Who else but a romantic would have answered the December 1981 letter from a highly articulate Englishwoman who described with eccentric charm part of a ruined castle in her backyard in the middle of Nova Scotia?"

- "The truth is that our conventionally woven carpet of Canada's history is so threadbare and so worn with holes where awkward evidence lurks under the rug that it has become embarrassing for informed, urbane, and sophisticated people who are yet expected to accept the conventional version of our national past and national identity.."

- "For some time I had been starting to suspect that the Book of Mormon wasn't just the ridiculous blasphemy that most non-Mormons thought it was, if and when they thought about it at all."

- "As we will see, the Holy Grail heresy was the dominant belief in much of Europe and some of the Middle East. It certainly affected all of Christendom. And it still does."

- "The greatest story ever told is a tale of unbelievable courage and supreme sacrifice, but it is also a chronicle of implacable hatred and inhuman cruelty."

- "So, the names Issa, Y'shua, Joshua, or Jesus had been applied to the Messiah as early as about 1350 BC."

- "I have always found it a bit curious that two of the most dominant personalities of the early Christian Era, the near-contemporaries Cleopatra and Jesus, are almost never mentioned in the same breath or sentence by historians."

- If there was a European community in Memphremagog region from about 1400 to 1550, what happened to it?"

- "So we see that the religion of the Holy Grail is really the same as the religion of true and original Christianity, reverence for the Great Goddess and her Good Shepherd husband-son consort."

I find I am distrustful of a number of the author's generalizations and hope they will not harm or hurt. The place for political correctness lies in human rights legislation; it should not appear between the covers of every book on every shelf in every bookstore or library. *Swords at Sunset* is politically incorrect; other charges could be directed against it too. Still, there has to be room to air unorthodox views and unpopular opinions. Bradley has taken leave to do that. It's a brave if foolhardy, act. Here are some statements I find hard to swallow:

- "Christianity had apparently originated on the Atlantic Coast of Europe, perhaps today's Brittany, or else had been brought there from islands out in the Atlantic of which only remnants still exist – Lyonesse and Atlantis have been names for this Atlantic civilization and its outposts."

- "The Caucasus Mountains were the last refuge of the Neanderthal genetic strain, or 'race' of people because the glacial climate to which the Neanderthals had adapted lingered in the Caucasus region after the last Ice Age had ended elsewhere in Europe and Western Asia."

13

- "The Old Testament also records the fact that many early Hebrews retained marked Neanderthal physical traits from their Caucasus Mountains origin."

- "I have suggested therefore that Neanderthal and 'highly Neanderthaloid' people had an 'inbred' or genetic tendency toward monotheism, the conception of just one God who created 'Everything.'"

- "Both Judaism and Islam were conceived and developed originally by very closely related Caucasus-steppe people."

I could continue but I believe the point has been made.

Elsewhere (in the foreword to *Holy Grail Across the Atlantic* and in the columns of *Mysterious Canada*), I have described Michael Bradley in a new way. I depicted him as a rehistorian, not as an historian, not even the historian as theorist – a systematizer like a Spengler, a Toynbee, or a Huntington. The word *rehistorian* is my coinage for someone who is a revisionist of the historical record, based on new readings of that record which has been augmented by myths, legends, folklore, urban lore, rumour, and a conception of human nature and social history decidedly at odds with conventional interpretations. The rehistorian thrives on supposition, association, and conjecture. The texts he writes are frankly speculative and often resemble pairs of socks in department stores that are labelled "fit-all." These speculations are nonetheless interesting for what they tell us about mankind, history, and the human desire to understand fate or destiny in broad but often mutually exclusive ways.

Michael Bradley is no Ripley; he is a book writer, not a cartoonist, but I think he would enjoy reading my copy of *Ripley's Believe It or Not!* Ripley famously wrote (quoting Napoleon) that "The Holy Roman Empire was not holy – nor Roman – nor an empire." I agree.

Bradley writes: "Armed with love, compassion and knowledge, one can cast off the cumbersome and crippling armour of religious dogma or political and economic dialectics to carve out, with supple and determined strokes, more appropriate social structures and a more rewarding human environment, using equally sharp edges of intellect and heart. That is what knights and heroines of the Grail have always done." Here I can wholeheartedly concur!

John Robert Colombo, author and anthologist, is known across Canada as "the Master Gatherer." He is the author of books of lore and literature, including *True Canadian Ghost Stories*, *True Canadian UFO Stories*, and *The Midnight Hour*.

Swords at Sunset

Last Stand of North America's Grail Knights

Michael Bradley
with
Joëlle Lauriol

Manor House Publishing Inc.

Manor House Publishing Inc.
452 Cottingham Crescent, Ancaster, Ontario, L9G 3V6
905-648-2193 www.manor-house.biz

1

The Golden Horseshoe of the Holy Grail

From the top of the Niagara Escarpment all of Ontario's famed "Golden Horseshoe" is spread out below you like a gigantic map or a satellite poster. Looking eastwards, the view is spectacular.

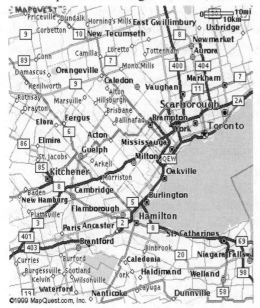

The angular western end of Lake Ontario is clearly evident. The steel town of Hamilton emits a haze of smog to your left. Even further to your left, Toronto's massive jumble of buildings makes a confused and indistinct smudge at the limit of visibility on the northern side of the lake, a smudge that is punctuated by the pin-like spire of the CN Tower. To your right, to the south, the long shoreline of upper New York State curves green into the east, looking downright pastoral compared with the giant metropolis of the Golden Horseshoe. But appearances, of course, can be deceptive. Buffalo with its factories at the terminus of the New York State Barge Canal – once much better known as the nation-building "Erie Canal" of the young United States – is behind you. Buffalo is out of sight, hidden by the Escarpment. But anyway, the Niagara Frontier is but one small part of mighty industrial America and is now even something of a backwater whereas the Golden Horseshoe remains virtually the heart and soul of industrial Canada.

As if to emphasise this proud if nearly unique conglomeration of Canadian hustle, bustle and wealth, traffic streams along the Queen Elizabeth Way between the U.S.A. and Toronto like an animated computer graphic of blood flow in a body politic. Each 18-wheeler represents some crucial kind of cell carrying economic oxygen. Cars scurry among the trucks like busy enzymes – commuting factory workers, executives, office workers, store clerks and salespeople all working hard to, well, make things work.

Lake Ontario disappears into the eastern distance in a cobalt blue panorama so vast that one can see the curvature of the earth. And this invitingly arched horizon of our beautiful azure planet will sometimes lead readers of *Swords at Sunset* seemingly over its edge. We will have intellectual journeys, at least, that will explore interrelated facts about the biblical Exodus, early Christianity, Ancient Egypt and even the last "Ice Age." And they have the greatest possible significance to our discoveries on the Niagara Escarpment. A surprising world of intimately connected concepts lies just over the beckoning horizon when you view it from high above the Golden Horseshoe in search of the Holy Grail.

If you happen to be looking eastwards from atop the Niagara Escarpment on a mid-August day in the late afternoon, this curving cyan arc of the earth's horizon is blurred with evaporation haze. The CN Tower wriggles in heat waves. And the windshields of cars and trucks wink and sparkle along the QEW as flashy as the jewels in one of Jean-Honoré Fragonard's more sycophantic court paintings.

Towards late afternoon, the many apartment blocks of the Golden Horseshoe resemble hundreds of sugar cubes scattered around the coast, all of them glowing dusty rose in the late light with crystallised icing reflecting off a myriad of windows. From the height of the Niagara Escarpment, they give the great lakeshore metropolis an almost Mediterranean look.

If the year were 2003 and you had been enjoying a Sunday drive somewhere west of Vineland and north of Grimsby in Ontario's Niagara Peninsula, you might have seen three people digging in a field near Highway 24.[1] Well, you might have seen two people working at archaeological excavation and one standing near the abrupt edge of the Escarpment trying to get some cooling breeze coming off Lake Ontario. My justification for laziness was that I had been on the trail of Grail-related evidence for almost a quarter of a century and in 2003 I was just barely on the sunny side of sixty. And, let's face it, excavating for late medieval artefacts in the August heat was getting to me.

That, at least, was my excuse for taking a long break to admire the view over the Golden Horseshoe. Within minutes, the stiff breeze coming over the rocky lip of the Escarpment had dried my sweat-drenched shirt in a fluttering and frenzied demonstration of textbook refrigeration through heat exchange. I was actually starting to get cold. My head and heart had stopped pounding.

Respectable publications have described me as an amateur historian, archaeologist and anthropologist.[2] But the bald truth of the matter is that I'm really only a curious romantic with embarrassingly threadbare credentials. And not only the truth is becoming bald.

Who else but a romantic would have answered the December 1981 letter from a highly articulate Englishwoman who described with eccentric charm part of a ruined castle in her backyard in the middle of Nova Scotia? Unfortunately for conventional Canadian history, after a careful investigation there did appear to be the ruins of some sort of pre-colonial stone-built construction on her property.

A three-year investigation of the site undertaken at the request of Nova Scotia's Ministry of Culture, Recreation and Fitness indicated that the structure had most probably been built by religious refugees in AD 1398. This colony of religious refugees had been established by "Prince" Henry Sinclair, Baron of Rosslyn in Scotland. Henry was also Earl of Orkney, a title and domain he held in fief to the king of Norway.

A long train of fairly convincing circumstantial evidence argued that these religious refugees had believed in a heretical form of Christianity much better known to almost everyone as the "Holy Grail". *Holy Grail Across the Atlantic* (Hounslow Publishing, Toronto, 1988) was my account of the Nova Scotia investigation.

This book was well received by ordinary readers, even if it was not always welcomed enthusiastically by professional academics and government officials. *Holy Grail Across the Atlantic* went through several printings and it inspired a virtual flood of letters. Over fifty pre-colonial – but obviously European – artefacts, sites and inscriptions were reported to me by informed and literate people. Some of these people were even professional academics, which is to say, they were university professors. However, it is also true to say that most of these academics were either retired and thus beyond the reach of retribution, or else they kept their traitorous letters to me carefully secret from their colleagues.

Not all of the reported artefacts and sites dated from late medieval or Renaissance times, however, and so they had little bearing on the fate of Henry Sinclair's colonists of AD 1398. These artefacts and inscriptions mostly dated from much earlier periods of history and even prehistory. Most of them had nothing to do with belief in the specific heresy of the Holy Grail.

But this deluge of letters did contribute to the rapidly accumulating data proving that Ancient Egyptians, Ancient Celts from Ireland, Ancient Celtiberians from North Africa and Iberia (Spain and Portugal), Phoenicians and Carthagenians had all conquered the Atlantic. Further, it seemed that even Ancient Hebrews from the Holy Land, Black Africans from south of the Sahara, Mycenaens, Greeks and Romans had also all crossed the Atlantic a thousand years and more before Columbus in 1492.

Then there were medieval Irish monks seeking solitude, medieval Moors seeking riches (of course) and safety from El Cid, medieval Norsemen seeking walrus hide, timber and grapes, medieval Spaniards and Portuguese seeking codfish, medieval Welsh[3] seeking relief from Norman-Plantagenet incursions and medieval Basques seeking whales. It is this latter group of motley medieval mariners that must be the focus of our attention for among them were medieval Grail Refugees seeking a transatlantic haven from their implacable foe, the Inquisition.

In fact, by Year 2000 so much evidence had been swept under the rug by conventional historians trying desperately to hang on to their world view that the carpet of our cosy historical living room had become unsightly with humps, bumps and lumps. As a sign of the times, the prestigious U.S. magazine *Atlantic Monthly* kicked off the new millennium with its January 2000 cover article "The Diffusionists Are Coming!" This piece gave an overview of all those who had crossed the Atlantic before Columbus. It also served notice on serious popular writers that toeing the conventional historical line would no longer be acceptable to informed American readers.

The same thing was true about informed Canadian readers too, of course, except that no Canadian magazine of prestige similar to *Atlantic Monthly* has yet dared to announce the truth. And the truth is that our conventionally woven carpet of Canada's history is so threadbare, and so worn with holes where awkward evidence lurks under the rug, that it has become embarrassing for informed, urbane and sophisticated people who are yet expected to accept the conventional version of our national past and national identity. *Canadian Geographic Magazine*, for example, has never dared publish any of the new data about the Lake Memphremagog artefacts even though the magazine was offered a detailed photo-feature. It isn't surprising, therefore, that Canadians eagerly grabbed *Holy Grail Across the Atlantic* when it became available in bookstores.

By 1991 I had received letters from people in Nova Scotia, New Brunswick, Quebec, Maine, New Hampshire, Vermont, New York State and Pennsylvania about seemingly genuine Grail-related evidence. It became possible to plot the explorations of Henry Sinclair's 1398 colonists and their descendants on a map. This evidence formed a pattern, or at least it seemed to. The original Nova Scotia religious refugees had probed inland along five major river routes between AD 1398 and about AD 1550 and these routes all converged on the Great Lakes.

It was easy enough to figure out a plausible reason for this. Henry Sinclair's late medieval colonists, whom I chose to call "Grail Refugees" for lack of a better term, required metal for the maintenance of their medieval lifestyle. The Great Lakes were, and are, the continent's metallic heartland. Copper nuggets had been mined by native people from about 3000 BC, while iron also abounds in the region. Much of this iron ore is easy to get at, too, because it lies near the surface and can be dug out of open pit mines that were within the capability of medieval technology.

That haze over Hamilton is mostly due these days to the smelting of Mesabi iron shipped from Minnesota on distinctive long-hulled lake freighters, but that wasn't always the case. The Niagara Escarpment once had its own rich veins of iron ore that were visible at the surface. These Niagara Escarpment iron deposits fed the first generation of colonial smelters and smithies. These Niagara Escarpment iron deposits had first established Hamilton as Canada's acknowledged steel town.

Grail Knights of North America (Dundurn Press, Toronto, 1998) traced the explorations of Sinclair's colonists and their descendants according to Grail-related evidence including a coin[4], a radiocarbon-dated dam[5], several sculptures[6] and some rock inscriptions.[7]

It became obvious from the geographic pattern of reported artefacts that, in addition to the original Nova Scotia settlement of 1398, these medieval Grail Refugees had established at least two inland concentrations of their population. One colony was in the Green Mountains on the present border of Quebec and Vermont in the immediate vicinity of Lake Memphremagog.

The other settlement was somewhere in the region I called "Niagara". It seemed reasonable to me that once they had discovered the St. Lawrence River, only one hundred kilometres or sixty miles from Lake Memphremagog, and shortly thereafter discovered Lake Ontario, then the Grail Refugees must also have discovered Niagara Falls fairly quickly. They would have realised immediately that they had to establish a settlement above the falls if they were to navigate on the upper Great Lakes. And these lakes were the keys to the treasures of a continent.

The French empire-builder, René-Robert de La Salle, had realised this when he built his full-rigged little ship, *Griffon*, in 1679 just above the falls beside a creek near Buffalo. The Americans realised this when they went to the immense labour of building the Erie Canal, completed in 1825, from New York Harbour to Lake Erie. In fact, the original termination of the Erie Canal may have been the very same stream in which the *Griffon* had been constructed 142 years earlier. Once on Lake Erie, it is possible to navigate to the western end of Lake Superior and, if you count Newfoundland as part of North America, this is in more than halfway to the Pacific Ocean. In *Grail Knights of North America*, I was unfortunately not able to say precisely where this "Niagara" settlement had been located. My best guess, based on reported artefacts, was the southern shore of Lake Erie. It had probably been in New York State near modern Jamestown on Lake Chautauqua, or so I thought – and in error, as it turned out.

I presented somewhat more definite evidence that, wherever it had once been located, the settlement had been called "Seguna" at the time of Jacques Cartier's visit to the future site of Montreal in AD 1535. The people of "Hachelaga" (Montreal) told Cartier that in the city of Seguna, which was some distance south-west of Hachelaga on the shore of a great waterway, the population dressed in woven cloth like Cartier himself.

Although I knew at the time (1991-1995) that "Seguna" was the first usage of later words like *Saguenay*, *Saginaw*, etc., it wasn't until April 1997 when I met Joëlle Lauriol that I learned what this curious word could once have meant. There are towns named Saginaw and Saguenay all over north-eastern North America. But this word, like Hachelaga, doesn't seem to have been an originally native Indian one. The possible or probable meaning of "Hochelaga" and "Seguna" has much relevance to the medieval legend of the Holy Grail.

The accumulated evidence in *Holy Grail Across the Atlantic* and advance photocopied proofs of *Grail Knights of North America* may not have convinced most Canadian historians, but they did at least intrigue some American television producers and fascinate some Quebec politicians. The interest of these two disparate and unlikely groups resulted in the filming of an Arts & Entertainment Network television documentary during October 31 to November 2, 1998.[8]

This hour-long documentary featured the C-14 dated dam near Lake Memphremagog that was constructed about AD 1500 or earlier and a carved granite medieval "gargoyle" found in the stream bed where the dam had been built. This gargoyle is of exquisite workmanship and artistry that was stylistically assigned to "Norse-Scottish" masonry and dated to about AD 1550. Both the dam and the sculpture were illustrated in *Grail Knights of North America*.

Obviously, only an established and relatively populous community needs a dam for a mill. And this particular dam is an ambitious sixty-foot span composed of roughly squared blocks of stone weighing up to a ton or more. Certainly, it had taken a couple of years to build. So, if the dam was radiocarbon dated at the University of Toronto's Isotech Labs to about AD 1500 (plus or minus) by hemlock-wood surveyor's stakes recovered by professional Quebec archaeologists, then the pioneer community that had built the dam must have been founded some years previously. Which is to say that there was a sizeable existing European community on the Vermont-Quebec border in the Green Mountain foothills before Columbus set sail in AD 1492 or John Cabot left Bristol in AD 1497.

As for the granite gargoyle, it at least argues a European community with trained artisans who had hard iron or steel tools. The gargoyle's mouth, eyes and teeth could not have been shaped without sharp metal chisels and good metal files. The detail is superb.

The on-camera hosts of this documentary were Dr. Gérard Leduc and me. Leduc is a retired professor of biology from Concordia University in Montreal. For some odd reason, professors of biology often turn to archaeology in later life. The famous (or infamous) Dr. Barry Fell of Harvard University is another example of this phenomenon. Gérard Leduc was one of my earliest Quebec correspondents. He'd read *Holy Grail Across the Atlantic* and it had inspired him to look for Grail-related artefacts along the St. Lawrence and to write his privately published *Templars in New France*. And, as irony would have it, it was during this A&E film shoot, while we stayed at Gérard's comfortable home in Mansonville, Quebec that dramatic new artefacts came to light.

First, almost indisputable evidence came from a Lake Memphremagog cottage owner that the dam and gargoyle must have been remains from a community that was, indeed, closely associated with Henry Sinclair. Second, new evidence of the Niagara community's exact location also became available during those few days of the film shoot.

But *Grail Knights of North America* was already on the press. It was too late to revise the book to include the new data.

Within two weeks after this A&E Network film shoot we had made three quick trips to the Niagara Peninsula in order to check out clues to the location of the Grail Refugees' settlement above the falls. By December 19, 1998, we were holding a summit meeting (of sorts, anyway) with several other maverick historical researchers at the Best Western hotel in Niagara Falls, Ontario.

Between one thing and another, the two regions of Niagara and Lake Memphremagog, some four hundred miles apart (about 600 kilometres), were to obsess our thoughts and drain much of our physical and financial resources from late 1998 until August 2003.

But maybe I should clarify this use of words like "we," "us," and "our" before going any further.

Readers of *Holy Grail Across the Atlantic* will know that in 1980 I travelled to Nova Scotia with Deanna Theilman-Bean, an old friend from my days doing perceptual research for the advertising industry. My marriage had broken up and my ex-wife had decided to remain in the Maritimes with our son, Jason. I'd promised to spend two years in Nova Scotia with Jason in order to help him over a difficult time of transition. But I didn't know how I was going to cope financially in the Maritimes. All my writing contacts were in Toronto and Los Angeles. Deanna had always liked Jason and so she threw in her lot with me to help *me* over a difficult time of transition and to be a sort of surrogate mother to Jason during our legally scheduled visits.

I have already recounted at length how, through a series of truly uncanny events and circumstances, our initially uncertain relocation to Nova Scotia became a fruitful, profitable and nearly magical experience. Almost immediately upon arrival I received the letter from the eccentric Englishwoman about her ridiculous ruined castle. The basic decision to respond to this letter, in spite of other seemingly much more serious concerns at the time introduced us to the reality of the Holy Grail. It may seem fanciful, but I tend to attribute everything that happened afterward to the mysterious power of the Grail.

Arriving with $500 and staying in a vacationing friend's apartment because we had no place of our own and couldn't afford one, within six weeks Deanna and I had not only registered a boat-building company called CanTraid Export but had a $98,000 contract with the Canadian International Development Agency. This contract was for building and testing prototypes of one of my boat designs intended to help impoverished, starving Third World fishermen.

Within two months of our arrival, Nova Scotia's Department of Development wanted to relocate our fledgling company out of Halifax to

24

a place called Kentville. We had never heard of the town. When we consulted a map to find out where exactly this Kentville was, we discovered that it was equidistant between Halifax (Jason, lawyers, business), New Ross (the absurd ruined castle) and Cape D'Or where, we were to discover, Henry Sinclair (a.k.a. "Glooscap") had spent the winter of AD 1398-1399.

And by the way, we relocated our meagre belongings to Kentville on the very day that our friend was scheduled to return to Halifax and reclaim his apartment. As Deanna remarked, it was lucky for us that we had *not* been able to rent a place of our own in Halifax.

In short, some unknown faith beyond our fears, wisdom beyond our ignorance and certainly governmental powers (and red tape) beyond our control had conspired to place Deanna and me in the only place where we could do every single thing on our two-year Nova Scotia agenda. We immediately bought a house trailer in Kentville, sold it two years later, and made a net profit, after taxes and lawyers, of $9.95. The Grail had given us everything we actually needed, with very little left over. When we left Nova Scotia, we were almost as poor as when we had arrived, but also immeasurably richer.

Deanna was so much help with the boat-building business, with Jason, with my initial emotional upset and with the castle research that I offered her a junior co-authorship of *Holy Grail Across the Atlantic* and a share of the book's income paid directly to her. It was no more, but no less either, than she deserved.

By the early 1990s, Deanna and I were inevitably, but very amicably, starting to have thoughts about returning to our separate life paths. She had learned a lot, thanks to me. I had learned a lot more, thanks to her. Jason was fast growing up and that time of transition was long past. Deanna and I structured our parting slowly and finally separated in an equitable and civilised fashion.

My next ten years were mainly occupied with writing novels, screenplays and newspaper articles punctuated by lengthy trips to check out Grail-related artefacts that had been reported to me in the many letters that had resulted from the book. I virtually lived in my B200 Dodge factory-built camper van and it took me into the Green Mountains on the Quebec-Vermont border, along the St. Lawrence and St. John Rivers, into New York State's Adirondack Mountains, to Lake Champlain and along the upper Hudson River, and into Pennsylvania's Tuscarora Mountains.

It was a time of camping during chilly mountain nights with the sole comfort of "the rough male kiss of blankets" as the British poet, Rupert

Brooke (1887-1915), once put it just before he died of blood poisoning in the World War I Aegean campaign.

It was a time of seeing medieval coins found in Nova Scotia, New Brunswick and Maine, dams and gargoyles in Quebec and Templar-inspired sculptures and petroglyphs in New York State and Pennsylvania. I walked steep logging road with good friends like Mike Twose of Toronto, Don Eckler of Houghton, New York, Bob Williams of Emporium, Pennsylvania and Gérard Leduc of Mansonville, Quebec. I recounted all this in *Grail Knights of North America*.

But I had also begun to suspect that there might be a final chapter to be written about the Grail Refugees in Canada and that this story had much to do with the Green Mountains and "Niagara."

And by 1996, I suddenly realised something else. I was getting fairly medieval or middle aged myself. The logging roads seemed a bit steeper, their ruts a little deeper, rough camping blankets seemed scratchier and the nights certainly seemed cooler. I knew what I wanted to do with my golden years and also knew that I didn't want to do it alone. And I didn't want to do it with bearded male companions either, however compatible they might be.

I wanted to finish this "Grail in North America" story if I could. And after that, if I could manage to live long enough, I wanted to go to Europe in order to uncover the deepest level of the Holy Grail – "The Legend which reaches back to the prime source of all legends", as Wolfram von Eschenbach had written in the greatest of all Grail epics, *Parzival*.

In early 1997, I advertised for a "Companion of the Grail", honestly stating my age, my already iffy health and at least most of my foibles, and listed my own requirements for a female research associate and domestic partner. This advertisement was discreetly distributed within certain circles that had come to my knowledge over many years of Grail-related research.

And once again, the power of the Grail apparently went to work.

A reply to my advertisement came almost immediately on one small sheet of quietly ostentatious cream-coloured stationery. The thick, heavy and expensive linen-based paper was adorned with a not-so-discreet blood red Templar cross. The writer was a mature woman at the top of a Rosicrucian Order (AMORC) CIRCES. She wrote briefly that she knew of a young woman, one who might just be a suitable "Companion of the

Grail" as per the advertisement's description. She had already given this young woman my contact information. A *young* woman? How young?

Joëlle Lauriol drove a fair distance to meet with me for the first time in April 1997. I was naturally a bit apprehensive and more than a bit curious. I had never advertised for a companion before and didn't know what to expect.

Joëlle Lauriol was like nothing and no one I had ever imagined. Physically, she proved to a somewhat mischievous brunette about five-foot-two with eyes of blue. But her eyes could change disconcertingly to a smoky blue-green when she became angry. Thankfully, Joëlle became angry only infrequently and never for long.

She was somewhat sturdily built with a more than generous bosom, definite hips and a ready smile. I was more or less managing to deal with all these curves that Joëlle was throwing when I was stunned to discover that she was almost twenty years my junior. Did this young woman know what she was getting herself into?

She explained that she could remember virtually nothing of her childhood or adolescence until the age of thirteen. This was possibly due to some trauma or abuse in infancy. She didn't know. She said that she was now more than ready for an intimate relationship, that she had been told about my age and health and that it didn't matter.

Joëlle had been born in Tonneins, France, a riverside town along the Garonne River. This Garonne River corridor across southern France was the very place I had earmarked to look for evidence of the Grail's deepest layer of meaning back in "Ice Age" times. Was this mere coincidence? Of course it was. Joëlle was a natural Francophone with an elegant French accent. But she'd been educated mostly in Canada and was therefore perfectly bilingual in English. She had degrees in Business Administration and Journalism. So she knew about both accounting and writing.

Her family name, Lauriol (i.e. "L'Auriol") meant "Halo" in English. Her family's publicly available genealogies went back to the seventh century of the Christian Era as reprinted in the 1982 international best seller *The Holy Blood and The Holy Grail*.[9] These genealogical records are now in the Bibliothèque Nationale, but they were once kept carefully hidden in the Bastille. France's national "Independence Day" is called "Bastille Day".

On July 14, 1789 a mob of revolutionaries stormed and took the fortress-like prison called the Bastille, an event that more or less officially marks the beginning of the French Revolution. However, according to *The Holy Blood and the Holy Grail*, some obscure documents of the Revolution indicate that the real purpose of attacking the Bastille wasn't so much the immediate establishment of Liberté, Egalité and Fraternité, but to get at the secret genealogies that were kept there. These genealogies included those of the Lauriols. Godfroi de Bouillon himself, whom we will meet soon, had sprung from Lauriol ancestors. There is a great deal of evidence that the French Revolution and the birth of most modern democratic ideals was, in fact, a democratic revolt engineered by believers in the Holy Grail heresy.

So much for the Lauriol family's publicly available genealogies going back to the seventh century, Godfroi de Bouillon, the French Revolution and all that. The Lauriol family's private genealogies, however, go back much further than the seventh century. These genealogies have never been published anywhere. And they never will be.

Joëlle had had a chequered religious past. Born the usual nominal Roman Catholic of southern France – and Roman Catholicism is much more "nominal" there than elsewhere, she had once become a Mormon and had spent eighteen months as a missionary in Haiti. There, she had added Intermediate Level Creole to her linguistic accomplishments.

Not much of all this was believable, of course. It was much too good to be true. Either that, or else somebody, somewhere was into kidnapping French girls, erasing their childhood memories, somehow programming them with a very definite personality and also providing them with a good education. Were Rosicrucians into that sort of thing? And, if so, why? I shuddered to speculate.

What bothered me the most was Joëlle's stint as a Mormon missionary in Haiti.

For some time I had been starting to suspect that the Book of Mormon wasn't just the ridiculous blasphemy that most non-Mormons thought it was, if and when they thought about it at all. Joseph Smith's history of the "Nephites" paralleled too closely the actual history of the Grail Refugees that I had managed to piece together over almost twenty years, from 1980 to 1997.

I doubted strongly that the "Prophet Smith" had been led by the angel Moroni to a record inscribed on golden plates, a record which Smith was then able to translate with the aid of divinely given spectacles. On the other hand, it seemed almost certain that Joseph Smith had found a genuine record of some sort, and it seemed to be suspiciously like the actual history of the Grail Refugees insofar as I had been able to reconstruct it. Perhaps this record had really been inscribed on *golden looking* copper plates, possibly old sheathing from a ship's hull. If this record had been written in a late medieval Scottish-English-Scandinavian dialect,[10] as I was already beginning to think, then Joseph Smith could have got the bare gist of it.

Me, although I was fascinated with the general story, I had always lacked the sheer courage to wade through the Book of Mormon's 561 pages of pseudo-biblical prose. But I was virtually certain that there would be crucial clues buried in that massive text that might shed some light on the more detailed history of the Grail Refugees and their ultimate fate in North America.

And here was a person – and a well-endowed young woman at that, who presumably knew the Book of Mormon, of all things, backwards and forwards. After all, she had been a Mormon missionary. Was this also mere coincidence? Well, of course it was. What else could it have been?

But I generally distrust coincidences, especially so many of them. Was Joëlle the Mormon idea of a honey trap? And what man wants to be stuck with a *Mormon* idea of a honey trap? Maybe such a contradiction in terms could only tempt another Mormon, which I wasn't. However, I did have another thought. And it was disturbing.

I had already been threatened with the Mormon death rite of "blood atonement," twice before 1997, by two separate Utah correspondents. They had both been outraged by the argument of *Holy Grail Across the Atlantic*. According to Mormons and their genealogies, Jesus had been married to at least two women: a woman named Anna and Mary Magdalene. Mormons believe that Anna and her children were and are "Israelite" and blessed, while Mary Magdalene and her children were and are "Canaanite" and forever cursed by blood taint.

Modern Mormons like to assure people that "The Church" has given up embarrassing customs like racial discrimination, "multiple marriage" and "blood atonement" but anyone who knows anything about the higher levels of the Mormon Church suspects that such progressiveness would be impossible for the truest believers. These practices are regarded as *divine injunctions*, and they definitely supersede mere man-made civil law. Ordinary Mormons have been given official Church dispensation to abide by civil law – under great pressure from the United States government, it should be added – but Elders of the Church still answer to what they consider to be a much higher authority. As Brigham Young once put it in an 1878 speech to the Utah State Legislature, "there is no higher service that a Canaanite can perform than to be killed and thus perform 'blood atonement.'"

Now, as it happened, one of my correspondents *was* a prominent Elder of the Mormon Church. Even I recognised his famous Mormon family name.[11] He was thus in a position to "suggest" a ritual killing and have it carried out without question by at least some Mormons even in 1997 (or in 2004, for that matter). Had Joëlle Lauriol been sent as curvaceously padded bait whose job it was to tempt me, somehow, into taking that final trip to Utah – for it would be *final*, I had been assured of *that*.

Canadian readers may choose to ridicule such suspicions. I can only say that it is a lot easier to nurture such ridicule in Canada than in Utah. Maybe readers who would blithely attribute my misgivings to paranoia should read the chillingly non-fiction book *The Mormon Murders* by Steven Naifeh and Gregory White Smith (Weidenfeld & Nicholson, New York, 1988). The Arts & Entertainment Network chose the three pipe bombing "blood atonements" for a 1994 one-hour television documentary on *City Confidential*.

We all tend to forget, especially those of us most "educated" in our contemporary universities, that three centuries ago *in Western Europe* people were still being burned at the stake because of religious conflict. And people were still being subjected to religious torture in New England. Religiously motivated murder and torture remain the rule, not the exception, everywhere else in the world today except Western Europe and North America. If nothing else, I hope that *Swords at Sunset* will show how shallow and vulnerable our cherished veneer of civil law and democracy really is because we very dangerously take it for granted. In fact, the more I have researched this book, the more I fear that the real religious war still raging beneath our thin layer of democracy is the actual cause of most of those humps, bumps and lumps under our threadbare carpet of history.

But I rather doubted Joëlle Lauriol could still be a Mormon that first evening in April 1997 because she was smoking a cigarette and eyeing my beer. On the other hand, it was always just barely possible that even instructors of Mormon missionaries at the Church school in Provo, Utah had lowered themselves to read John Le Carré. Maybe they had picked up contemporary ideas about what a proper honey trap should be. Did this smiling and too-comfortably built young woman have "blood atonement" planned for me at some time in the future, especially since two other Mormons had failed previously?

But coincidences abound in Grail Country – and, besides, I trusted the higher levels of the Rosicrucians' security screenings. I also remembered those Lauriol genealogies and I had even greater faith in the ethical integrity of the Holy Blood. I decided to live dangerously. Since time was going by, I would let the fundamental things apply in order to enrich my remaining golden years: five-foot-two, eyes of blue, Joëlle's relative youth and, well, her other accoutrements.

I was also to learn fairly soon that some of Joëlle's proclivities regarding appropriate attire for dancing, swimming, sunbathing and archaeological digging reflected – sometimes rather shockingly for some people – extreme southern French values rather than extreme Mormon ones. I accepted this as the Mormon Church's loss and my gain.

So, Joëlle and I together constituted the "we" that discovered new evidence during the A&E film shoot, the "we" that visited the Niagara region several times in late 1998 and the "we" who arranged a summit meeting of maverick researchers at the Niagara Falls, Ontario hotel.

Joëlle and I had cello-taped the large-scale government topographical maps to the top of the large banquet-sized table that the hotel staff had brought into our room. They showed the Niagara Peninsula in various degrees of magnification, as it were. One map had a scale small enough to show Lakes Ontario and Erie to either side. One map of a certain area had a scale large enough to depict individual houses and buildings.

Four, five and sometimes six people had pored over these maps during the course of the past two days. A carafe of coffee had always been close by and many cups had been thoughtfully drunk and distractedly cleared away after much musing. Besides the maps, the table was littered with notes, photos, newspaper clippings, a magnifying glass and a copy of the Book of Mormon.

Don Eckler, a tall and stolid microscope technician from Houghton, New York and friend of several previous adventures in New York State and Pennsylvania, dwarfed Joëlle as he stood beside her at the table pointing down at a mid-scale map. Don had, two days before, brought photographs and microphotographs of a bronze axe head that had been discovered along the banks of the Genesee River. Crystallography indicated that this axe had most probably been cast in a mould, an indication of European technology.[12]

"Bert Wheeler" – I will not give his real name here because he is employed by the Niagara Parks Commission – looked where Don was pointing.

Bert had contributed his special collection of newspaper clippings from the Niagara Frontier to our amateur historical symposium. These clippings ranged from an article in a New York State newspaper of 1823 called *The Western Farmer* to the St. Catharines, Ontario *The Standard* newspaper of 1988, but all the clippings had one thing in common.

They were all about discoveries of metal artefacts, house sites, stone foundations and puzzling human remains that had been found along both sides of the Niagara Frontier. The next few pages carry samples from more than 60 clippings.

—The *Batavian* recalls the fact that about two miles west of Shelby Center, Orleans Co., there can now be seen the ruins of an ancient fort. The two rows of intrenchments, from 14 to 16 feet in width, enclosing about three acres, seemingly in a perfect circle, are particularly discernible. Relics of pottery, flints, arrowheads.etc.,have been found there this summer. There is also a burying ground a short distance from the fort, where it is claimed skeletons have been found which measured in the neighborhood of seven feet. N FG. SEPT. 18/1878

Niagara Falls Gazette. (NY)

"Mormon Plates" Work of Joker

By Associated Press

Rochester, April 27.—Closer examination of the plates found on Mormon Hill, Palmyra, the inscriptions on which bore refutations of the tenets of Mormanism, according to the discoverer, Rev. Charles E. Driver, has revealed that they are the work of a practical joker, it was learned today. The plates were discovered last Friday and the Greek inscriptions punched into the metal with a shoemaker's awl, were revealed at a church service last night. The translation read:

"Repent ye," and "Ye must be born again."

A plumber's shears left unmistakable evidence of the newness of the metal. The plates were found under a pile of soil and rock by the evangelist. The holes in the plates showed no dirt imbedded. These discoveries led the skeptical to believe the plates were "planted" to stir up animosity against the Mormons, who plan to journey to Palmyra for an investigation in the autumn.

Niagara Falls Gazette (N
27 APRIL 1923

A Battle of the Remote Past.

To Editor of the Democrat and Chronicle:

Sir: The late Judge Arad Thomas, of Albion, N. Y., in his "Pioneer History of Orleans County," mentions the fact that when the first white settlers discovered the mound or combined mound and fortress near the present village of Shelby Center and learned that it contained human skeletons they could obtain no information from the Indians then living and roaming in the vicinity in regard to the people who had supposedly been victims of a general massacre.

The condition of the skeletons at that date, a century or more ago, seemed to prove that they had lain underground at least a century then. Inquiry among the Indians in various parts of the country was in every case fruitless. Those whose remains lay covered there left no record whatever except the remnants of their tools and weapons, which were similar to those used by most if not all Indian tribes. In all probability their history will be an unsolved problem for all time to come, and the extreme antiquity of the battle and massacre effectually does away with any supposition that they were the victims of white settlers or soldiers. The general public, where not ignorant of the existence of the remains, has never seemed very much interested.

Local interest in the matter was heightened, however, when Dr. Cushing, of the town of Barre, settled in and began the practice of his profession in Medina in the late seventies. With him came his son Frank, a slim, high-browed young man not yet out of his teens, who was a born naturalist and student of antiques. That mound or demolished fort in Shelby drew him like a powerful magnet, and many a night accompanied by George Kennan, the Siberian explorer and author, who then lived in Medina, the pair built brush and bark fires by the mound and industrously dug after long-buried bones and weapons and tools of the forgotten race. Frank investigated industriously, made frequent visits to the Tonawanda reservation, picked up an amazing knowledge of their legends and language, and in the end learned no more of the beginning or ending of the burial tribe than when he started. It is not altogether unlikely that in the experience just mentioned he received the impulses that later led to his visit to and adoption by the Zuni Indians and his long connection with the Smithsonian Institute.

J. B. SWEET.

Rochester, N. Y. June 5, 1909.

DEMOCRAT + CHRONICLE

33

Find Skull, Sword On Isle

Workmen on Grand Island unearth remains believed to be those of Indian, together with a sword; Historians asked to visit spot

6 SEPT. 34

NIAGARA FALLS, N. Y. Sept. 6 — A steamshovel excavating for the roadway between the south and north Grand Island bridges, unearthed a skull, a sword and a heap of bones yesterday afternoon. The discovery was made about 1,500 feet south of Burnt Ship Creek, which separates Grand Island from Buckhorn Island.

Herbert H. Murpay, 619 McKinley Parkway, superintendent of the construction company which is building the road, said he believes the skull to be that of an Indian.

In the belief that the bones and sword are of historical importance local historians will be asked to visit the spot to investigate. Numerous engagements between Indians, British and Americans have taken place on Grand Island, but old settlers on the island have said that many graveyards of early white settlers have been overgrown by underbrush and forgotten.

Some favor, others oppose a new white dial for "Big Ben," famous clock of the British House of Commons, the present dial having been punctured in a number of places by shrapnel during air raids in the World War.

Niagara Falls Evening Review 6 Spt. '34
(CONT.)

34

5/28/09

The gruesome spectacle which confronted Mr. Sweeney of Orangeport, in unearthing the skeletons of a large number of Indians, while in the act of digging a peach tree from his farm, an account of which appeared in this paper last week, has attracted the attention of the government officials at Washington, and it is expected they will visit the place in a few days. Large numbers of visitors are daily flocking to the place. But as yet no one has given any valuable data as to the origin of the mass of human bones.

It can be readily seen upon examination of the position of the skeletons that they were all placed there after the flesh had been removed from the body. In what manner this came about is undermined by the vast number of curious people who have made a personal visit to the scene the horrible grave-like trench.

It was discovered that the bodies lie in tiers and are composed of infants and adults. Male and female are also buried in the heap. It appears very much as if many of them were tied together in bundle fashion and pitched in the large hole which was prepared for them.

While some theories have been advanced as to a pre-historic existence, others aver a historical knowledge of a race of Indians inhabiting these parts in the year 1639. Many contradictory statements are made and it is yet a mystery. Perhaps a great naturalist might possibly throw some light on the subject and probably solve the perplexing problem.

Adjoining one section of the pit is a semblance of charred bones and ashes which give rise to the belief that cremation was the means used in destroying the bodies. As this is not a custom with the Indians, another important question arises in regard to the probable nationality or type of human being living in that day.

There is about one thousand skeletons in all in the trench, as every available space has been used in storing the bodies away. The surface of the hole covers an area of thirty-two feet and it is estimated to be approximately five feet deep.

What is believed to be the cause of death of such a large number is that a war must have ensued between two tribes living at that time, and men, women and children were massacred relentlessly. After the affray was over the bodies were pitched in the pit in a heap.

Many visitors have gathered relics in the shape of skulls and bones for souvenirs. It is expected that the entire space may be dug up and all of the bones taken away.

May 28, 1909
Rochester DEMOCRAT
AND CHRONICLE ?

The clippings had another thing in common. Almost invariably the discoverers had pleaded for some expert to come and have a look at the artefacts and to explain what they were. And almost invariably, too, no expert had investigated and the artefacts were simply ignored. Sometimes there were follow-up articles showing that some of the discoveries had been ignored for years. Don Eckler's axe would have fitted right into this collection except that its discovery had never been reported to any newspaper. This had been a purposeful lapse. The experts

35

now have yet another way of getting rid of awkward artefacts besides just ignoring them until they are lost or forgotten. They are "repatriated" to a local Indian Reservation because today's dogma of political correctness insists they *must* be of Aboriginal origin. And the Aboriginals are quick to get rid of any artefact that is pre-Columbus and European.

The most recent example, which actually did cause something of a public and media outcry in spite of the dogma of political correctness, was the "repatriation" of Kennewick Man's entire 9,500-year-old Caucasoid skeleton. The bones have now been buried according to ancient tribal rites in a secret location known only to Washington State Indian elders. Kennewick Man's embarrassing Caucasian racial traits can no longer puzzle anthropologists or challenge Indian myths. A detailed account of the Kennewick Man saga and its implications can be found in Elaine Dewar's *Bones*.

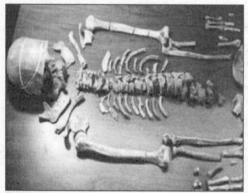 

The bones, left, and facial reconstruction, right, of Kennewick Man.

Using Bert's newspaper clippings, Don's personal stories, Bob William's careful notes, archaeologist Ron Williamson's book *Legacy of Stone*,[13] archaeologist Bill Fitzgerald's work at Neutral Indian sites, and my own bibliographic research and personal discoveries, we had plotted all the Niagara Frontier artefacts we'd ever heard about on the maps.

I had created two major categories of artefacts: "Aboriginal" and "European." Mind you, I had not always agreed with the archaeologists, including Ron Williamson and Bill Fitzgerald, as to which artefacts belonged in which category. But every artefact was presumably pre-colonial. There were also several sub-categories each represented by different coloured little sticky discs that we had bought from a nearby Grand & Toy office supply store. The resulting splotches and corridors of colour formed a distinct pattern. The vast majority of the reported

"European" artefacts clustered along the line of the Welland Feeder Canal in the Niagara Peninsula of Canada, crossed the mouth of the Niagara River and straggled along the southern shore of Lake Ontario before petering out.

The vast majority of artefacts assigned to the "Aboriginal" category were more randomly distributed on both the American and Canadian sides of the Niagara Frontier. There was, however, a notable statistical increase in the Aboriginal artefacts at the Kingsport condominium site and along the line of the Niagara River, especially on Grand Island and both sides of it just above the falls.

Eckler picked up the magnifying glass for the umpteenth time. Maybe it helped focus his thoughts, no pun intended. After all, he was a microscope technician. But this time he actually peered through it.

All along the line of the dead-straight Welland Feeder Canal, in addition to the coloured discs representing European artefacts, there were also curious little lakes. Joëlle had first spotted them.

They were like little doughnuts about two hundred to four hundred metres in diameter, according to the scale. Some were complete circles. Some were deteriorated but had clearly once been nearly circular before being eroded so that the map showed them as tiny horseshoes. They were little circles of water each with an island in the middle.

"Homesteads protected by moats," Eckler mumbled.

"And they correlate with the European things." Wheeler.

"And they are all connected to the feeder canal," contributed Joëlle. "Or, at least they once were. That or the Beaver River."

"We call it Beaver Creek," Bert grinned. "Have you actually seen these lakes?" Bert asked me.

"Not yet. Joey only noticed them on the map last month up in Mansonville at Gérard's place." Then I paused, remembering. "But, you know, I did see one back in 1995 when Zoë Nickerson and I made a quick day trip from Welland just to get the feel of the land. Only back then I didn't know what I was looking at," I added. I paused again. "And I didn't know what I was looking for, either."

Gerard's house has heated *floors*," Joëlle remarked to no one in particular. "So civilised," she mused. Then she shrugged. "Of course, he's French," she finished, as if that explained it all. And actually, Gérard Leduc's heated floors *had* pretty well explained it all, in a manner of speaking anyway.

Six weeks earlier Gérard and I had returned to his house after a long day filming in intermittent sleet and biting wind off the Green Mountains. We had actually been chilled to the bone by early morning, but A&E's Producer-Director, Joshua Alper from Los Angeles, kept insisting that we walk around in mere long-sleeved lumberjack shirts as if it were early autumn in, say, northern California. We walked for about ten hours more – after we were already frozen but thankfully were beginning to get numb – often doing the same scene several times in seemingly endless replays. "Look comfortable!" was Joshua's constant command. He had an expensive wind-proof down-filled parka. Yeah, right.

At last, we came shivering into the living room after the season's early nightfall. By then, the miserable weather had begun to bother even Joshua. We found Joëlle stretched out in a negligée on the (heated) floor's shag area rug in front of a cosy fire. She looked up from maps and a confusion of file cards. A multi-coloured Accent Highlighter was poised in her hand. I habitually carried my collection of maps and my always-handy portable research kit wherever I went. Joëlle, with nothing much to do while Gérard and I were out filming in the sleet and wind, had managed to do just about the most valuable thing imaginable in terms of North American Grail-related research.

Gérard and I naturally headed straight for the fireplace and, en route, we couldn't help but see what Joëlle was doing and had done. Using my card file of artefacts from the Niagara Region, she had plotted their locations on my maps of the area using dots of Highlighter. The file of artefacts was not nearly so complete as Bert Wheeler's collection that we used about six weeks later and my card files referred only to "European" items. And the maps were only gas station road maps. Still, even so, the pattern was crystal clear. And while doing this careful plotting with her Highlighter, Joëlle had seen and marked the little doughnut lakes. I had never even noticed them before.

I was brought back to the present by Eckler's comment. "Those features will be covered with snow and maybe ice within a week," grunted Don. He was right. Snow was already swirling outside the hotel's bay windows.

"Maybe so. But we know where to dig in the spring." This was from Wheeler, the Niagara Parks Commission officer. Part of his job was to keep track of unauthorised archaeological excavations. I raised one eyebrow. He grinned. And shrugged.

"Why the hell hasn't anyone done this before?" Eckler tapped the map angrily with the rim of the magnifying glass. He gestured at the little coloured discs. "This alone proves the case."

"No one wants to know." This came from Joëlle. And after all, perhaps she knew it best.

"You can say that again," muttered Don, looking around for the coffee carafe.

"Something else proves the case," I said. "Almost, anyway." I ran a forefinger along the line of little doughnut lakes. "If this scale is accurate, these things – the moats – are only about twenty-five to fifty yards wide. Or metres. That means that the Europeans didn't have to worry about powerful bows in the hands of potential attackers. And it means that they only had bows or crossbows themselves, but more powerful ones."

"The Book of Mormon states specifically that the bows of the Nephites were made out of steel," Joëlle put in.

"That's interesting," I said. "I never knew that. But it means that the Nephites were using crossbows, not longbows. No one has ever made a *longbow* out of steel. Not that I know about, anyway. It also means that their crossbows were based on post-Crusader technology, after the Europeans learned about Damascus steel. It was the only known medieval steel springy enough for crossbows."

"And that possibly indicates that the second category of Templars were involved here," said Eckler. Don Eckler and I both knew that the second rank of Knights Templar were all crossbow experts with steel-bowed weapons adopted the hard way from the Saracens in the Holy Land. That placed the indicated technology after about AD 1200, but before about AD 1600.

"Well, I don't think we're talking firearms here. There's no provision in this pattern for long-range fields of fire," I continued.

"Seems to be a valid point," said Bert.

"Maybe," Eckler conceded with a dubious grunt. "But based on an awful lot of suppositions." He poured coffee.

"I think this general distribution of homestead also shows something else," I carried on. "These homesteads, if that's what they really are, are surrounded by moats but they're also isolated. There's no single concentration of European artefacts that would indicate a stronghold or a really centralised defensive strategy." I pointed my finger at several widely separated doughnut lakes.

"That's right," came from Bert Wheeler as he scanned the map carefully.

Don Eckler bent over the map too. "Okay," he said. "I'll buy that."

"These people had confidence in their technological superiority over their immediate Indian neighbours," I continued, "even if it was only the relative superiority of European armour, bows, crossbows and swords and not the absolute superiority that reliable firearms would give. I think we're talking late medieval Europeans here for sure. Before sixteen hundred."

"Maybe the Europeans were also bigger than the Indians, on average," Bert said. "There are plenty of Iroquois legends and myths about the 'stone giants' that once came into their land."

"Stone giants, Bert?" Eckler was interested. "Never heard of that."

"An old Iroquois legend, Don… Maybe not so old," Wheeler mused. "Well, anyway, the arrows of the Indians were ineffective against them." Bert shrugged. "So the Indians concluded these giants must have been made of stone. There's quite a few Iroquois rock drawings showing these 'stone giants' with arrows bouncing off them."

"How old are these rock drawings? Anybody know?" Don asked.

"Back in the 1930s," Bert continued, "Dr. Albert H. Hooker got interested in these legends because Hooker thought that these stories were about medieval Europeans. Hooker was a chemist, not an historian. But he was a respected amateur historian and lectured in Buffalo during 1934 and 1935. Hooker founded the company that was later involved in the Love Canal pollution scandal. Anyway, he thought that the 'stone giants' were Scandinavians from the Icelandic Republic."

"That's Sinclair's ballpark in terms of time, the 1200s to about 1390," I said. "Sinclair was a Scandinavian too, at least officially. He was a Jarl of Norway. And he came with about five hundred ex-Templar knights, or their descendants. No difference between Sinclair's people and quote Scandinavians unquote, given the terminology of the times. Six of one and half dozen of the other."

"Hooker thought that the 'stone giants' had come about 1350 and that some of their descendants were alive when Cartier came in 1534."

"Bingo," said Don Eckler, thumping the map.

"Hooker also thought that these Europeans had intermarried with the Iroquois and that political ideas of the Icelandic Republic had been transplanted into the Iroquois Confederacy," Wheeler continued. "Just like you wrote in *Grail Knights*." I'd given both Don and Bert brand new copies the day before, hot off the press.

"He said it before I did. I wish I'd known."

"Joseph Smith's 'Lamanites' would have been Iroquois," Joëlle said.

Don laughed and smiled toward Joëlle. "Do you know what the word 'Leman' means, honey?"

I knew what it meant. But thinking seriously through her English vocabulary, which probably didn't include many archaic Scottish and English words, Joëlle finally shook her head. She smiled prettily, but her eyes had turned that dangerous smoky blue-green colour. It had been Don's harmless and unconscious use of the Americanism 'honey' – meaning any young woman – which had miffed her.

"It's an old English and Scottish word for a lover. A companion, but not a Church-approved husband or wife," said Don Eckler.

Joëlle's eyes widened. "So that may be where Smith got his word 'Lamanites' from." He nodded, grinning.

She paused. "And did *you* know, Don, *mon bon bougre*, that your Genesee River is an obvious corruption of the French for word the biblical Genesis, *Genèse*? I wonder how the local Iroquois learned that one?"

"Oh, I never knew that. That's interesting... *Joëlle*." I notice that he never asked what *mon bon bougre* might have meant, but I never doubted that he'd gotten the gist. Don and Joëlle got along fine after that.

After another few hours of discussion and rehashing all the data that confronted us, we decided to call it a night. We agreed to meet for breakfast and work out a plan of shared research and a strategy for actual fieldwork. My experience in "small group dynamics", whether it is a meeting of advertising execs or of maverick historians, is that people feel more comfortable whenever they have a proposal in writing. At least they have something to hold in their hands, something that can be modified and changed because there's already a structure.

While Joëlle went to bed, I stayed up most of the night on the computer writing out a proposed strategy for both research and in-the-field excavations. Occasionally, to stretch my back and when thinking about how best to phrase something, I walked over to the window to watch the snow falling. The city of Niagara Falls would have a white Christmas, but then Niagara normally got a lot more snow than Toronto.

It was almost five years later that I turned back from the edge of the Niagara Escarpment on a hot August day in 2003. Since 1998 we had found a lot of things along the line of the Welland Feeder Canal and among those doughnut lakes. Maybe three dozen arrowheads. A brass plate inscribed with Hebrew, Latin and Greek characters (shades of Joseph Smith!). Bert Wheeler had found part of a sword blade that *wasn't* from the War of 1812 but was much earlier. The War of 1812, I learned quickly, was the favoured expert explanation for almost any odd European artefact that was found anywhere on the Niagara Peninsula.

Ron Williamson, a professional archaeologist, had discovered *seven thousand* arrowheads at the Kingsport Condominium site. He had prudently assigned them to an "Archaic Flint Industry". No one could argue with that. These arrowheads, no matter why they had once been shot in such great profusion at that particular place *had* once been made by an "Archaic Flint Industry". And did Williamson's use of *Archaic* refer to the recognised Great Lakes (Shield) Archaic Period, or did it just mean "old". Ron told me that some of the arrowheads were "Late Woodland" (not Shield Archaic) in style, but this may have begged too many questions that were too awkward to answer.

Bert Wheeler stood up from his hole, peering around like a weary woodchuck. He stretched his back and then bent down again to retrieve his trowel, brushes, a collection of Ziploc bags holding the day's archaeological catch – I could see that all the items were small – and finally the Glad Zipper Sandwich Bag box as well. Bert had shed his shirt and picked it up in a limp bundle. "Let's knock off, Joey," he called as he passed by her assigned plot.

Joëlle emerged from her excavation like a finalist in a wet T-shirt contest. She was sleek with perspiration. But she was a contender who would have been disqualified. For, like Bert, she had also shed her shirt and had its arms tied around her waist. Bert had long since become acclimatised to Joëlle. He didn't bother to grin or even to look he was so weary. But he did wait patiently while she gathered her gear and then offered a hand to help her jiggle up out of the shallow dig.

I could see that her day's catch had been archaeological small fry too. But one of Joëlle's Ziplocs, the one bearing the neat label "8-17-03, J2" did have a scrap of five interlocked iron or crude steel rings – they were badly rusted, that seemed to have once been chain mail.

"Hey, that's interesting," said Bert with at least a spark of animation as sweat dripped off his chin. Mind if I have a look?" he asked as he reached for the sandwich bag that Joëlle then held out dangling between a dainty, dirty thumb and forefinger. He took it just as carefully and peered through the plastic. "A piece of something larger. But the rings look too delicate for armour to me." He handed the bag to me.

I peered through the slightly hazy plastic too. "That depends. The first chain mail had fairly large and heavy links. Like Crusaders' mail. Clumsy stuff. But later the work got much finer, almost decorative. Much more supple and less uncomfortable to wear. I've seen work like this before, but only from the late fourteenth century and the fifteenth."

"We could send it to the ROM," Joëlle suggested, wiping sweat from her brow. Streaks of perspiration channelled trickling down the middle of her chest.

"And have it disappeared?" We had all picked up the terminology of the Human Rights Violations in Guatemala, Panama, Rwanda, Chile, Argentina and too many other places.[14] Bert glanced at me.

"Maybe Oxford or Cambridge would be safer," I said.

"Or the Sorbonne," Joëlle spoke up, forever French and always loyal.

"Or the Sorbonne." I agreed. Anywhere except a North American university, and certainly not any Canadian one. "But maybe we can do something to avoid wasting time at Oxford, Cambridge... or the Sorbonne..." I smiled at Joëlle.

"What?" This was Bert.

"Well, we can take a careful look at these rings under a microscope, especially the inside of the rods or wires. If the inside is iron and there's only a thin coating of Austenitic steel on the surface, that will roughly date this thing." I looked up from my peering at interlocked rings to find Joëlle and Bert looking questions at me. "Real steel, steel all the way through, was only made after about AD 1500 and only in Europe – in any quantity, that is. Before that, only a thin coating of steel over an iron core could be made.[15] That coating was what is called Austenitic steel, and it has a different molecular structure from iron. It also a different colour, a kind of slivery-looking grey.

43

There's usually a distinct boundary between the steel coating and the black iron core." "How did they make this steel coating?"

"You don't want to know, Joey."

"Yes, I do."

"The smith would take a white hot blade of iron and plunge it into something that was rich in carbon. Something that had a lot of body fat because fat is mostly carbon and water – carbohydrates, and all that. That combination of hot iron and carbon-rich tissue added carbon molecules to the iron molecules. The ionic differences between the two elements caused a re-arrangement of both sets of molecules into a tight and rigid geometric structure. Austenitic steel. But it could be only a surface coating of steel maybe a millimetre or two thick because the iron cooled relatively quickly to a temperature where the molecular bonding couldn't take place. No one knew the chemistry back then, of course, but they knew that the technique worked."

"When's back then?" Wheeler asked.

"I think that the first known steel coating manufactured by plunging hot iron into living flesh method had been produced about 1500 BC by the Harappa and Mohenjo-daro cultures of the Indus River. They got an Austenitic layer of steel over their iron plough shares that was about two millimetres thick and surprisingly consistent over a fairly large surface. They probably used something pretty large, like a Brahma bull or a Kouprey ox."

"When did this steel-making method get to Europe? Joëlle paused. "And why did you say I wouldn't want to know?"

"I guess this technology travelled fairly rapidly from India to Europe, from smith to smith, but I don't really know any dates. The Assyrians are supposed to have had lots of iron by 600 BC, so they could probably have made this thin steel coating too."

I hesitated, then went on. "I said you wouldn't want to know because they used slaves whenever possible. Generally animals don't have as much body fat as people, but sometimes the smiths and their warrior customers had to make do with a cow or pig they needed to eat anyway."

"Jesus," said Bert.

"But think of the problems of making a long iron blade into steel," I said. "Sword blades were the major product absolutely requiring steel. Use your imagination."

"Impaling," Joëlle said.

"Exactly. And the best steel-making candidate was always a plump or pregnant woman. More body fat. And, maybe, with luck there would be a lot of carbon-rich liquid, amniotic fluid, in her womb. There was, of course, quick... er... access from the forge lengthways up into the body with no bones in the way, so that the blade would remain hotter longer and the resulting steel coating could be thicker."

We were all silent for a while. "Wouldn't a person die instantly from that kind of shock?" Bert asked.

"Hopefully, but not necessarily. I imagine that some slaves lived for hours, hearing their flesh cook and sizzle inside them around the blades."

Joelle looked a little sick and absently began to untie her shirt from around her waist. She stretched into the damp arms of the shirt and wrapped it around her chest before she said anything. We all started walking back to our cars that were parked in the farmer's private drive. "A hideous way to die," Joëlle commented. "Skewered between the legs and then cooked on a hot spit deep inside."

"That's probably why medieval swords had such dramatic names," I said. "Ogier the Dane's sword was supposedly called *Ormstunga*, 'Worm's Tongue' - meaning a pronged dragon's tongue. A dragon's bite was considered both excruciatingly painful and always fatal. Another chap's sword – I forget whose – was named *Skraelingar*, 'The Screamer'. Shrieks extracted from luckless slaves during the blade's birth were deemed to be an indication of its potential prowess in battle."

"I see," said Joëlle very quietly, now possibly imbued with a new or renewed commitment to feminism, the possible domestic repercussions of which I didn't want to contemplate so late in the day. "But how would steel chain mail have been made?" she asked, indicating the Ziploc baggie I still carried.

"I've read," I said, "that the inter-connected iron rings were forged first. Probably in small pieces. Then the iron mail was wrapped just once around an iron bar, heated as white hot as possible, and then shoved into a body cavity. That way the single layer of iron mail would have a chance to turn into steel. This would have to be done many, many times in order to get enough Austenitic steel mail for a complete suit of armour, of course."

"Were there enough slaves for this?"

"Jesus," said Bert.

"In some cultures there were probably enough slaves. But I would think that in medieval Europe, especially in northern Europe, animals must have been mostly used for this process, especially after Christianity had been introduced. Except maybe for sword blades, of course."

Trying to end the dissertation on a more positive note, I said: "I would think that in northern Europe, the body cavity was opened in the normal course of slaughtering an animal's carcass for cooking meat. The meat was just cooked on both sides. From the inside as well as the outside. So, if these links seem to be Austenitic steel – I held up the Ziploc bag again – "then the date should be after about AD 1000 and before 1500. Christianity had been introduced almost all over northern Europe by AD 1000. Fairly good steel was available after 1500."

Soon we'd reached our cars. Within a few minutes we were ourselves on the Queen Elizabeth Way. Bert Wheeler was headed toward Niagara Falls, a fairly short drive. We were headed in the opposite direction, toward Toronto about ninety kilometres or fifty-five miles away. At the QEW cloverleaf, we transmuted into enzymes ourselves. Maybe our investigations, if they resulted in a book, would play its small part in contributing to the Golden Horseshoe's continued commercial wellbeing.

Nonetheless, as we entered into the drive back to Toronto in the gathering dusk I was increasingly pervaded by a sense of disappointment and even frustration. Sure, the past five years since 1998 had steadily yielded the bread-and-butter-fare of true archaeology, the small and non-dramatic finds that allowed a vanished people's lifestyle to be reconstructed with fairly confident accuracy.

But who had ever accused me of being a real archaeologist? By temperament, I was a romantic. A relic hunter, tomb-raider and grave-robber. My spirit has more in common with Heinrich Schliemann than with Carl Blegan. What was so wrong about Schliemann's re-naming his young Greek wife "Helen", dressing her in a hoard of jewellery discovered in the ruins of Troy III and then photographing her wearing them as "Helen's" gorgeous trinkets?

For that matter, I'd like to have discovered that gold death mask at Mycenae and to have telegraphed the Royal Society with Schliemann's dramatic message: "I have gazed into the face of Agamemnon."

On the Niagara Escarpment I had been hoping for an unlikely and dramatic discovery that would have symbolised the last of the Grail Refugees in one haunting, unforgettable and evocative artefact. Just as Heinrich Schliemann had (probably in error) dramatised the ancient Mycenaean Civilisation in just that way with Helen's bogus jewellery and a death mask from Mycenae that had probably immortalised some other Mycenaean ruler, not Agamemnon. I was starting to appreciate the wisdom of Canadian historian, Farley Mowat, when he had complained that "the facts always seem to be getting in the way of the truth." Was it not true that the Grail was much more central to Western civilisation than a bunch of Mycenaean or Achaean overlords? And was it not also true that the Holy Grail had been the inspiration for Western civilisation's earliest literature, far older than *The Iliad* and *The Odyssey*?[6] Why couldn't Bert Wheeler, Joëlle Lauriol or I have come up out of our assigned excavation plots with a complete late fifteenth century sword, hardly rusted at all, that could have been held aloft in triumph against the flaming sunset of a dying August day?

Naturally, I'd always imagined Joëlle in this role.[7] Was not the personification of France's La Liberté always a sword-wielding woman with at least one breast bared? Even Britain's version of La Liberté, Britannia, boasted at least some cleavage. Only America's Columbia had always been depicted fully draped with typical American decency – or prudery. Joëlle, holding a perfect sword in the manner of a crucifix against a blood-hued sunset would have symbolised the Last Stand of the Grail Knights in a poignant, heroic vignette fit for the cover of a book. She could have supplied subliminal intimations of La Liberté, too. That would make a good book cover, especially for a book about the final chapter in the most evocative and romantic episode of Western history. It has been called the greatest story ever told.

Notes to Chapter 1

[1] I have slightly disguised the real location for reasons that will become obvious.

[2] My biography has been in the University of Toronto's *Canadian Who's Who* since 1993 under my original name "de Sackville, Michael".

[3] On March 9, 2004, Professor Alan Wilson of Cardiff University and Professor Baram Blackett from Newcastle University jointly announced that Welsh voyages may have crossed the Atlantic even earlier than the generally accepted expedition of Prince Madoc, the son of Owen Gynedd (King of North Wales), circa AD 1170. According to Wilson and Blackett, there is evidence that an earlier "Madoc", Prince Madoc Morfan of South Wales, made a transatlantic voyage in AD 562. "There are old-style Welsh hill forts around the Ohio River valley that are patterned as they are in Britain," said Wilson. Most readers of this book will know such announcements are nothing new. Indeed, since the 1950s, the evidence has become overwhelming (and rather boring) attesting to all sorts of transatlantic voyages before Columbus.

[4] Illustrated on page 284 of *Grail Knights of North America*.

[5] Illustrated on pages 296 and 297 of *Grail Knights of North America*.

6. The Quebec "gargoyle" is illustrated on page 300 of *Grail Knights of North America*. The carved head from Pennsylvania is illustrated on page 389 of *Grail Knights of North America*.

[7] A Pennsylvania "Baphomet" rock inscription or carving is illustrated on page 388 of *Grail Knights of North America*.

[8] Produced for the Arts & Entertainment Network by Greystone Productions of Los Angeles.

[9] *The Holy Blood and the Holy Grail*, page 236.

[10] I first suggested this on pages 338-358 of *Grail Knights of North America*.

[11] Some readers may be interested that this same Mormon family was intimately involved in the "9/11" so-called terrorist attacks. Further, it may also be interesting that Sen. Orrin Hatch of Utah, in a televised interview with Dan Rather, was the first person to my knowledge (and I was glued to the television all that day) to say that he had "proof" that Osama bin Laden had been responsible for the attacks. This "proof" was never discussed further, or examined, but within a few days it had become "common knowledge" that bin Laden's "Al Qaeda" had masterminded 9/11. The Winter Olympics were held in Salt Lake City in February 2002. How much would Olympics-related travel have assisted terrorist planning in the autumn of 2001?

[12] Illustrated (photo) on page 350 of *Grail Knights of North America*.

[13] *Legacy of Stone*, Eastendbooks, 1998.

[14] This usage seems to have come from the Spanish *desaparecidos* meaning "the disappeared" which was applied to those who vanished through massacre or imprisonment during the civil war in Guatemala 1962-1996.

[15] Fisher, Douglas Alan, *Steel, from the Iron Age to the Space Age*, Harper, 1967.

[16] The Swiss Egyptologist Marthe Chambrun-Ruspoli in her *L'épervier divin* ("The Divine Falcon"), argues convincingly (in my opinion) that the famous Egyptian "Books of the Dead" deal with the so-called "Osirian Religion" of Osiris, Isis and their son Horus. This first "Holy Family" became the basis of the Holy Grail legend as well as the template for Joseph, Mary and Jesus in the much later New Testament. Since Egyptian "Books of the Dead" date from at least 3600 BC and the Trojan War traditionally took place about 1225 BC but Homer is supposed to have lived about 800 BC, then this Holy Grail tradition actually ranks as the earliest Western literature. It is about 2,800 years older than *The Odyssey* and *Iliad*.

[17] For some years, about ten to fifteen, I've gradually developed the notion through observation that women's breasts are some kind of "social sensory organs." As most of my readers know, I have a fair amount of zoological and anthropological training (under Dr. Carlton Coon, among others). It would make sense, around a tribal fire, for women's breasts to be able to "pick up" and transmit the "social vibes" of the group, especially of possibly aggressive males (and females) in the group. I have even conducted some "semi-scientific" research on this idea using Duke University's card system. A topless woman seeing a card and then "sending the image" to another topless woman who "receives" the symbol mentally, results in scores higher than chance. And I've tried all combinations of topless sender, topless receiver, various symbols and more complex messages. The size of the breast doesn't seem to matter so much (although bigger breasts seem to "receive" a bit better), but what really *does* matter seems to be the nipple. Big nipples with a

definite teat work better than "little girl"-type nipples. Redheads (with redder nipples) seem to work better than other skin complexions. I think this may be the source of "women's intuition" and maybe also the origin of some Wiccan lore. *This has helped me to find artefacts* because some of my women friends could walk over terrain and tell me where they felt "emotional vibes" -- a battle, or much sadness or misery. And where any human tragedy happens, you're likely to find artefacts. The woman doesn't have to be completely topless, but the breasts can only be covered by a thin layer of non-synthetic material. But you do get more definite "vibes" with bare breasts. In 1995, before I met Joëlle in 1997, I went to the Escarpment with a tall (taller than me), biggish-breasted redheaded woman named Zoë N. (from Nova Scotia), the wife of a good friend of mine, Bob Hall, a special effects artist in the film business. Bob had been working on a film shoot for six solid weeks, night and day, and Zoë was bored stiff and had hardly seen him. So I invited her for a day trip on the Escarpment to give her something to do. This area had always intrigued me because it just looked "lived in" by Europeans for a long time. It was at the Welland Feeder Canal that Zoë got such strong vibes of sadness that she began to cry. I told her then what I suspected (*Swords at Sunset*) about the area. And I also told her what I suspected about breasts and why, perhaps, she had started crying. Being an uninhibited and Bohemian girl, Zoë took off her bra and held her T-shirt clear of her nipples and walked all around this part of the canal banks. She pinpointed a "grave" and I dug. I did not find a burial, but I found a half-dozen arrowheads around a rusted iron "battle-axe" blade. Several of these "battle-axe-looking" blades have been found in the Escarpment area, the last about 15 years ago in Stony Creek. You read about these discoveries every few years or so. Since the experience with Zoë, I've always taken a woman along to Escarpment areas, and preferably a woman who was somewhat "exhibitionist" (that's a man's term). I think women were and are designed to go topless because they get valuable information that way, and "clothing them decently" according to Judaic-based religions is a purposeful attempt to blunt their sensory input, their birthright. Now, researching with Joëlle on the Escarpment, there was never any problem (in the summer) because of her topless proclivities. And I think that's one of the reasons we found so many artefacts. I knew where to go, generally, by the "lay of the land" and the history I had worked out, and Joëlle could then pinpoint where to dig. Now, she may have been correct 100% of the time for all I know, but we found some anomalous artefact about 30%-50% of the time. This is better, much better, than the usual archaeological dig. This is why I also wanted to include a semi-nude photo of Joëlle in Chapter 1 of *Swords at Sunset*. Besides "titillation" (pun intended) her proclivities contributed materially to our success! **I think that a book about finding old artefacts, combined with tasteful photos of topless researchers and Wiccan commentary, would probably be a bestseller in itself. Aside from that, some very valuable additional evidence of pre-colonial Europeans on the Escarpment might be found.** Now the "Cooley" site at Ancaster, Ontario (near Hamilton) was a known early and small colonial cemetery where archaeologists expected to find 6-12 interments. Instead, over 100 were found. The archaeologists have clammed up, but it is possible that some of the "extra" bodies may have been pre-colonial Europeans. Early colonial settlers may have accidentally discovered this cemetery and used it themselves. About 20-30 years ago, it seems to me, Elaine Morgan wrote a book called *The Descent of Woman*. She basically took Sir Alastair Hardy's Oxford theory of human evolution and applied it to the evolution of women only. It was very popular in some feminist and New Age circles, but physical anthropologists (both male and female) were either amused or outraged by it. Although it is simply a fact that only human females among the primates (or *any* mammals) have breasts that protrude all year around and not just when nursing, Elaine Morgan denied this. She didn't like the current anthropological explanation that human female breasts had developed as "sexual aggression-displacement mechanisms" in addition, of course, as a means of nurturing babies. Morgan went on to assert that manatees also had human-like breasts. They do not. Morgan would have been better off to have met me and talked with me. Although human female breasts are undoubtedly *both* "sexual aggression-displacement mechanisms" *and* "secondary sexual attractants" (and mammary glands), I think they are *also* and perhaps more significantly for human evolution some sort of "social sensory organs." I find it odd that human female breasts must have developed rather suddenly, and then in response to a fairly large leap in intelligence that characterized the transition between Australopithecines (thought to be like Chimpanzees – no breasts) and true "humans", although very primitive humans. I call these "not quite human" or "very primitive human" creatures "Australo-homo-pithecines," and there were apparently many different kinds of them. On some, like the *Sedepa* described from Sumatra, the females are reported to have small but definite breasts. And this *Sedepa* is only on the very barest threshold of being fully "human." All "modern humans" known to be living today, even groups so primitive as the Ulele pygmies of the Congo and the *hantu Sakai* of former Malaysia, have definite female breasts. They also all have at least a rudimentary form of *religion._*To me, there's nothing remotely "mystical" or "spiritual" about religion. Religion has a biological and evolutionary function. It is to assert the conception of "territory in the dimension of time" as a valid human environment to be inhabited and "exploited", but this all-important concept is really what separates us from other "animals." *Human breasts seem to have developed in step with the conception of religion*. This is because of the higher level of aggression required of humans by yet *another* kind of "territory" (in addition to real territory and the social territory of dominance) to be inhabited, defended and asserted. Females, women, above all had to be able to assess the stage of this higher level of aggression at any given time and to decide whether it posed an immediate threat to themselves and their children. I have some reproducible evidence for this opinion. I would like to explore this possibility, get more indisputable evidence of it, and do a book about it. I would suggest reading *Esau's Empire II* on my website, "The Psychobiology of Religion". It is basically the gist of my first book, *The Cronos Complex*. This book earned me several Nobel Prize nominations and may well win it some day.

2

The Greatest Story Ever Told

The greatest story ever told in the Western world is usually regarded as the drama surrounding the nativity, life and sacrifice of Jesus Christ.

At least, Hollywood produced an epic film with that title. The real problem is *which* story of the advent and life of Jesus Christ should we use? For that matter, which story can we trust?

Most modern Christians have no problem. They use the King James Version of the New Testament and most modern Christians recite the Nicean Creed that confirms the basic events related in the New Testament as facts that they *must* believe if they are to be considered true Christians. I have heard some modern televangelists thump the King James Bible and intone sincerely and gravely to the TV audience: "This bible was good enough for Jesus and it's good enough for me."

That is an interesting statement in view of the fact that the first version of the New Testament, called "Marcion's Canon" by biblical scholars, wasn't codified until a century and a half after the scriptural death of Jesus. The King James translation of the original Greek, Aramaic and Hebrew renditions of the story was made a millennium and a half after that.

Jesus could never have read the present canonical New Testament. This becomes quite obvious with just a bit of thought. The New Testament consists of four individual remembrances of his own life and death, plus some letters that offer interpretations of what his message meant. Jesus was too harried to have read accounts of his own teaching during his brief ministry and he certainly couldn't have read them later.

The truth of the matter is that very earliest Christians, those closest in time to the actual events, did not believe in the New Testament story. It didn't yet exist. In fact, they seem not to have known what to believe.

Had Jesus been just a man? Had he been a god? Had he been *the* God? Had he been the "Son of God"?

Some people were not even sure that any *God* was involved. Many early Christians believed in the great *Goddess*, and believed that Jesus

51

had been *her* Son. Although this notion may seem particularly blasphemous today, modern Christians might ask why the "Holy Ghost" or Divine Spirit is female in gender, not male.

This isn't so apparent in the English-language King James Bible, but in Latin and all the Romance languages, the two genders are differentiated by different endings on the respective words. Masculine Latin words end in "-us" and modern Romance-language masculine words end in "-o".

Feminine Latin and Romance words mostly end in "-a" or the French "-é", which re-creates and emphasises the original Latin "long 'a'" sound. A good example is the abstract noun "Liberty" – *La Liberté*, which we have already had reason to note. Most abstract nouns in all Indo-European languages, including English, are feminine although English has simply lost almost all its original inflexions.

This loss of gender-revealing inflexions, or word endings, is evident from the English word "ship", for example. It was once feminine in gender and so ships are still referred to as "she" even though in modern English there are no word-endings, or inflexions, to indicate this.

Thus, the "Holy Ghost" in Latin is *Sancta Sophia* – feminine. Roman Catholics, especially in Ireland and around the Mediterranean coasts and islands, still call Virgin Mary the "Mother of God" which is surely an odd way of expressing the totality of the situation described in the New Testament. Unless, that is, "Mother of God" is a cherished phrase referring to the beloved Great Goddess of times long before the first century of the so-called "Christian Era". And unless it was *Her* divine spirit that filled Jesus, making him more than an ordinary man.

In short, there were early Christians who believed in nearly every conceivable interpretation of Jesus' life and nature, and they generally had some written record to support their point of view.

All this changed when Constantine the Great (AD 274 or AD 288 to AD 337) became the sole Emperor of Rome in AD 312 after defeating several rival claimants. Constantine was a believer in Mithras during most of his life, but he at least tolerated Christianity. Most of his Imperial predecessors had persecuted Christians.

Constantine convened, or at least he endorsed, the Council of Nicea in AD 325 and this was when an "orthodox" form of Christianity was first codified. Being a Roman Emperor himself, Constantine either had genuine sympathy for, or was influenced by, the Bishops of Rome and their view of what a true Christian should believe and had to believe.

More probably, Constantine really had no deep Christian convictions of his own – his coins were struck with a depiction of Sol Invictus ("Invincible Sun"), the symbol of Mithras worship. But, as a Roman Emperor, and one who had had to contend with three other rivals, he valued order, authority and enforced obedience to a well-defined and solidly structured hierarchy.

There were dissident voices raised at the Council of Nicea, but they were quelled by sheer Roman power, the soldiers that Constantine had provided, ostensibly for security. The "Nicean Creed", of course, came out of this Council. Every other dissenting Christian viewpoint instantly became a heresy after the Council of Nicea. As America's controversial and outspoken Episcopalian Bishop of Newark, New Jersey, John Spong, has said: "Orthodoxy is orthodoxy because it won, not because it is true."[1]

Ironically, therefore, it came to pass that the hated Romans of the New Testament became, through the Church of Rome, the nominal leaders of Christianity.

Nonetheless, even with the Roman Empire's protection, Nicean orthodoxy had a difficult time becoming dominant outside the immediate vicinity of Rome. This was because the Roman Empire itself was crumbling under the weight of both its own corruption and invasion by barbarians called Visigoths, Ostrogoths, Vandals and Lombards. These barbarians, in turn, frightened Europe's Celtic and Teutonic peoples into desperate migrations.

But we now know that the truly basic cause of all these migrations into Europe, and then the resulting domino-effect migrations by people already within Europe, was a numerous and ferocious tribe of steppe people called Huns.

They had come from the Caucasus Mountains and were representatives of an ancient and once much more widespread European Ice Age population called "Neanderthals" by modern physical anthropologists. Under the pressure of more numerous people coming into Europe from the Atlantic Coast and North Africa, people usually called "Cro-Magnons" by anthropologists; these Neanderthals had retreated into and settled the higher elevations. The cold climate to which they had adapted lingered longer in mountainous regions.

But because the Caucasus Mountains and other mountainous regions around the Black Sea could support only a limited number of people, their excess population spread out onto the steppes beyond the foothills of these mountains. This was lush territory for both herdsmen and agriculturists, as humanity evolved out of the Palaeolithic ("Old Stone

Age", a purely hunting-gathering culture) and into the "Neolithic" ("New Stone Age", an increasingly agricultural human economy). The mountains, foothills and steppes of the Caucasus and related mountains tended to encourage cycles of rapid population growth and expansion, separated by quiet centuries until the population overflowed again.

The Huns were first described by Greek writers in AD 272 as inhabiting the area where the Volga River flows into the Caspian Sea. The Greeks had compiled their reports from refugee Visigoths who were fleeing from the Huns. These Visigoths had suddenly appeared in force in northern Greece, that is, in Thrace and Macedonia. Not much was known about these Huns except for Visigothic stories about their ferocity so savage and their atrocities so unspeakable that it was best not even to utter their name.

This time of history at and near the end of Rome's dominion is often called the "Dark Ages" or "The Migrations of Peoples". Pushed ultimately by the Huns, Teutonic Angles, Saxons and Jutes crossed the North Sea and began invading the British Isles by about AD 400. Sicambrian Franks, who were originally settled in Austria along the Danube, were pushed into modern France – then known as Gaul – as of about AD 350 and by AD 400 had reached the English Channel.[2]

In an attempt to save itself and to concentrate its defensive strength, Rome abandoned fringe provinces like Britain and recalled its legions home. Rome even recalled troops from Gaul, virtually next door to Italy. But the end was near. Visigoths under the leadership of their High King, Alaric, sacked Rome in AD 410. The Roman Empire, which had once ruled much of Europe and the entire coast all around the Mediterranean Sea, did not even control the city of Rome itself after AD 410. The Roman Empire had ended.[3]

Then, like a long-dreaded nightmare, the Huns themselves under their High King, Attila, arrived in Western Europe in AD 449. Attila spared Rome, in romantic myth because he was offered the Roman princess Honoria in marriage, but mainly and simply because Rome was no longer worth the trouble of taking.

A desperate coalition of Celtic, Teutonic, Roman and Visigothic forces met and somewhat miraculously defeated Attila at the Battle of Chalons in AD 451, about 140 miles from Paris, in France. After their defeat, the Huns retreated back through Europe along much the same route they had used for invasion. Attila died two years later, in AD 453, at his capital of Kazaran-Itil near the mouth of the Volga.

By about AD 455 to AD 500, Vandals had over-run the remaining pockets of Greco-Roman civilisation in North Africa. By AD 550 to

AD 600, the Lombards had taken most of Italy except the immediate vicinity of Rome itself. The Eternal City was still being defended by mostly Visigothic princes and warlords who had become "Romans" by courtesy.

In my first Grail book, *Holy Grail Across the Atlantic*, I had begun with a chapter called "The Christmas King of Camelot" about King Arthur's lifelong struggle to rally the remnant of Romano-Celtic Britain against the incursions of the Angles, Saxons and Jutes. I did this because King Arthur is known to almost everyone in the English-speaking world. Everyone also knows that he supposedly had some connection with the "Holy Grail". King Arthur therefore provided a convenient character with which to introduce an unfamiliar story.

But for all Arthur's courage and the aura of romance that still clothes him, his faithless wife Guinevere, Lancelot and Camelot in the shimmering garments of beloved and poignant legend, Arthur's struggle was merely a foredoomed military action in a geopolitical backwater.

Swords at Sunset must begin to introduce a larger view of the Holy Grail. This forces me to paint on a canvas that is larger than Arthur's Britain and even larger than medieval France. Indeed, the entire picture must extend all the way to western India, encompassing the Caucasus Mountains particularly, but also the directly contiguous mountain ranges of the Elburz, Zagros, Hindu Kush and Pamirs. As we will see, the Holy Grail heresy was the dominant belief in much of Europe and some of the Middle East. It certainly affected all of Christendom. And it still does. *Swords at Sunset* must therefore take a much wider view of Western religion in order to show what this great religious struggle has been, and still is, all about.

But this wider view is also one permitting less detail. Readers are referred to *Holy Grail Across the Atlantic* and *Grail Knights of North America* for a closer look at the myths, legends, traditions and stories that allow history to nurture the heart as well as challenge the mind. *Swords at Sunset* cannot afford that luxury.

Around the year AD 622, the Vandals were reinvigorated by the emergence of a new religion that included some aspects of the Old Testament and the New Testament, but also claimed new revelations about God's nature and divine expectations from "His" final Prophet – Mohammed.

The modern Western scholar, H.A.R. Gibb, has shown in various writings that many of the Koran's Suras (Chapters) of Mohammed's so-called "Medina Period" seem actually to have been written down by Jewish scribes. They did not hesitate to write the Old Testament's Jewish patriarchs into the Koran and to imbue the Koran with Judaic ideas of God's injunctions. Gibb has also demonstrated some influence of Syriac Christianity on the Koran. Therefore, fundamentalist or "orthodox" Islam – or so-called "Koranic Islam" – might better and more accurately be termed "Judeo-Islam".

Under Islam or "Judeo-Islam", the Vandalised people of the southern Middle East and North Africa found an astonishing new vitality. As "Arabs", "Berbers" and "Moors" they expanded toward western India, including modern Pakistan and large portions of the Indian Ocean, and completed their conquest of North Africa to the Atlantic Coast at Morocco.

Although *Swords at Sunset* cannot deal with Islam in the detail it deserves, it is very much worth noting that the further Islam was taken from the Caucasus Mountain homeland of its Vandalised inventors, the less fundamentalist or strictly "Koranic" it became. The Moslems of the southern Sahara in African Mali, and the Moslems around the Indian Ocean (modern Indonesia and Malaysia), were and are much less fanatical and fundamentalist than "Judeo-Moslems" of the Middle East. And this more or less parallels a similar situation with orthodox Judeo-Christianity. We will have occasion to return to this fascinating and important observation in the final chapter.

In AD 711, the Berber Chieftain, Tarik, crossed the Straits of Gibraltar and invaded Spain and Portugal that had formerly been held by Rome since the time of Julius Caesar. But, because Rome had fallen to the Barbarians 301 years earlier, Tarik met the local Visigoths' more-or-less Christian King, Roderick II, and defeated him.

Within a decade these North Africans, usually called simply "Moors" by Europeans because of their dark skins, had crossed the Pyrénées into what is now France. The Moorish army under Abd-er-Rahman was defeated and stopped by Charles Martel at the Battle of Poitiers, near modern Tours in southern France, in the year AD 732. But the Moors always threatened to cross the Pyrénées again and France struggled against the onslaught of Islam for another four and a half centuries.

During these Dark Ages after the fall of Rome, thousands of historical records were lost because many of the few existing libraries had been sacked by barbarians. Vandals, for example, used the pages of priceless ancient manuscripts for fuelling their cooking fires. Our word "vandalism" still means ignorant and wanton destruction.

Social cohesion and the bonding memory of shared history were lost all over Europe and the Mediterranean world. This made it somewhat easier for the Church of Rome to offer a sense of salvation from despair

– which relief, of course, went hand in hand with the imposition of Nicean orthodoxy based on the New Testament. That was the up side for orthodox Christianity. But the down side of the Dark Ages for the Church of Rome was more serious.

There had simply not been sufficient time for Christian heretics to be rooted out of Europe before pagan barbarians had confused the issue by inundating Europe with thousands of new people who believed in all sorts of gods and goddesses. And, in some cases at least, early Christian beliefs were closer to some barbarian beliefs than they were to the Roman Church's New Testament orthodoxy. The Roman Church was forced to pick and choose its most dangerous rivals very carefully.

Ordinary pagans didn't bother the Roman Church unduly. Some Christian celebrations were made to coincide, roughly, with some established pagan celebrations and the Roman Church knew very well that sooner or later the simple "pagans in the fields" would gradually become "acceptable" orthodox Christians through ingrained habit.

But heresies – that is to say, variations of Christianity itself – were much worse for the Church of Rome than mere paganism. Heresies called for greater subtlety in negotiation or outright confrontation. For example, the long-established Celtic Church of Ireland, Scotland, parts of England and parts of France could not be allowed to co-exist with the Church of Rome. Celtic Church priests were allowed to marry, had different robes, tonsures, dogma and dates for religious celebrations than Rome. The Celtic Church represented a cohesive and visible Christian alternative to orthodoxy, not mere pagan loyalty to old gods and goddesses who were rapidly being transformed into Christian saints anyway.

Worse, the Celtic Church possessed documents, and had founded some of its practices upon them, that referred to a Saviour named "Yesu" who had lived long before the first century – and he had not lived in Palestine, either.

The Synod of Whitby in AD 664 peacefully settled the outstanding disagreements in favour of the Roman Church in a debate adjudicated by English nobles. The major reason for the victory of Rome was not so much the doctrinal truth or otherwise of the Celtic Church's departures from Nicean orthodoxy. The major consideration, as the *Catholic Encyclopedia* freely admits, was that the Celtic Church – like most other early Christian congregations – was a loosely organised community of believers who took little part in geopolitical events of the day.

But English nobles wanted an authoritarian Church that could and would actively encourage the common peoples' allegiance and loyalty to the prevailing secular powers, that is, themselves. The Roman Church had long before learned this valuable lesson from Constantine's own motivations and concerns, had made organisation its strong suit and had thus found favour with the local feudal nobility that had everywhere replaced Rome's long-gone Empire in Europe.

The Celtic Church's documents referring to ancient "Yesu" did not figure in the debate at Whitby, as it turned out, and no one knows – at least, it was never recorded – what became of these writings.

Meanwhile, during the four centuries between the Crucifixion and the fall of Rome, what was to become the most dangerous heresy of all was quietly gaining adherents in southern France.

It took deepest root along that Garonne River corridor that I had previously earmarked for my golden years research. The heresy flourished along major tributaries of the Garonne, too, like the Tarn River that reaches into Provence almost to the mouth of the Rhône River near Marseilles. This was the unorthodox form of Christianity that was to become known as the "Holy Grail".

Simply put, some early Christians believed that Jesus had been an ordinary man, although one filled with divine essence. And, as an ordinary man, Jesus had been married. The wife of Jesus had been Mary Magdalene of the New Testament's account of his life and Ministry. They had had children that survived to grow up and marry into European nobility and royalty. This "Holy Bloodline" was the "Holy Grail".

The "Holy Grail" was a cup, chalice or vase only in a symbolic or poetic sense. It was really a human lineage that "contained" the Holy Blood. The phrase "Holy Grail" first appears in southern French poetry as the words "*Saint Graal*". But this is only a pun on two much more common French words with similar pronunciation, *Sang Réal* or "Holy Blood."

This secret "holy" lineage had been known for centuries after the Crucifixion among some of the noble and royal families of southern France who had joined with it in marriage. The "L'Auriol" ("Halo") family, one living representative of which we have already seen a great deal of... or maybe "encountered" would be a better word... was just one of many bloodlines boasting a degree of relationship to Jesus and Mary Magdalene.

But the Lauriols and many other families kept their momentous secret from the general public for almost two thousand years.

The Grail became a much more open secret in post-war France because various scions of the Holy Lineage had played a leading part in the World War II Resistance, the Free French and the Liberation. They were heroes, and post-war France desperately needed heroes. The more that journalists and writers dug relentlessly into the past histories of their wartime subjects, the more an unbelievable story emerged. Among these heroes were people like Pierre Plantard de Saint-Clair (i.e. "Sinclair"), Alain Poher and Charles de Gaulle. Roland Lauriol had fought in Algeria. And, at some point, or so it appeared, the past of all these people merged into the "Holy Blood". During the 1950s and early 1960s, the secret of the Holy Grail started to become revealed, at least for French-language readers of books like *Le Trésor Maudit* or *La Race Fabuleuse* and magazines like *Le Charivari*.

Finally, the story became available to the English-speaking world when a BBC writer-producer named Henry Lincoln happened to spend his 1960 vacation in southern France. Lincoln picked up a popular paperback, *Le Trésor Maudit* (*"The Accursed Treasure"*) by Gérard de Sède, to read for light entertainment. Instead of the frothy summertime diversion he had expected, Henry Lincoln was stunned. Lincoln spent the next twenty years researching what Gérard de Sède had asserted in that book and Lincoln also read and checked out many other sources.

Lincoln then teamed up with writers Richard Leigh and Michael Baigent to produce the smash international bestseller *The Holy Blood and the Holy Grail* in 1982. This book reprinted some genealogies, including those of the "L'Auriols", purporting to trace a lineage from Jesus and Mary Magdalene.

Since the publication of *The Holy Blood and the Holy Grail*, which was based largely on the work of French-language writers Jean-Marie Angébert, Fernand Neil, Maurice Magre and Gérard de Sède, there has been a spate of English-language books purporting to flesh out the details of the Holy Grail story.

Since 1982, readers have seen the publication of *The Tomb of God, The Holy Place, The Arcadian Cipher, The Bloodline of the Holy Grail, King Arthur, The Woman with the Alabaster Jar, The Sword and the Grail, The Labyrinth of the Grail* and many more Grail-related books. To be frank, in my view many of these books have really been non-books, mere band-wagoneering on the Grail Craze without adding anything substantial and demonstrable to the story of the Holy Grail.

But maybe people in glass houses shouldn't throw stones. Some critics, especially academics, have said the very same thing about my *Holy Grail Across the Atlantic* and *Grail Knights of North America*.

It can only be said in my defence that I have been in contact with at least one of the original authors of *The Holy Blood and the Holy Grail*, Michael Baigent. And Baigent vehemently blamed his own obtuseness for missing clues published *in his own book* that there was a genuine North American chapter of the Holy Grail story. Baigent therefore allowed me to reprint some of his photos in my *Holy Grail Across the Atlantic* manuscript even though at that time, 1986, we were both in competition for the same publisher, Jonathan Cape of London.

Baigent has never extended this courtesy to any other book author that I know of, and certainly not for free. Michael Baigent not only refused to charge any fee for these photos, but he supplied top-quality glossies at no cost. When he sent the photos, Baigent also suggested in his covering letter that he and I should collaborate on a book about Templar cartographers on Mallorca.

I like to think that my books have been genuine efforts to uncover the Holy Grail's adventures in North America, but you the reader must be the judge.

Anyway, on with the story. And the story goes that after the Crucifixion of Jesus, Mary Magdalene, the Virgin Mary and Joseph of Arimathaea were rounded up by Jewish authorities in the Holy Land and set adrift in a small boat. Here's the legend as recounted by Katherine Esty, author of *The Gypsies: Wanderers in Time*:

> Pilgrimages are nothing new to the Gypsies, of course... For the last seventy-five years, though, *the* Gypsy pilgrimage has been to Les Saintes Maries. There is a widely known Gypsy legend which explains both the name of the village and why it is a pilgrimage spot. According to legend, after the death of Jesus, the Jews gathered together all those closest to Jesus, forced them into a small boat – without oars, sails, food or water – and pushed them out to sea. Death seemed certain for this pious crew... but gentle winds pushed them westwards until they approached the shores of the Rhône delta. Black Sara, Queen of the local tribe of Gypsies, swam out to guide them in. The Marys converted her to Christianity at once and she spent the rest of her life helping the saints. Traditionally, the pilgrimage centred around the showing of the relics, the bones of the two Marys.[4]

This legend exists in literally hundreds of variations that refer to almost as many locations. There are even fairly exact southern French word-for-word accounts of sermons that "the Marys" gave in order to convert local people to Christianity.

There is an actual historical circumstance that argues strongly that the closest of Jesus' relatives would have ended up in southern France in the area around Marseilles. The region was called Septimania in Roman times because it had been set aside as a retirement colony for veterans of the Seventh Legion. Septimania was an established place of exile for persons who were out of favour with the Empire for one reason or another, but had not committed any capital offence.

Pontius Pilate, prominent in the New Testament, of course, was exiled to Septimania because of his bungling of the "Jesus Affair" under pressure of the Jewish Sanhedrin.[5] It isn't at all unlikely that "the Marys", Joseph of Arimathaea and any of Jesus' offspring would have ended up in the same convenient place. Loyal veterans of the Seventh Legion in Septimania could keep an eye on them.

And it was also protective custody of a sort because these people were certainly *persona non grata* among the Jews of Palestine. The Romans wanted no part of any further avoidable incidents in Judea because they already had more than enough trouble there. So, in this instance we don't have to blame the Jews for casting the "pious crew" adrift. They were much more probably taken from Palestine to Marseilles, just like Pilate himself, by Imperial decree.

Barbara Thiering, an Australian theologian, has scoured obscure sources and has concluded that at least one daughter was born of Jesus and Mary Magdalene in the Holy Land, or more probably in Alexandria. This girl's name was Tamar ("Palm Tree" in both Hebrew and Egyptian). Alexandria would also have made a more probable port of embarkation for Marseilles than Jaffa in Palestine because of its much greater volume of shipping.

Thiering cites evidence for another daughter and a son born to Jesus and Mary Magdalene. Other authorities cite two sons and one daughter.

However many children of Jesus and Mary Magdalene there really were – and no indisputable proof for *any* children has been made publicly available so far – it would have been easy for them to have ended up in southern France for reasons already discussed.

And now we immediately run into a problem in tracing the Holy Blood: Glastonbury in England has a rival tradition, backed by some hard evidence that Joseph of Arimathaea came to Glastonbury with the "Holy Grail" and founded the first Church in all Christendom there about AD 40. I have covered the Glastonbury legends in some detail, and illustrated *Holy Grail Across the Atlantic* with some photos I'd taken in Glastonbury in 1983.[6] But interested readers can also consult *The Quest for Arthur's Britain* (edited by Geoffrey Ashe)[1] and several other books.

The most probable explanation is that the Holy Blood was established in both places, initially in southern France, but that Joseph of Arimathaea then travelled on to Glastonbury with one or more of the "Holy Children" in order to find an even safer refuge. Southern France, with its huge seaport of Marseilles and its large Jewish community, wasn't safe for Jesus' relatives and associates. There might be possible future changes in Roman policies and certainly the Holy Bloodline was not safe in the Marseilles area from the implacable constancy of Jewish antipathy.

Glastonbury, on the other hand, was on the very western fringe of Roman civilisation and could have had no large Jewish community. In Glastonbury, then, the Holy Grail survived to intermarry into the existing Romano-Celtic nobility and royalty. About four hundred years later, when Rome abandoned Britain under the mounting pressure of barbarian incursions all around the Empire, these Holy Blood-enhanced families of Romano-Celtic nobility and royalty undertook the task of protecting what they could of Britain from invasions by Angles, Saxons and Jutes. This effort culminated in King Arthur, lasted for about fifty years while the light of Camelot blazed defiance in the growing darkness and was finally extinguished beneath the inundation of "Saxons".

It is recorded, however, that some effort was made to evacuate the Holy Grail to "Armorica" (sometimes written "Amorica"), to present Brittany. This was the territory of the Sicambrian Franks, soon to known as "Merovingians". In fact, there is hard archaeological evidence from Britain's Cadbury Hill, the almost undoubted site of Camelot, in the form of Merovingian glass shards that Arthurians and Merovingians had already negotiated defensive and possibly marital pacts.

The end of Arthurian Britain is usually put at the year AD 542. This was the ultimate Battle of Camlann in which Arthur's son, Mordred or Medraut, allied himself with Saxons in order to usurp Arthur's throne in Camelot. According to tradition, the Battle of Camlann was a bloody draw. Arthur succeeded in killing his traitorous son Mordred, but was fatally wounded himself. Sir Kay, Sir Gawain, Sir Galahad and Sir Bedivere (i.e. Celtic "Bedwyr", sometimes identified with Lancelot) also fell at Camlann.

As Geoffrey of Monmouth told it in his *Historia regnum Britanniae* (*"The History of the Kings of Britain"*):

Even the renowned king Arthur himself was wounded deadly and borne thence to the island of Avalon for the healing of his wounds, where he gave up the crown to his kinsman, Constantine, son of Cador in AD 542.[7]

King Mark of Cornwall fought for several decades more in an attempt to keep his domain free of Saxons. But "Arthurian Britain" was finished and to get some aid and assistance, King Mark tried to ally himself with the High King of Ireland by arranging a marriage with the king's daughter, Iseult or Isold, naturally the most beautiful woman in Ireland. And (naturally), King Mark made the mistake of sending his son (or nephew) and most handsome and proven warrior, Prince Tristram, to collect the beautiful Irish princess and to escort her home. No one can be very surprised that King Mark waited a long time for Tristram's ship. It never arrived in Cornwall.

The Romance of Tristram and Iseult informs us, however, that although they were consumed by passion for each other at first sight, both Tristram and Iseult were determined to keep their various vows. Unfortunately for the couple's virtue, however, there happened to be a flask of love potion on board that had been intended as a wedding present pick-me-up for ageing King Mark. Naturally they were forced, against their wills, to drink from it when they ran out of water at sea. Under the circumstances, the lovers decided that it was more politic, and certainly safer, to head for Armorica rather than Cornwall.

From scraps of Romances like this, we get a blurred picture of what went on after Arthur failed in Britain. It is interesting that a variant spelling of Armorica is *Amorica,* which, if it means anything, could mean roughly "the land of lovers" in Latin. Tristram is also described in several versions of the story as a Prince of "Lyonesse", not of Cornwall. For that matter, Arthur's own father, Uther Pendragon, was also styled High King of Lyonesse rather than Britain (in some sources) and King Mark of Cornwall is sometimes presented as a King of Lyonesse too.

In *Holy Grail Across the Atlantic*, and emphasised strongly in *Grail Knights of North America*, I suggested that some researcher simply has to look deeply into this matter of Lyonesse. Traditionally, Lyonesse was a group of fairly large islands that were once scattered between modern Cornwall and modern Brittany. We know that such islands once existed because some of them sank as late as the seventh and eighth centuries and the events were recorded. Some still existing islands seem to be remnants of Lyonesse that never subsided, like the Scilly Isles off Cornwall and the islands of Hoedic and Belle Isle off Brittany. Some shallow fishing banks in the area are obviously islands that did sink, but as yet not very deeply.

Lyonesse is more than plausible. From a geological point of view, the English Channel is just the post-glacial mouth of the Rhine River. When the Rhine started to flow at the end of the last "Ice Age" about 11,500 BC, and its first flow was a giant spate, a great deal of glacial detritus formed islands in the Rhine's estuary or "delta". These islands and this detritus were Lyonesse. It was gradually washed away by the fact that the "Ice Age" glaciers began to melt and this raised the world's sea level by some three hundred feet over the next six thousand years by about 5600 BC. Also, the Gulf Stream began to flow all the way to Northwest Europe at the end of the "Ice Age" and it, combined with the ever-increasing sea level contributed to the progressive eroding away of Lyonesse.

Lyonesse as it still existed just before and after the Christian Era was never, apparently, conquered by the Romans. Lyonesse isn't mentioned in Caesar's *Gallic Wars*. Lyonesse would therefore have been a perfect location for an independent Celtic kingdom, a better refuge for Joseph of Arimathaea and his "Holy Grail" than Glastonbury and a strategic place from which to oppose Angles, Saxons and Jutes.

There is a rather dubious medieval map purporting to be a map of the Kingdom of Lyonesse. It shows the largest island labelled "Avvalon", which is suggestive, to say the least. Is it possible that names like Avalon and Caer Sidi, the Celtic name for Glastonbury, were originally places in Lyonesse and whose names were transplanted to places in Britain and Brittany after Lyonesse mostly sank?[8]

So, Romances like *Tristram and Iseult* may reflect larger geopolitical and geological events that were encapsulated or personalised in a love story. The word "Romance", by the way, is still with us and usually refers to a wistful and always threatened love. The word comes from the word "Rome" and we see just how much emotional and cultural impact the fall of Rome still has on our modern society.

Sometime around the year AD 470 or so, or probably during the early reign of Arthur's father Uther Pendragon across the Channel in Britain, a Sicambrian Frankish king named Merovée married a mysterious woman. She was described as a "sea creature". No one really knows what this means, at least the meaning has never been publicly recorded for historians.[9]

But because the name Mary means "of the sea" and the first Christian symbol was "the sign of the fish", Grail researchers have assumed that this sea creature who enhanced the Frankish kingship was a poetic way of referring to a descendant of Jesus and Mary Magdalene. We do not know whether this woman came from the Holy Grail that Joseph of Arimathaea took to Glastonbury, or whether she descended from the Holy Bloodline that had been established in southern France.

In any event, whoever she really was, this bride bequeathed such prestige to this obscure Frankish king that Merovée's dynasty thereafter became known as "Merovingians". These Merovingians ruled most of France, through two and sometimes three nominally separate kingdoms, for slightly less than three hundred years, from about AD 470 until AD 754. To commemorate their descent from this "sea creature", the Merovingians adorned their battle-banners with an amphibious frog, of all things. This is possibly why the French are sometimes, and less than politely, called "frogs" in Anglo-Saxon slang to this day.

After the fall of Rome in AD 410, the Roman Church looked desperately around for a cohesive military power with which it could ally itself. Around AD 470, the Merovingians emerged as that power. The problem: Most of these Sicambrian Franks, or Merovingians, were still pagans. But they were not barbarians. Some had been Roman citizens and Rome had even had several Sicambrian consuls in its recent history. Being somewhat literate in Latin, and at least quasi-civilised, they could be converted and the Church spent a quarter century of effort to do it.

The story goes, and it is greatly elaborated in *Holy Grail Across the Atlantic*[1], that the Roman Church made a "perpetual pact" with the Merovingians. They would be the Church-approved secular power in Europe, and even in the Church's view, of the world, while the Roman Church would, of course, remain the supreme spiritual power. Accordingly, the Merovingian High King of the time, powerful Clovis, was converted and baptised by St. Rémy in AD 496. This was taken to be the birth of a new sort of Roman Empire, but one directed by the Church, a sort of "Holy Roman Empire".

After Clovis, however, the Merovingians seemed increasingly to lose their martial prowess. The vitality of the line seemed gradually to diminish. French history knows the later Merovingians as "enfeebled kings". Another subsidiary lineage of nobility, the "Mayors of the Palace," increasingly took over real power while Merovingians slumped on the throne. This line of subsidiary nobility is usually called the "Carolingian Dynasty" because, in the fullness of time Carolus Magnus, much better known as Charlemagne or "Charles the Great", was to spring from it. It was Charles Martel, a Carolingian Mayor of the Place, and not the nominal Merovingian High King, who won the Battle of Poitiers and stopped the Moors in AD 732.

Perhaps the last Merovingian King to rule with any actual authority was Dagobert II. He was murdered by Carolingian henchmen while he was out hunting near the town of Stanay. Dagobert II's son and heir, Prince Sigisbert IV, was confidently thought to have been killed too, but the boy was taken to safety by loyal retainers to the Duchy of Razès (pronounced "Razz" or "Race") in the Pyrénées. In medieval times, the modern town of Rennes-le-Château was the capital of the Visigothic dukedom of Razès and was then called Reddis, Rhedae or "Royal Rhedae".

It must be said here that the mysteries of Rennes-le-Château really started the contemporary "Holy Grail Craze". Gérard de Sède's *Le Trésor Maudit* was about the accursed treasure that supposedly haunted the town's church dedicated to Mary Magdalene and that also both haunted and sanctified the surrounding area. When Henry Lincoln read this book during his vacation in 1960, he happened to be near enough to the town to investigate some of de Sède's claims. This story is much too complicated to go into here. It was a major part of *The Holy Blood and the Holy Grail*. I have already dealt with it in reasonable detail in both *Holy Grail Across the Atlantic* and even more fully in *Grail Knights of North America*.

But literally dozens of books have been written about Rennes-le-Château alone, of which Henry Lincoln's *The Holy Place* is probably the best. Lionel and Patricia Fanthorpe's *Rennes-le-Château* provides a simple and popularly written introduction to the mysteries. *The Tomb of God* certainly gives a provocative interpretation of the curious clues at Rennes-le-Château, while *The Arcadian Cipher* claims the discovery of the tombs of Jesus and Mary Magdalene nearby.

In brief, the idea is that the Holy Bloodline, represented by Dagobert II's son, Prince Sigisbert IV, found refuge in Rennes-le-Château when both the Carolingian Mayors of the Palace and the Roman Church had confidently thought it had been wiped out. The Holy Blood sheltered in the foothills of the Pyrénées for almost three hundred years before it emerged into the light of history and geopolitical affairs again. Only the fact that these mountains were a no-man's-land between the French and the Moors made this possible. It was a region that was dominated neither by the Roman Church nor by the Moslems, but consisted of dozens of politically and religiously independent "kingdoms", principalities, duchies and counties. The tiny principality of Andorra in the Pyrénées, sandwiched between France and Spain, is the last modern survivor of dozens of similar medieval polities. Today, Andorra mostly exports stamps for collectors all over the world.

The Roman Church was quick to repudiate its "perpetual pact" with the Merovingians. A descendant of Charles Martel, Pepin the Short, was crowned King of France in AD 754. And the Church of Rome realised its great medieval dream by officially crowning Charlemagne as the first Holy Roman Emperor in AD 800.

But in southern France, south of the Garonne River in the foothills of the Pyrénées, a unique civilisation was coalescing around belief in the Holy Grail. This has sometimes been called the "Provençal Civilisation" because it extended as far north as the Rhône River and Provence, but its heartland was the French region still called Languedoc. Attractive travel posters all over France today advertise *Languedoc, pays des Cathares* ("Languedoc, country of the Cathars"). This civilisation drew on Celtic, Roman, Visigothic, Moorish and Jewish cultures in more or less equal proportions and was advanced – for the times – in literature, arts, science and commerce. The language of this civilisation was Provençal French, a dialect of medieval French with much Arabic admixture. An intriguing line of troubadour poetry will give the sound and a little taste of the flavour of this language:

"Al cap des set cen ans, verdegeo el laurel."
"At the end of seven hundred years, the laurel will be green again."

This means that at the end of seven hundred years, this twelfth century poet is predicting a rebirth of literature. More specifically, the context of the poem makes it clear that the poet is predicting a renaissance in an understanding of the Holy Grail. Since these lines were penned in AD 1244 in the aftermath of the terrible "Albigensian Crusade", the prediction was remarkably accurate. Seven hundred years comes to 1944, almost the end of World War II. And, as we have seen, the secret of the Grail started to unravel in post-war France.

The population of the Provençal Civilisation included orthodox Christians, Moslems and Jews, as well as lingering pagans, but the majority of the population, plus the higher classes and most of the nobility, believed in a religion called "Catharism" that derived ultimately from belief in the Holy Grail. By the year AD 1100, there were Roman Churches in which a mass had not been said for decades. The Roman Church sent St. Bernard to Languedoc in order to do something about the situation, but he reported of these heretics: "No sermons are more Christian than theirs and their morals are pure." Because of later events, some modern Grail researchers tend to think that St. Bernard became a Cathar heretic instead of converting them.

Cathars did not have a hierarchy of ordained clerics. Cathar preachers were called *perfecti* in Latin or *parfaits* in French, both meaning "perfected ones". They were vowed to chastity, poverty, celibacy and, apparently, vegetarianism. They were not ordained by any "laying on of hands" by a bishop, but were simply recognised by acclamation. Cathar *parfaits* could be, and were, both men and women. They preached precepts for ethical living in this world, not hope of salvation in the next.

They preached reverence for, but not worship of, Jesus and Mary Magdalene.

Possibly because of the equal status of Mary Magdalene in the Cathar scheme of things, Magda Bogin in *The Women Troubadours* has shown by an examination of actual legal documents from Languedoc that southern French women enjoyed a much higher status than in Roman Catholic Europe. In addition to being *parfaits*, women could also be military commanders. The most famous was Esclarmonde de Foix.

Godfroi de Bouillon emerged from this civilisation.

Today, few people even recognise his name but he was once the most famous warrior and monarch in Christendom. On some medieval decks of playing cards, he is depicted among the kings along with David, Alexander and Julius Caesar. Godfroi de Bouillon was one of the leaders of the First Crusade, AD 1096 to AD 1099, which succeeded in taking Jerusalem from the Saracens. Godfroi was elected to be King of Jerusalem "by an anonymous conclave of clerics and secular leaders", apparently because he could produce genealogies showing that he descended – through the L'Auriols – from Jesus and Mary Magdalene.

Godfroi did not accept the kingship because he knew that he was dying. He had been mauled by a bear en route to the Holy Land and his injuries had become infected. Godfroi accepted only the title "Protector of the Holy Sepulchre" and he supposedly founded the "Order of Sion". Readers can learn much more about the Order of Sion in *The Holy Blood and the Holy Grail*, *The Holy Place*, *Holy Grail Across the Atlantic* or *Grail Knights of North America*.

When Godfroi died in February 1100, his younger brother, Baudoin ("Baldwin") became the first Frankish King of Jerusalem. In AD 1114 (or 1118?), Baudoin founded two new orders of knighthood which have inspired more fascination than even Godfroi's mysterious genealogies. The most famous was the Order of the Poor Knights of the Temple of Solomon, much better known to most people as simply the "Knights Templar". The second was the Order of the Knights of St. John of Jerusalem, Hospitalliers. There is some scant evidence that the Knights of St. John had existed as early as the eighth century, but in any case Baudoin reconstituted the order to ensure its loyalty to de Bouillon interests.

There are hundreds of books on the Templars and the Knights of St. John, including *The Holy Blood and the Holy Grail*, Barber's *The Trial of the Templars* and my own Grail books. But very generally, although their roles overlapped a bit, the Templars were the sword arm of the Holy

Blood in mainland Europe itself, while the Knights of St. John defended Holy Blood interests in the Mediterranean and outside of Europe.

Also, in non-military matters, the Templars specialised in revitalising European banking, which had virtually ceased with the fall of Rome, while the Knights of St. John focussed on hospital work – including the investigation and promotion of sanitation and basic public health.

Although they were supposedly at the apex of chivalry, in retrospect it can be seen that the Templars and Knights of St. John actually struck at the foundations of feudalism upon which the Roman Church depended. Templar banking very rapidly stimulated the growth of commercialism that supported the first beginnings of a "middle class" of artisans and business people between the serfs and the aristocracy. The Knights of St. John tried to ameliorate the squalor of Europe with medicine and sanitation whereas the Church had always challenged disease and death with faith alone.

In the year AD 1187, the Saracens under Saladin launched a successful counter-offensive in the Holy Land. Moslems retook Jerusalem and, one by one, European conquests in the Middle East were revenged and reversed. Although it is something of an over-simplification, it may be accurate enough to say that the "de Bouillon Complex" fell back to its natural geopolitical power base in southern France. Their Templars went with them. The Knights of St. John stayed in the Holy Land and the Mediterranean, but they were driven from the mainland. They first occupied the island of Rhodes and later relocated to the island of Malta. They are therefore better known today as the "Knights of Malta," and the "St. John's Ambulance" organisation is their modern-day legacy, direct from the medieval era.

With the loss of Jerusalem, the de Bouillons lost the immense prestige that had cowed the Church of Rome from taking any overt action against the Holy Grail. They lost their security.

In AD 1209, the Vatican called for a "Crusade" against the Cathar heretics of southern France. This was only twenty-two years after the loss of Jerusalem to the Saracens. The "Albigensian Crusade", so called because the town of Albi was a centre of Cathar reverence, raged in southern France until AD 1244. It was one of the most savage religious wars in European history. The last major heretic stronghold, the mountaintop citadel of Montségur where the Holy Grail was kept, commanded (some say) by Esclarmonde de Foix, fell on March 16, 1244.

But it is said that the Holy Grail had been taken out of the doomed castle three days previously by four knights who climbed down the steep sides of the mountain. Their names are renowned in Grail and Templar histories. Genealogies hidden in the altar supports of the church at Rennes-le-Château traced the Holy Bloodline from AD 1244 until AD 1644. So, some descendants of Jesus and Mary Magdalene had apparently survived the ordeal of the Albigensian Crusade.

The Inquisition had been established specifically in order to find out what the Holy Grail was and where descendants of the Holy Blood were hiding. All of the two hundred surviving defenders of Montségur were tortured hideously, but they did not reveal the whereabouts of the Holy Grail. It is said that those who could still speak after enduring the horrors of the Inquisition sang at their stakes as they were burned alive. It is said that the soul of Esclarmonde de Foix ascended into the air in the form of a smoky dove. The place where Montségur's defenders were burned is still called *Le Champ des Crémants* ("The Field of the Burning Ones"). French people still leave anonymous bunches of flowers on the grass there.

For a while, their sheer military and financial power protected the Templars. But on Friday, October 13, 1307, the French King Philippe IV, ordered simultaneous dawn raids against all Templar priories within his domain. Hundreds of Templars were taken, and they were subjected to the most horrible tortures that the Inquisition could devise. But the secret of the Holy Grail was supposedly not revealed by these agonised men.

However, the Templar fleet of thirteen vessels, headquartered at the Biscay port of La Rochelle, got advance warning of the raids and put to sea. It is said that much of the treasure that the Templars had amassed was thus taken out of France along with the Holy Grail. Descendants of the Holy Bloodline had been hiding among the Templars at La Rochelle and at the nearby fortress of Angoulême.

Philippe IV pressured Pope Clement V into disbanding the Templars in AD 1312. The Last Grand Master of the Templars, Jacques de Molay, suffered years of torture without revealing the location of the Grail or other Templar secrets. Finally, in AD 1314 de Molay was granted the mercy of being roasted to death over a slow fire by order of the king and pope.

This cruelty was never to be forgotten. During the French Revolution, several witnesses recorded an odd vignette. As a group of priests was being herded toward the guillotine in 1791, a man shoved out of the crowd carrying a whip and began to beat the priests mercilessly as they stumbled toward their deaths. "There's one for the Cathars!" and "There's one for the Templars!" he cried with each blow that he rained upon them.

There were Templars outside of France that Philippe IV couldn't reach, and some Templars even within France managed to escape. Not only the Holy Blood, but also the Templars themselves, desperately required a refuge from the Inquisition. No place in Europe was safe because the Roman Church had become completely dominant. The only safe places were the lands across the Atlantic, which were even then being whispered about in every busy European seaport.

Refugee Templars headed for the Atlantic fringes of Europe, to Portugal, to Scotland, even to Spain – headquarters of the Inquisition itself. Can it be mere coincidence transatlantic voyages of discovery were soon launched from these very places?

In both *Holy Grail Across the Atlantic* and in *Grail Knights of North America* I presented evidence, including the maps themselves and late medieval references to them, proving that explorers like Columbus, Magellan and Henry Sinclair had been supplied with maps showing their transatlantic discoveries in advance. This can no longer be reasonably doubted, although it can still be ignored. The map of Columbus is mentioned in his own Log. The map used by Magellan was mentioned by one of the expedition's navigators, Pigafetta. The map used by Henry Sinclair had been drawn by his Venetian navigator, Antonio Zeno, about AD 1400 and it has not only been preserved, it has been analysed by the U.S. Air Force Strategic Air Command's 8th Reconnaissance Wing.

It has been judged to be a genuine product of the mid-to-late fourteenth century in terms of the ink and paper used. But the geography it depicts and the map's geographical *concepts* must date from the last so-called "Ice Age". Another map, this one from Damascus and drawn by the Arabic cartographer, Hadji Ahmed, exhibits the same "impossibilities". I have spent many pages discussing these maps (and others) in *Holy Grail Across the Atlantic* and *Grail Knights of North America*.

The common conventional tactic of simply ignoring the existence of these maps postpones, for a while, the necessity of explaining where these maps came from and how they got to Europe in order to inspire voyages of discovery. The answers are easy. The maps originally came from the Middle East. They had been stolen from the archives of Middle Eastern cities that had been taken by Templars. The Templars had then brought these maps back to southern France, initially, after the fall of Jerusalem in AD 1187. But after the Albigensian Crusade and the Templars' own dispersal, Templars took their precious maps to seafaring nations around the fringes of Europe in order to promote voyages that might discover a safe transatlantic haven from the Inquisition.

The answers are easy enough. The trouble is that they start to unravel threads of the story of the Holy Blood and the Holy Grail. People will be faced with the uncomfortable fact a secret history, a heretical religion *and the preservation of extremely ancient knowledge* have all formed much of the recent Western history that they only *think* they know.[1]

The Templars were welcomed in Portugal and did not even have to maintain a low profile. They changed their name to the "Knights of Christ" and were welcomed in AD 1314 as allies in the struggle to separate Portugal from Spain. Voyages of discovery across the Atlantic were quickly launched, beginning in AD 1325, by King Alfonso IV.

The Templars were just as welcome in Scotland, too, because enough of them had arrived by June 20, 1314 to win the Battle of Bannockburn for Robert the Bruce. This victory guaranteed Scotland's independence from England for almost four centuries. Robert the Bruce had been excommunicated and would have likely welcomed excommunicated Templars on his right flank. There, they faced the English knights who were thoroughly awed by the reputation of the Templars.

The Templars in Scotland gravitated to Rosslyn, the family seat of the noble Saint-Clairs, or Sinclairs. Sinclairs had intermarried with the de Bouillons and, in fact, Henri de Saint-Clair had been handpicked as Godfroi de Bouillon's battle companion for the final hand-to-hand street fight for Jerusalem in 1099.

Nonetheless, these Templars, although invaluable at Bannockburn where they had largely swung the fortunes of the day, were something of a long-term liability. Scotland was more vulnerable than Portugal to Vatican pressure applied through English monarchs who were actively trying to conquer Scotland anyway. The too-obvious presence of Templars in Scotland might inspire the Vatican to call for another crusade that English kings and nobles might endorse with enthusiasm.

Thus, the Templars at Rosslyn (there are plenty of Templar tombstones there)[1] lived quietly, did not form another order of knighthood as in Portugal and there is evidence they transformed themselves into the secret society called Freemasonry. One Masonic document on record specifically names the Sinclairs as hereditary leaders of the organisation. But the Sinclairs and the refugee Templars themselves really knew that the best solution for everyone was for these excommunicated soldiers to be relocated across the Atlantic.

And here we come to the AD 1398 voyage which I described in *Holy Grail Across the Atlantic*. This voyage transported Rosslyn's Templar descendants from Scotland to Nova Scotia – there could not have been many (or any) of the first generation Templars alive in AD 1398. The record of this voyage is called the "Zeno Narrative" by most historians because it originally consisted of letters written by Sinclair's navigators, Niccolo and Antonio Zeno of Venice, to their brother Carlo "The Lion" of Venice. Although I quoted the entire text of the narrative in the previous books, I can afford space for only relevant snippets here. The "I" in this text is Antonio because Niccolo had perished in Sinclair's service on a voyage to Greenland in AD 1394.[10]

> This nobleman, Sinclair, is therefore resolved to send forth with a fleet towards those parts, and there are so many who desire to join in the expedition on account of the novelty and strangeness of the thing, that I think we shall be very strongly appointed without any public expense at all... I set sail with a considerable number of vessels and men, but had not the chief command, as I expected to have, because Sinclair went in his own person.

> Our great preparations for the voyage to Estotiland were begun in an unlucky hour; for exactly three day before our departure, the fisherman died who was to have been our guide. Nevertheless, Sinclair would not give up the enterprise, but in lieu of the deceased fisherman, took some of the sailors who had come out with him from the island.

> Steering westwards, we sighted on some islands subject to Frisland and passing certain shoals, came to Ledovo, where we stayed seven days to refresh ourselves and to take on necessaries. Departing thence, we arrived on the first of April at the island of Ilofe, and as the wind was full in our favour, pushed on. But not long thereafter, when on the open ocean, there arose so great a storm that for eight days we were continuously in toil and driven we knew not where, and a considerable number of vessels were lost to each other. At length, when the storm had abated, we gathered together the scattered vessels and sailing with a prosperous wind, sighted land on the west.[11]

This proved to be the island of Newfoundland, as modern scholars like Bernard G. Hoffman, author of *From Cabot to Cartier,* have concluded from the narrative's detailed descriptions. The inhabitants were hostile and Sinclair's fleet could find no secure place to come ashore for provisions, much less think about founding a settlement. Sinclair's expedition circumnavigated Newfoundland completely, thereby establishing it was an island.

> Wherefore, Sinclair, seeing that he could do nothing... took his departure with a fair wind and sailed six days to the westwards, but the wind thereafter shifting to the southwest, and the sea becoming rough, we sailed 4 days with the wind aft [i.e. north-east – Author] and finally sighted land.

...Some of the crew pulled ashore and returned with great joy with news that they found an excellent country and a still better harbour. We brought our barks and our boats to land, and on entering an excellent harbour, we saw in the distance a great hill which poured forth smoke which gave us hope that we should find some inhabitants in the island.

Neither would Sinclair rest, though it was a great way off, without sending 100 soldiers to explore the country...

While were at anchor there, the month of June came in and air in the island was mild and pleasant beyond description; but as we saw nobody, we began to suspect that this pleasant place was uninhabited.

To the harbour we gave the name of Trin and the headland into the sea was called Cape Trin.

After eight days the 100 soldiers returned, and brought word that they had been through the island and up to the hill, and that the smoke was a natural proceeding from a great fire in the bottom of the hill and that there was a spring from which issued a certain substance like pitch, which ran into the sea, and that thereabouts dwelt a great many people, half wild, and living in caves. They were of small stature and very timid.When Sinclair heard this, and noticed and pure atmosphere, fertile soil, good rivers, and so many other conveniences, he conceived the idea of founding a settlement.

As early as 1951, William Herbert Hobbs, a geologist at the University of Michigan, had noted that there are only three open pitch deposits in the Americas. One is in Trinidad off the coast of South America; another is the famous Los Angeles "La Brea" tar pits and the third and last is the pitch deposits of Stellarton, Nova Scotia – the only possible candidate here.

The "smoking hill" must have been Mount Adams that was aligned between the burning pitch and the "excellent" harbour. Therefore, the geographic descriptions of "The Zeno Narrative" were not only accurate when applied to Nova Scotia, but pinpointed Sinclair's landfall. Guysborough Harbour satisfies the description "a still better harbour" and Cape Canso, the most definitive cape in Nova Scotia, extends out into the Atlantic just north of the harbour.

The only date for Trinity Sunday that works within the chronology of Sinclair's life and this voyage is June 2, 1398 and that is the date accepted by both the *Encyclopedia Americana* and the *Encyclopaedia Britannica* as the day Henry Sinclair reached North America. This is 99 years before John Cabot and 94 years before Christopher Columbus.

But his people, fatigued, began to murmur, and say that they wished to return to their homes for the winter was not far off and if they allowed it once to set in, they would not be able to get away before the following summer. He therefore retained only boats propelled by oars, and such of his people who were willing to stay, and sent the rest away in ships, appointing me, against my will, to be their captain.

Having no choice, therefore, I departed and sailed 20 days to the eastward without any sight of land; then turning my course toward the southeast, in 5 days I sighted on land and found myself on the island of Neome and knowing the country, I perceived I was past Iceland; and as the inhabitants were subject to Sinclair, I took in fresh stores and sailed in 3 days to Frislanda, where the people, who thought they had lost their Prince, in consequence of his long absence on the voyage we had made, received us with a hearty welcome... Concerning those things you desire to know of me, as to the people and their habits, the animals, and countries adjoining, I have written about it all in a separate book, which please God, I shall bring with me. In it, I have described the country, the monstrous fishes, the customs and laws of Frisland, of Iceland, of Shetland, the Kingdom of Norway, Estotiland and Drogeo; and lastly, I have written... the life and exploits of Sinclair, a Prince as worthy of immortal memory as any that ever lived, for his great bravery and remarkable goodness.

Holy Grail Across the Atlantic was about the settlement Henry Sinclair founded in Nova Scotia almost a century before Cabot and Columbus crossed the Atlantic. Antonio says that he set sail with "a considerable number of ships and men" and that Sinclair had been able to send "100 soldiers" on a reconnaissance expedition to the smoking hill. In 1991, I re-read "The Zeno Narrative" and realised just how large this expedition had been. Consulting with experts in medieval warfare, I learned Sinclair must have had at least 500 men at his disposal, whom Antonio calls "soldiers." These fighting men could only have been the remaining greybeard Templars from Rosslyn and their descendants. The medieval Barony of Rosslyn and Earldom of Orkney could not have raised a feudal levy of fighting men of that size. This number of men could have immediately begun explorations of the new land they had found and to which they were effectively exiled for political reasons.

Sinclair "retained only boats propelled by oars" when Antonio left with the fleet, but it's certain he returned to Scotland. Henry fell in a skirmish in August 1400 (some records state 1404). He built a small ship in Advocate Harbour, Nova Scotia. The ship is remembered as a "stone canoe" with "trees growing from it" in Mi'kmaq (formerly "Micmac") Indian legends of the culture hero named "Glooscap."

During the mid-1950s, 1960s and 1970s the Sinclair expedition to North America was generally accepted, perhaps simply because its immense relevance to unravelling the Holy Grail and true Christianity wasn't known or suspected. The *Encyclopedia Americana* and the *Encyclopaedia Britannica* both accepted the fact of the voyage and both

75

had entries about it. Up until 1988, the Royal Nova Scotia Museum in Halifax had a panorama illustrating Prince Henry's landing "somewhere" on the coast of the province.

But with the publication of *Holy Grail Across the Atlantic* in 1988, a concerted effort seems to have been made to deny and ignore Henry Sinclair. There are even historians who now deny every word of "The Zeno Narrative" in spite of the mention of the open pit deposits and the "smoking hill" in line with Pictou behind it that could only be Mount Adams. The Royal Nova Scotia Museum's former Henry Sinclair panorama has been replaced and the two encyclopaedias have deleted Henry Sinclair entries in more modern editions.

The problem with all this is that perhaps the most important single piece of Sinclair-related evidence wasn't discovered until the 1990s. A Scottish historian and one who has been featured several times on History Channel television documentaries, Robert Philip Brydon, found unarguable evidence, literally carved in stone, that the Sinclairs of Rosslyn knew about the New World before Columbus or Cabot. Brydon found and photographed a stone doorway in Rosslyn Chapel that was decorated in the carved motif of ears of American corn, or maize. American corn is generally conceded by historians to have been unknown in Europe before Columbus. Rosslyn chapel was begun in AD 1441 and was completed in 1485. I reproduced this photograph in *Grail Knights of North America*, but it has also been published in *The Hiram Key* and several other books.

No one can reasonably argue that the Sinclair voyage of AD 1398 did take place. The fact that people continue do so, and even more vehemently than before 1988, is only an indication of how much this particular episode threatens the foundations of modern Western society. The Sinclair expedition not only challenges the myths of John Cabot and Christopher Columbus, but because of Henry Sinclair's "Holy Grail" and Templar associations the expedition's "smoking hill" is more like a smoking gun. Delving too deeply into Henry Sinclair is a thread that, if pulled too strongly, will unravel the myths of modern Judeo-Christianity upon which our Western civilisation is supposedly based. The Holy Grail had come to North America. This adventure must be considered a minor event in the long saga of the Holy Blood, but it was nonetheless a crucial one. If a transatlantic haven from the Inquisition had not been found when it was so desperately needed, then the Holy Grail would almost certainly have perished. The greatest story ever told is a tale of unbelievable courage and supreme sacrifice, but it is also a chronicle of implacable hatred and inhuman cruelty. Gérard de Sède was right. The

Holy Blood and the Holy Grail is a treasure belonging to Western humanity, but it is in many ways an accursed one.

Notes for Chapter 2

[1] Spong, John Shelby, *Rescuing the Bible from Fundamentalism*, Harper, San Francisco, 1991, page 21.

[2] I have covered this in *Holy Grail Across the Atlantic* and *Grail Knights of North America* in great detail, mostly based on standard European histories and *The Holy Blood and the Holy Grail*. However, for *Swords at Sunset*, the publisher requested a shorter book and so this detail cannot be repeated.

[3] There were apparently some attempts to protect Britain until AD 418 as described in *Holy Grail Across the Atlantic*.

[4] Katherine Esty, *Gypsies, Wanderers in Time*, Victore Gollancz, London 1962, page 124.

[5] Peter Blake, and Paul S. Blezard, *The Arcadian Cipher*, Sidgwick & Jackson, London, 2000, page 69.

[6] *Holy Grail Across the Atlantic*, pages 25-29.

[7] Geoffrey Ashe, (Ed.), *The Quest For Arthur's Britain*, Granada Publishing Limited, London, 1968.

[8] Geoffrey de Monmouth, *History of the Kings of Britain*, ed. and trans. Lewis Thorpe, Penguin, Harmondsworth and Baltimore, 1966.

[9] A dubious map of Lyonesse by Giraldus Cambrensis circa AD 1200 shows these place-names in "Lyonesse".

[10] But her name is recorded as being "Melusine".

[11] See *Holy Grail Across the Atlantic*, pages 183-197.

[12] See *Holy Grail Across the Atlantic* pages 96 –112 and *Grail Knights of North America*, pages 51-72.

[13] See *Holy Grail Across the Atlantic*, pages 157-159.

[14] The earlier "Niccolo Zeno" had, indeed, perished on a voyage to Greenland in Sinclair's service in AD 1394, but his later ancestor and namesake, another Niccolo Zeno, published "The Zeno Narrative" in Venice in AD 1558.

[15] This, and all other quotes from "The Zeno Narrative", are derived from Frederick Pohl's *Prince Henry Sinclair*, Clarkson N. Potter, New York, 1974, pages 110-115.

3

The Greatest Story Never Told

On November 26, 1922, British archaeologist Howard Carter, his sponsor Lord Carnarvon (the fifth Earl of Carnarvon at Highclere), Carnarvon's daughter Lady Evelyn and a British railroad engineer named Arthur "Pecky" Callender (a close friend and professional colleague of Carter), first entered the famous tomb of Tutankhamun.[1]

It had been suspected by Egyptologists, from clues in papyrus records, that Tutankhamun was a pharaoh of the Eighteenth Dynasty and had lived about 1350 BC. Carter, funded by Carnarvon's money, had been searching for the crypt for seven fruitless years, ever since 1915.

Rather miraculously, the tomb had not been completely robbed and destroyed in antiquity, although tomb raiders had apparently entered it twice during the intervening 3,300 years.[2]

It still contained dazzling riches in the form of sculptures, furniture, a chariot, and jewellery – much of it made of silver, gold and gold plate – the exquisite work of Ancient Egyptian artisans.

The American Egyptologist, James H. Breasted, said: "The best Greek artists were mere hacks compared with the craftsmen who adorned Tutankhamun's tomb." Variously valued at some £15 million sterling by 1933, the tomb's contents actually proved to be a priceless treasure trove of Ancient Egyptian artistic virtuosity and cultural sophistication.

Newspapers of the day gave the discovery almost continual coverage in orchidaceous prose, even though *The Times* of London had supposedly purchased the exclusive right from Lord Carnarvon to report on the excavation of the tomb.[3] This massive publicity unleashed the world's first wave of what has been called "Tutmania."

The fashion industry was first to respond to Tutmania when Russicks, a Fifth Avenue, New York furrier, offered an "Egyptian-embroidered" bisque squirrel-collared coat in 1923. Warned Alexandre M. Grean, president of the United Cloak and Suit Designers of America, a year later in 1924: "Tutankhamun is a dangerous theme. Do not exaggerate it," he cautioned. "Modify it, and choose the beautiful parts only."[4]

Nonetheless, King Tut had captivated the popular imagination, at least that of the more affluent classes of people. And by 1925 the

Parisian fashion house of Bakst was offering its "Isis Collection" of women's dresses based on the four diaphanously-clad protective goddesses (Neith, Selkit, Nepenthys and Isis)[5] that had been excavated from around the perimeter of King Tutankhamun's sarcophagus.

The second onset of Tutmania started in 1976, roughly half a century later, when the treasures of King Tut's tomb were sent first to the United States – for America's bicentennial celebrations – and then went on tour to museums in all major Western countries. This was a cog in the Egyptian President, Anwar Sadat's, strategy for better relations with a pro-Israel U.S. and some resolution to the ongoing Middle Eastern crisis.

But 50 years had passed since the last seizure of King Tut madness and the Western world had become more populist, more egalitarian and much coarser. Tutmania commercialism of the late 70s was predictably more vulgar. Perhaps naturally, a southern California automotive manufacturer offered a customized "Tutmobile" with a reproduction of Tutankhamun's exquisitely crafted death mask on its grille. Harley-Davidson marketed a two-tank motorcycle for longer cruising range, prompting the warning: "Keep your hands off my Tuts." [6]

Nonetheless, the sheer drawing-power of the Tutankhamun Exhibition in 1976 America proved that the pharaoh had lost none of his fascination in the public's imagination. In New Orleans, for example, more people viewed the Tutankhamun Exhibition *in* that city than actually *resided* in the city.[7] If people only knew the truth.

If people knew the truth, there'd be a third outbreak of Tutmania that would shake the Western world's fundamental religious beliefs. For the tomb's real treasures were not gold and silver. The real treasures were minor artifacts and clothing showing that King Tutankhamun had been a Christian, and probably a priest. These items have not been displayed.

In 1922, Howard Carter discovered the first artistic rendition of "The Father, the Son and the (female) Holy Spirit" depicted on Tutankhamun's tomb walls.[8] He'd also discovered a depiction of baptism where the water of life, in the form of a flow of tiny ankh ("life") symbols, poured onto the pharaoh and his wife from a jug.[9] He'd found the first known example of a Christian priestly vestment called a "Dalmatic." Tutankhamun had a pair of gloves decorated in a fish-scale pattern, identical to gloves that were still being used by some Christian bishops of Carter's day when pontificating, or speaking *ex cathedra*. Carter had found flabelli (ostrich feather fans) identical to those used in papal processions. Tutankhamun had also worn, on occasion, a ceremonial apron identical to the aprons of modern Freemasons.[10] Carter did not find an example of the Christian cross for the very good reason that the cross had been adopted by the Roman Church only in the sixth century AD. Carter and Carnarvon were quite naturally stunned.

Further, when the tomb of Tutankhamun was first opened in 1922, Egyptologists and other archaeologists, like Sir Charles Leonard Woolley who was then working at the site of Ur in Mesopotamia, expected that papyri would be found somewhere in King Tut's sepulchre.

Undoubtedly, it was thought, papyrus scrolls would be discovered inside the massive stone sarcophagus, opened in 1925, or else within the three wooden mummiform coffins inside the sarcophagus that more intimately protected the king's mortal remains.

These three "mummy cases" had been opened and the king's body had been X-rayed by November 1925. The king's papyrus scrolls would doubtless tell something about the king's life and greatness, his immediate ancestors, his wife and his descendants.

Tutankhamun's successors had made every effort to efface his memory, a fate that had also befallen several other pharaohs, but his own burial papyri would surely reveal at least *something* about his place in Ancient Egyptian history and in his own Eighteenth Dynasty. This was important for Egyptology because the tumultuous XVIII Dynasty was a time of profound crisis in Ancient Egyptian life and culture.

But, to everyone's surprise, no papyrus scrolls were reported from the tomb of Tutankhamun. There was no record of the king's place in the XVIII Dynasty and no account of his achievements.

Howard Carter's rather pedantic record of his famous discovery, his massive three-volume *The Tomb of Tutankhamun* (Cassel, London, 1923, 1927 and 1933), makes no mention of any papyrus documents discovered in the final resting place of King Tut. However, rather coyly, a photograph of the tomb's ante-chamber, one of the first illustrations in the three-volume book, actually shows rolled-up papyrus scrolls in the foreground. The hieroglyphic symbols on the scrolls cannot be missed.

But there were rumours from the beginning that papyrus scrolls *had* been discovered in Tutankhamun's tomb. And these rumours came from the highest possible source, none other than Lord Carnarvon himself, financial backer of the seven-year search for Tutankhamun's tomb.

On December 1, 1922, just eight days after Lord Carnarvon and Howard Carter first looked into the antechamber of Tutankhamun's crypt, Carnarvon wrote to Sir E.A. Wallis Budge, Keeper of Egyptian Antiquities at the British Museum. Carnarvon stressed to Budge that he wanted to write just "one line to tell you that *we have found the most remarkable 'find' that has ever been made, I expect, in Egypt or elsewhere* [author's Italics]."[11]

This is a remarkable statement, and Carnarvon was not given to flights of hyperbole. Carnarvon then described what he had seen, in company with his daughter Lady Evelyn and Howard Carter, to Sir Wallis in the same letter. "I have not opened the boxes, and don't know what is in them", he wrote, "*but there are some papyri letters*, faience, jewellery, bouquets, candles in ankh candlesticks. All this is in [the] front chamber, besides lots of stuff you can't see [author's Italics]."[12]

By "papyri letters," Carnarvon meant "papyri *documents*" because Lord Carnarvon himself could not read hieroglyphs. However, Carter and Carnarvon's personal secretary, Sir Richard Bethell, were fluent in reading hieroglyphs and within days had given their rough translations of some of the documents to Lord Carnarvon. This record apparently told a very different version of the Exodus than the one in the Bible.

As early as December 5, 1922, an unnamed British consular official in Cairo paid a visit to the site of the tomb's excavation. He then warned Howard Carter and Lord Carnarvon, according to some of Carter's letters, that the British government wanted no mention of Tutankhamun's Christian associations or of papyrus records that gave a different account of the biblical Exodus. For this would, in the official's words, "destabilise the three great Western religions and undermine the integrity of Britain's Balfour Declaration."[13]

The Balfour Declaration was the 1917 letter to Lord Rothschild stating the British government's agreement-in-principle to the Zionist effort to establish a Jewish "traditional homeland" in Palestine.

The problem was that both Howard Carter and Lord Carnarvon were so excited by the dramatic nature of their tomb discoveries that *they had already told some of their close relatives and their closest colleagues about the Christian artifacts and the papyrus records*.

In Carnarvon's December 1, 1922 letter to Sir Wallis Budge at the British Museum, for example, we see reference to "the most remarkable find that has ever been made... in Egypt... or elsewhere." Thankfully for Wallis Budge, Carnarvon had not said *exactly* what had been found, and so the esteemed Sir Wallis survived what was to come. Sir Wallis Budge lived to become a revered doyen of British archaeology.

The famous and ridiculous "Curse of the Mummy" solved the problem of Western civilisation's most world-shattering leaks. Lord Carnarvon was its first victim. In early 1923, Carnarvon supposedly suffered an odd "insect bite" that refused to heal and he fell seriously ill with blood poisoning.

Carnarvon's wife, Lady Almina (Victoria Marie Alexandra Wombwell) rushed from England to Cairo to nurse her husband back to health. Lord Carnarvon actually seemed to be on the mend before she left England, but he died on April 5, 1923 – within a week after her arrival at his Cairo hotel. Lady Almina was an illegitimate daughter of the same Lord Rothschild to whom the Balfour Declaration had been addressed.

Howard Carter was in the same Cairo hotel and was also afflicted with some strange malady. But shortly after Lady Almina arrived, and as decently as possible after Carnarvon was actually dead, Carter went back to the site of the tomb on the fringe of the desert where he had the protection of his Bedouin guards. He therefore survived the immediate crisis. When he returned to England, however, he began to suffer symptoms of "slow arsenic poisoning", as he put it, and spent the last six years of his life in progressively greater agony. But he managed to finish the three volumes of *The Tomb of Tutankhamun*.

The first volume, published in 1923, was co-authored with Arthur C. Mace of the Metropolitan Museum of Art in New York. Mace also fell ill at the same time as Lord Carnarvon and explained before his death on April 6, 1928 that his illness was due to arsenic poisoning.[14]

Lord Carnarvon's personal secretary, Sir Richard Bethell, also died within five years of Carnarvon at age 47. Bethell's father, in London, either fell or was pushed from a window three months after his son's death. Lord Carnarvon's sister also died from a mysterious "insect bite." Lord Carnarvon's half brother, an expert yachtsman, managed to fall off his yacht and drown in the Nile. All told, 20 to 30 people had succumbed to the "Mummy's Curse" by 1933. In retrospect, it becomes clear that all these people had been in a position to know about Tutankhamun's Christian associations and to know the message of the papyrus records.

As for Lady Almina, she remarried within eight months and moved to the United States. The papyrus records, which were thought to have been most probably secreted at Carnarvon's estate of Highclere, vanished.

The London *Daily Mail's* August 3, 5 and 6, 2002 advance excerpts of the book, *Tutankhamun: The Exodus Conspiracy* (Virgin Books, London) by Andrew Collins and Chris Ogilvie-Herald, caused a storm of controversy in Europe. This revelation of an 80-year old scandal has played its part in eroding the British public's support for Tony Blair's seemingly unconditional alliance with U.S. policy in the Middle East, including the March 2003 invasion of Iraq. *Tutankhamun: The Exodus Conspiracy* has hardly been mentioned in North American media.

Based on private and unpublished letters and documents from the Carnarvon and Carter families, *Tutankhamun: The Exodus Conspiracy* contends that archaeologist Howard Carter was either induced or coerced into suppressing the fact that papyrus records had been discovered in the tomb of Tutankhamun. And these records, Carter maintained, would undermine both the Jewish so-called "history" recounted in the Old Testament and also the Christian story told in the New Testament.

The "Curse of the Mummy" was real, all right, the ruthless serial murders of people closest to Howard Carter and Lord Carnarvon who were in a position to have known about the papyrus records concerning the Exodus and to have known about Tutankhamun's Christian associations. Since the revelation of *Tutankhamun: The Exodus Conspiracy*, published on September 5, 2002, three British Members of Parliament have called for the exhumation of some of the "mummy's" victims to determine whether the cause of death was mundane arsenic poisoning rather than ancient mystic incantations. And did Zionist agents or British ones administer the poison?

We do not have to rely upon *Tutankhamun: The Exodus Conspiracy* to arrive at a fairly clear picture of Tutankhamun's importance. And this importance does not relate merely to his own XVIII Dynasty of Ancient Egypt. It is equally relevant to the deepest meaning of the Holy Grail legend, as well as to Middle East geopolitical conflict and terrorism today. The work of Egyptologists, linguists and archaeologists since Howard Carter's discovery of the tomb of Tutankhamun in 1922 fills out the world-shaking picture more than clearly enough.

Kamal Salibi, linguist at the American University of Beirut and author of *The Bible Came from Arabia*; Dr. Kathleen Kenyon of the University of London's School of Archaeology; Dr. Alexander Badawy; Dr. Ahmed Fakhry of the Egyptian Antiquities Service; Dr. Donald B. Redford, Canadian director of the University of Pennsylvania's "Ikhnaton Project" and, above all, London-based Egyptologist Ahmed Osman, author of *Stranger in the Valley of the Kings*, *Out of Egypt* (1998), etc., have together made the chronology and events of the Eighteenth Dynasty at least relatively clear. Naturally, however, this chronology and history of the XVIII Dynasty of Ancient Egypt is still disputed by some authorities. Depending on how one chooses to add them up – does Queen Hatshepset count as a "pharaoh"? – Amenhotep III is thought to have been either the seventh or eighth ruler of the XVIII Dynasty that began the "New Kingdom" of Ancient Egypt. He married his sister, Sitamun, in 1405 BC[15] in order to gain the throne of Egypt according to traditional Egyptian custom. But Sitamun may have been only three years old at the time of this dynastic union.

But, in "Year Two" of Amenhotep III's reign, or 1403 BC, a girl named Tiye, "Daughter of Yuya and Tuya," is described as being "The Great Royal Wife"[16] – that is, the mother of any heirs to the throne of Egypt sired by Amenhotep III. Tiye must have been about eight years old at the time of this marriage. She seems to have been a Hebrew girl, one of the Israelites residing in "Goshen," as the Bible would have it, the extreme north-eastern part of the Nile Delta and not officially in Egypt proper. She may have believed in the "One God" *Aten*.

Aten the "One God" had certainly taken intellectual shape in the minds of "His" followers by this time – that is, before the birth of Akenaten. We know this because Amenhotep III gave his new wife Tiye a pleasure barge as a wedding present, and the name of this barge was *Aten Gleams*.[17] And further, we know that this barge operated on Lake Zawr, which was artificially enlarged by Amenhotep III to give larger scope for cruises. Lake Zawr was one of the lakes of Goshen.

These lakes presently occupy the geological depression through which the Suez Canal was dug and they still form lateral extensions of the canal in places. Goshen was about the only place in Egypt that could boast any lakes. The Bible says the Hebrews settled in Goshen and so it's reasonable to conclude Tiye was a Hebrew girl. That she was believer in the "One God" *Aten* also seems reasonable because of the suggestive name of the barge that her doting husband gave her as a wedding present.

Therefore, the "first monotheism" based on worship of *Aten* may have been a genuine and original conception of the Hebrew refugees brought into Goshen by biblical Joseph so that the Israelites could survive a famine. As Vizier of Egypt, as the Bible tells us, Joseph could bring the Hebrews *almost* into Egypt and within range of Egyptian bounty, but could not bring them into Egypt proper. This is because – as the Bible does *not* tell us – the Egyptians hated "Asiatic" herdsmen. The Hyksos, or "Shepherd Kings," had invaded Egypt from Palestine some three centuries earlier and had instituted a reign of terror and torture in the northern part of Egypt. The Hyksos were finally defeated by Amasis I (sometimes spelled "Amose I"), Amenhotep III's direct ancestor, the founder of the Eighteenth Dynasty and the New Kingdom.[18]

Therefore, Joseph could bring his Hebrew relatives into the land of Goshen on the edge of Egypt, but not into Egypt proper. But perhaps the Bible has given this episode of Joseph a Hebrew spin. It's possible the Hebrews in Goshen were actually already there, a remnant population of Hyksos shepherds who had settled on the borders of Egypt. The citadel of Zawr on the shore of Lake Zawr was once the Hyksos capital Avaris.[19]

The Egyptian word for "Joseph" may have been "Yuya-sef," from which the Arabic "Yusef" was to evolve in the course of time. Therefore,

Tiye may well have been the daughter of biblical Joseph himself by his Egyptian wife. Tiye was described as "the daughter of Yuya and Tuya" and the text infers that this "Yuya and Tuya" were well enough known to need no further introduction or explanation.

But the conception of monotheism may also have been an even earlier Egyptian development of some Nile Delta cult with whom the Hyksos or Goshen Hebrews came into contact during their sojourn there. There is presently insufficient evidence to decide this question.

Akenaten was probably born in 1395 BC. And, as Ahmed Osman conjectures from the timing of things as suggested by a ceremonial Scarab issued in "Year Eight" of Amenhotep III's reign, he may well have been conceived aboard the barge *Aten Gleams* cruising on the enlarged Lake Zawr. Amenhotep III would have been about twenty-two years of age at the time. Tiye may have been barely fourteen or fifteen. Because Amenhotep III had broken with Egyptian tradition to reject his sister-wife Sitamun and make Tiye his "Great Royal Wife" instead, he knew that there might well be trouble with the royal succession.

Amenhotep III gave orders for the child to be killed if it proved to be a boy, because a son by Tiye would be a potential and unorthodox non-Egyptian claimant to the throne of Egypt. Akenaten was born, was hidden by his mother Tiye among her Hebrew relatives in Goshen, and survived to claim the Egyptian throne at age 16 or 17. Akenaten is almost certainly the biblical "Moses," as Sigmund Freud suspected in his last book, *Moses and Monotheism* (1939) and as Ahmed Osman has virtually proved in several books published during the 1990s.[20]

Accepted as a legitimate claimant, Akenaten ascended to the throne of Egypt as "Amenhotep IV." Because of his father Amenhotep III's advanced age of 54 – most people then only lived to age 40 – a system of co-kingship was apparently arranged by Akenaten's mother, Queen Tiye.

She also arranged Akenaten's marriage to his half-sister, the exquisitely beautiful Nefertiti, thought to have been the daughter of Sitamun and his father Amenhotep III.

Co-ruling with his father until Amenhotep III died about 1367 BC, Akenaten remained tolerant of Egyptian worship of the old gods and goddesses, including the principal Egyptian sun god Amun – or "Amen" – and Christians might wonder why they intone "Amen" after a prayer!

But after the death of Amenhotep III, Akenaten ruled alone and he immediately exhibited his fanaticism, imposing belief in his own "One God" *Aten*. He destroyed the images of all other Egyptian gods and goddesses, disenfranchised their priesthoods and ruined their temples. I won't enter the controversy over Akenaten's personality and possible metabolic and physical abnormalities. This is a matter that has been discussed by the Scottish Egyptologist Cyril Aldred, Ahmed Osman, Kay Kenyon and many other experts. Did Akenaten have Froelich's Syndrome? Did he also maybe suffer from Marfan's Syndrome?

After roughly six years of Akenaten's intolerance there was a popular revolt about 1361 BC and Aye,[21] head of the crack chariot corps, could no longer guarantee the Pharaoh's safety. Akenaten either abdicated or was driven into exile, or both. He had some followers, of course, in spite of his general unpopularity. There's evidence, not proof, Nefertiti may have been killed, a casualty in the popular uprising against Akenaten.

There is also evidence, not proof, that Akenaten's mother, Queen Tiye went into exile with him. Again, there is evidence short of proof that they fled first to the northern part of the Sinai Peninsula, right next to Goshen, where the Egyptians had long operated turquoise mines and had some religious shrines. A finely carved figurine of Queen Tiye was discovered in the northern Sinai during the 1950s and was illustrated in Osman's *Out of Egypt*. This enforced exile of Akenaten and his followers seems to have been the "Exodus" of the Hebrew Bible's Old Testament.

The core group of *Aten*-worshippers may have been the relatively few Hebrews residing in Goshen, but probably the majority of *Aten*-worshippers consisted of Egyptian converts. No one really knows.

Akenaten's immediate successor seems to have been named Smenkhkare but very little is presently known about him.[22] For many years he was not even considered to be a successor of Akenaten at all – and future research may still support this older opinion. After four years or less of Smenkhkare's rule, Tutankhaten, came to the throne (1361 BC?) with the military support of chariot corps commander, Aye.

This young king married Ankhsenpa-Aten, his sister or "step-sister" (?), the youngest of the six daughters of Akenaten and Nefertiti. He also quickly changed his name to *Tutankhamun* in order to show his respect for, or at least tolerance of, Egypt's traditional gods and goddesses. His reign was one of reconciliation and tolerance.

From the time that Howard Carter first opened his tomb, there had been no doubt among knowledgeable experts that Tutankhamun had possessed, let's say, "Christian associations," even if the public remained blissfully ignorant. Most people had not read Carter's massive three-volume work, *The Tomb of Tutankhamun*. Most popular condensations of it did not mention, and still don't, the Christian artifacts, garments and frescoes that had been discovered in Tutankhamun's crypt.

Besides, the public was fascinated with the glitz of Tutmania and with the morbid appeal of the "mummy's curse" that quickly became a favoured Hollywood theme. As no reader needs to be told, the mummy's curse is still a major Hollywood theme with the remakes of *The Mummy* and *The Mummy Returns* of 1999-2002. No reader needs to be told, either, that these two popular modern films took the opportunity to present large doses of anti-Arab and anti-Egyptian propaganda. Imhotep, actually an architect, physician and poet, was presented as a vicious thug. The Egyptian jackal god Anubis, the peaceful guardian of Egyptian eternity, was presented as the leader of terrible "Anubis warriors."

As a pharaoh and having all those priestly Christian trappings and garments in his tomb, Tutankhamun had probably – or undoubtedly – been a priest of the cult. He had himself been a "Jesus figure."

Ahmed Osman, a London-based Islamic Egyptologist, takes these undoubted Christian connections further. Osman has given disconcerting evidence that because of Tutankhamun's reign of tolerance and reconciliation, he was *the* Jesus figure reflected in the New Testament.[23]

Tutankhamun restored the old temples and re-enfranchised the traditional priesthoods. However, it's clear from his tomb's frescoes and decorations that Tutankhamun himself continued to be a worshipper of monotheistic *Aten* until his death. Reciprocating his tolerance, the restored Egyptian priests of the necropolis furnished and decorated Tutankhamun's tomb in the style and manner of an *Aten*-worshipper.

How did Tutankhamun die?

Ahmed Osman (*Out of Egypt*, 1998) presents evidence Tutankhamun went into the Sinai Peninsula to try to attempt religious reconciliation with his exiled predecessor, Akenaten. But he encountered Akenaten's implacable fanaticism instead and was murdered. His mummy shows that he was virtually dismembered by the Hebrew method of execution[24] – being hung on a tree, bush (or cross) and beaten by metal rods. This execution was supervised by Panhesy, Akenaten's Chief Priest of *Aten*.[25]

The incident is mentioned, but spin-doctored, in the Old Testament, as Sigmund Freud was one of the first to perceive.

Chariot corps commander Aye attacked the exiles' camp in the northern Sinai on the borders of Goshen, inflicted severe casualties upon them, and recovered the mutilated body of Tutankhamun for return to Egypt and burial. The Bible describes this incident as a "plague" shortly after the Exodus that took "24,000 lives," but this is likely to be a gross exaggeration of the actual casualties. Young Tutankhamun apparently died without known issue, but no one can be sure of this.

Any good map of north-eastern Egypt and the Suez depression, once containing the lakes of Goshen, will indicate clearly that no group of exiles living in the northern Sinai next to Goshen, and being pursued by Egyptian the chariot corps, could have entered the Sinai Peninsula itself.

Also, no large group of people with flocks and herds would have entered that waterless moonscape under any circumstances. There's nothing to eat or drink. Ahmed Osman has illustrated his books, notably *Out of Egypt*, with just such detailed maps of north-eastern Egypt, Goshen, the northern Sinai and adjoining Palestine.

Kamal Salibi, linguist at the American University of Beirut, has presented much evidence that the exiled Hebrews under Akenaten/Moses were harried along the top, or northern part, of the Sinai Peninsula to the modern Gulf of Aqaba. The refugee horde then crossed the Gulf of Aqaba near its head – the biblical crossing of the "Red Sea" – or the *Jam Suf* as it reads literally, the "Sea of Reeds."

If they were still pursued by Egyptian chariots, doubtful in view of the distance from Aye's headquarters, the "Israelite" horde was then harried southward along the north-eastern, or Arabian, shore of the Red Sea. In any event, once across the Gulf of Aqaba, they had no choice but to head that way. They couldn't go back.

Eventually, according to Salibi, they reached the modern Arabian region called Hijaz on the northern border of modern Yemen.[26] This is a trek of about 500 miles, and might well have required the biblical "forty years" in the wilderness for a migrating horde with flocks and herds.

But more important, this route is at least possible because the Arabian coastal strip is still reasonably fertile today and was even more fertile back then before the climate suddenly became drier about 600 BC.

Hijaz is still the garden of modern Arabia, insofar as it can be said to have one, and presently produces melons, tomatoes, lettuce and so on. These are all thirsty plants requiring a reasonable amount of water.

To try to be scrupulously fair to everyone, no one knows for certain where the "Israelites" (if we can call them that at this very early time) went during the Exodus. The Bible has it that the Hebrews under Moses went into the land of Midian or "land of the Midianites" – where Moses, according to the Bible, had once lived and had once married. But is this biblical story just an attempted spin in order to distance Moses as much as possible from Egypt and Akenaten? And Nefertiti? This "Land of the Midianites" is known, however, to have been in the extreme eastern part of today's Jordan, centred roughly on the ancient city of Petra.

But there is no natural boundary between this territory and Hijaz further south comprising today's Arabian province of Hijaz and today's northern Yemen. In fact, up until June 1918 the governor of what is now modern Jordan was the Emir of Hijaz, Feisal ibn Hussein, the Hashemite leader of the Arab Revolt under the famous T.E. Lawrence "of Arabia." There wasn't much in this desert territory from eastern Jordan to northern Yemen that could differentiate geographic regions.

Somewhere between modern eastern Jordan, Hijaz and northern, coastal Yemen was really the "Promised Land," and it is no accident that the earliest "proto-Hebrew" inscriptions have been found there, around Petra and south-east to today's Yemen. The Hebrews of the Exodus did not enter Palestine in force because it was too strongly held by the resident Canaanites. Besides, there were strong Egyptian garrisons between Goshen and Palestine, which would have precluded the refugees' going that way. There is no archaeological evidence, and no other tribal histories, to substantiate the biblical account of Joshua's supposed conquest of Canaan as the "Promised Land".

Some Hebrews did drop out of the main exile horde during the brutal crossing of the northern Sinai Peninsula's desert, and they gradually trickled northward into Palestine. They lived quietly as an ethnic minority among the Philistines in the region around Jerusalem, according to Israeli archaeologist Dr. Ze'ev Herzog of Tel Aviv University. Our modern word "Palestine" derives from *Philistine*, the dominant ruling people of the area until the Persian conquests of Cyrus the Great about 530 BC. There was never any Israelite kingdom of David and Solomon *in Palestine*, again, in the view of Ze'ev Herzog.

David and Solomon may however, have been or become consorts of Midianite or Yemeni queens. It is now known that there was a matriarchal "queendom" called Saba, the "Sheba" of the Bible, that once occupied this very stretch of territory from eastern Jordan to northern Yemen. Jewish history given in the Bible apparently claimed this known queendom as David and Solomon's Israelite kingdom.[27]

When the climate became drier about 600 BC, the Arabian deserts encroached to the Red Sea coast and isolated Saba or "Sheba." Although the major part of Hebrew history had apparently taken place there from the time of the Exodus, news from Sheba came only sporadically to the few compatriot Hebrews in the region around Jerusalem.

This was thanks only to the domestication of the camel. According to the archaeological evidence of bones, camel domestication began on an experimental and small scale about 1500 BC. By about 600 BC, camel domestication had become an important cultural foundation of the Arabian Peninsula and the drier parts of the Middle East.

Even so, it is probably fair to say that no one has ever really *liked* camels. Aside from being notoriously bad-tempered and difficult to tame or train, their natural gait made them a most uncomfortable mount for riders. Camels are one of the few mammals that *amble* (move both legs of one side at once). Nonetheless, thanks to camels, at least some caravans could cross the Arabian deserts, from about 900 BC onwards.

Roughly at the same period of history, about 750 to 600 BC, first the Assyrians, then the Babylonians and then the Persians attacked Palestine and regional authorities and histories were disrupted. During the so-called "Babylonian Captivity," the priests and scribes of Jerusalem decided to transplant the major part of Hebrew history and culture from Sheba to Palestine. But Kamal Salibi has shown that many linguistic, geographic, botanical and zoological mistakes were made in the Bible, terms that still refer to the region of Hijaz and northern Yemen. The words "Jordan," "Ramah," David's "Bathsheba" (girl or woman of Saba) and even Solomon's "Queen of Sheba" all refer to the geography of modern Hijaz and Yemen.[28]

This is the real curse of Tutankhamun's mummy. King Tut's reconstructed life, based on archaeological and linguistic facts, undermines the veracity of orthodox Judaic, Judeo-Christian and Judeo-Islamic canonical scriptures and these, unfortunately, still mould the Western world's and Arab world's foreign policy in the Middle East.

Is it possible Jesus lived around 1350 BC in Egypt, not in first century Palestine? As strange as it may seem to modern Christians, the story of the advent and life of Jesus is much older, than even Tutankhamun. Some "Early Christian Fathers" knew it well, but this wisdom was gradually forgotten under the onslaught of New Testament orthodoxy.

True or original Christianity was the basic belief in a Neolithic "good shepherd" or "teacher of righteousness." He was traditionally put to death y being hung on a bush (or "tree" or "cross") by a "Wicked Priest."

And, by the way, obviously even the very concept of a "good shepherd" is possible only within a culture that had achieved the domestication of sheep. And also, because sheep and lambs are relatively vulnerable, the idea of a "good shepherd" would probably be among the very first conceptions of a Neolithic culture that had managed to domesticate this species. But the notion and necessary reality of shepherds inevitably leads to certain "Christian" principles and moral values: the strong protecting the weak, the need to heal sick and injured "lambs," the obligation of selfless leadership and so on.

It is easy to show that these associations attached to the Neolithic Good Shepherd thousands of years before either the Old Testament or the New Testament was written.

Egyptian-educated Bishop Eusebius (AD 263-339?), usually accorded the epithet "Father of Church History," seems to have known something of the very ancient origins of Christianity. He wrote "Christianity is nothing new and outlandish," but was the oldest religion in the world. St. Augustine (AD 354-430), a former North African pagan who eventually became the Bishop of Hippo in modern Algeria, elaborated on the above-quoted comment by Eusebius: *That which is called the Christian Religion existed among the Ancients, and never did not exist, from the beginning of the human race until Christ came in the flesh, at which time the true religion which already existed began to be called Christianity.*

There is mounting evidence this prehistoric and Neolithic "saviour" was held to be the consort of the Great Fertility Goddess, he was her continually regenerated husband-son. The Neolithic Good Shepherd and consort-son of the Great Goddess was doomed to be ritually sacrificed and replaced by a new "king" at various intervals of months or years, depending on the specific Neolithic cultural group or "tribe."

Both Sir James Fraser in *The Golden Bough* and Robert Graves in *The White Goddess* have discussed this custom in great detail. It might have been inevitable that the Good Shepherd himself would come to be equated and associated with his own lambs. Thus it was written many thousands of years later that Jesus came to his fate "like a lamb to the slaughter" and a metaphor for Jesus is "the Lamb of God," and so on.

The first known name of the Great Goddess seems to have been Dana, although Robert Graves says it was Anna. She was known in Egypt as Isis and to the Greco-Romans as Aphrodite-Venus. In the Middle East, she was also called Cybele, Astarte, Ishtar, and had many other names in many languages extending into western India. The first Grail was her womb, a vessel that continually regenerated humanity and the whole world. And, ultimately, all subsequent historical representations of the Holy Grail referred back to this ancient symbolic motif.[29]

There are some purely zoological reasons for thinking that this belief in the Great Goddess and her Good Shepherd consort-son seems to have originated "somewhere" out in the Atlantic Ocean or on the Atlantic Coast of Europe. Or, perhaps more probably, it may have originated on the now-sunken islands of lost Lyonesse off the coast of modern Brittany. This location of Lyonesse may explain why, in Roman Catholic oral tradition – for it is not written in any known New Testament source – "St. Ann of Brittany" is held to be the mother of Virgin Mary. That is, "St. Ann of Brittany" was held to be the maternal grandmother of Jesus.

This folk belief is something of a minor puzzle in itself because it is difficult to imagine how orthodox early Christians in the Middle East, Greece and Rome could even have learned of far-away Brittany. And why choose a woman from Brittany, of all places, as the mother of supposedly Palestinian Mary?

But "St. Ann of Brittany" may be an allegorical personification of the very first phases of Neolithic development, a time before even Good Shepherds became widely known and generally necessary. "St. Ann" may symbolise a time when the domesti-cation of sheep had just barely been accomplished and it may have been an achievement that was first introduced in Brittany. There are, in fact, several intriguing linguistic reasons for thinking so.[30]

The religion of the Neolithic Earth Goddess and her Good Shepherd consort-son apparently appeared in Northwest Europe first and quickly travelled through southern France. Then it went with Neolithic colonists from the Viols-le-Fort, presently the oldest Neolithic site in the world, and the Narbonne region of France on across the Mediterranean Sea via the islands of Corsica, Sardinia, Sicily and Malta by about 7000 BC.

An important centre of this belief was established in the region of the northern Adriatic Sea – today's Balkan states of Slovenia, Serbia, Croatia, Albania, etc. – within the maritime so-called "Danilo-Hvar Culture" by 7000 BC. And it was here, apparently, the Great Goddess began to be worshipped as a "fish goddess" similar to the fish goddesses of the Danubian Vinca and Lepinski Vir cultures. The problem is that we don't know whether this idea of Isis was inspired by Danubian fish goddesses, or whether the cultural borrowing went the other way around.

From the northern Adriatic, this form of Goddess worship and "true Christianity" was taken even further south and east to Crete, Cyprus, Egypt and elsewhere on the mainland Middle East. We know this, or we can more or less safely conjecture it, because "Balkan-style" sheep and goats from the northern Adriatic arrived in the Nile Delta at the same time as the basic Christian story.[31] And in the Nile Delta, the Great Goddess was simultaneously and very firmly established as "Isis," originally a fish goddess, by about 6000 BC.[32]

An intriguing question, but one that may never be answered and one that is well beyond the specific focus of this book, is the origin of the Great Goddess as "Isis," who eventually transmuted into the Virgin Mary. Was this fishy and maritime notion of the Great Goddess conceived somewhere out on the Atlantic Ocean, or on the Atlantic Coast of Northwest Europe? Or, on the northern Adriatic Sea coast in close proximity to Danubian cultures? No one knows.

We know only that "Isis" was the identity by which the Neolithic and megalithic Great Goddess was known in Egypt from at least 6000 BC. We can also safely conjecture that "Isis" was brought directly to Egypt by maritime colonists from the northern Adriatic's so-called "Danilo-Hvar Culture". But we do not know where belief in "Isis" originated.

It should also be mentioned that at some time, may be between about 7000 BC and perhaps 4000 BC, the Neolithic belief in true Christianity of the Goddess and the Good Shepherd extended all the way to western India. This accounts for the many uncanny similarities between Jesus Christ, Lord Krishna and even Buddha as "good shepherds" and "teachers of righteousness."

Greek Sculpture of Apollo-like Good Shepherd, from 3rd Century BC.   **Indian sculpture of Boddisattva as Good Sheppard, also from 3rd Century BC.**

Scholars of comparative religion have long noted that teachings, parables and sayings attributed to Jesus, Buddha and Krishna are not just generally similar. Given the uncertainties of translation, they seem actually to be identical in literally scores of instances. Some esoteric groups, notably the Rosicrucians, have tried to explain the situation by speculating that Jesus must have travelled to India in his youth in order to teach and to learn before he began his ministry in Palestine. But this assumption cannot, of course, explain why the many statues of the Good Shepherd are pre-Christian by centuries.

The "Atlantean," or (at least) Atlantic, origin of this "true Christianity" may be hinted by a rite that was performed even as late as the 1920s in some parts of India. Here's an interesting story told by the famous British novelist, E.M. Forster. He was once a secretary and general factotum for a minor Indian raja and was charged with organizing the local religious celebrations. Forster recounts that the ten days commemorating the birth of Lord Krishna culminated in the ceremony of sinking a mud-built model of a city in a pond.

This incident is related in Forster's little known collection of letters entitled *The Hill at Devi* (1927),[33] written long before his much more famous novel, *A Passage to India*. Did this ancient but so recently living custom reflect some localised Indian flooding? Or, did it reflect Plato's version of the end of Atlantis? Did it recall the similar sinking, on a smaller scale, of the lost islands of Lyonesse? Perhaps it is only coincidence the traditional capital city of Lyonesse was most anciently called "Kris." Is this where the word "Christ" came from, meaning a rightfully anointed king, whose capital city was once sunken Kris on Lyonesse? Is this really the deepest origin of the word "Christianity?" It is a fascinating thought, but will probably never be a provable one.

It is very much worth noting that people believing in the Old Religion or "true Christianity" were remarkably peaceful by our present standards. What Dr. Marija Gimbutas has termed the "Civilization of the Goddess" once extended from Ireland to India between about 10,000 BC and about 4500 BC when Indo-European Language speakers from the Caucasus-steppes of "Russia" began to encroach upon it.

By the fall of 2003, over 100 sites of this Goddess-worshipping culture had been excavated in Northwest Europe, the Mediterranean coasts of France, Italy, the Balkans, Greece and a scattering of sites through Syria, Iraq, Iran and on into western India. In August 2002, the discovery of the "oldest city in the world" underwater just off the Kathiawar Peninsula of extreme western India was somewhat over-enthusiastically announced. It has so far been dated to about 7500 BC, but that is 2500 years younger than Viols-le-Fort in France.

There were no empires, although there was a definite and cohesive religious conception among these far-flung people and many cultural affinities from one site to the next. They lived in apparently independent townships, some of which could accommodate up to 10,000 people. In some places they constructed stone-built houses or cottages laid out along identifiable streets, as at Viols-le-Fort, Rennes-le-Château and many sites in the Balkans. In other places, they built wooden houses. There are always megalithic structures near their settlements and dotting the countryside between villages.

There could have been very little organised warfare during this 10,000 BC to 4500 BC era because weapons represent less than 1 per cent of the tens of thousands of artifacts so far recovered. During this long period from 10,000 BC to 4500 BC in Europe and Western Asia, not one walled town or city has so far been discovered.[26] They were peaceful artisans, farmers, orchard-tenders, herdsmen, beekeepers and, above all, traders by both land and sea. The bulk of artifacts, some 65 per cent presently tabulated, consist of wooden, stone, copper and some-times bronze tools and implements (including boat paddles with long handles). About 30 percent of the artifacts are personal adornments and some items have not been identified.

City and town sites are predominantly coastal or located on navigable rivers leading to the sea. It is very evident that people of this Old European Civilisation much preferred to settle on islands near a mainland whenever possible. Groups that penetrated inland even built artificial islands out in lakes – large wooden platforms supported on wooden pylons with only a narrow bridge to the shore.

Literally tens of thousands of clay-moulded votive offerings to the Great Goddess have been recovered from the period 10,000 to 4500 BC, the majority of them clustering around 6500 to 4500 BC, a fact that seems to indicate the heyday of the Old European Civilisation. The Great Goddess is always depicted naked, sometimes reclining and sometimes in the process of giving birth. She has wide hips and hefty breasts, and there may well be a definite cultural affinity with, and evolution from, the "Venus figurines" of some Upper Paleolithic European hunting cultures of the last "Ice Age" about 23,000 BC. Votive offerings of the Neolithic Good Shepherd usually show him with a proud erection and swollen testicles appropriate for the consort of a fertility goddess.

It may be that Hesiod, a Greek poet who was a near contemporary of Homer, was referring to folk memories of this Old European Civilisation when he wrote of a past "Golden Age" of humanity. During this Golden Age, he wrote, "men then lived on honey and acorn-bread and were subject to their mothers their whole life long, but at least they did not make war upon one another."

There are now over 100 Neolithic-megalithic sites, most with nearby museums, on Corsica, Sardinia, Sicily, Malta and Hvar where hundreds of artifacts of this Old European Civilisation of the Goddess can be seen. Archaeologists began to realise with great excitement back in the 1970s that an entirely new civilisation had been discovered. The previous lost civilisations of Minoan Crete and Mycenaean Greece, not to mention the excavation of Homer's Troy, had generated immense fascination among scholars and the general public. But the very recently discovered

"Civilisation of the Goddess" was immeasurably older than Minoa, Mycenae or Troy and was the deepest taproot of Western culture.

French anthropologists Marcel Griaule and Germaine Dieterlen have documented the fact that the basic Christian story had come to predynastic Egypt by at least 6000 BC.[35] By 1400 or 1350 BC in Egypt, specific motifs of recognisable modern Christianity had evolved. These motifs included initial baptism with the "water of life", the Triune nature of the Divinity – the Father, Son and a *female* Holy Spirit – and the similarly triune "Holy Family". We have seen how Howard Carter discovered these elements in the tomb of Tutankhamun in 1922.

The Egyptian Saviour was called the *meseh*, or "crocodile", because he was ritually anointed with crocodile oil. He "became" a crocodile. Personally, I suspect that his association with crocodiles was because of the obvious fact that crocodiles are voracious predators of fish. They seemed eager and determined, therefore, to fill themselves (in a way, that is) with the divine essence of the Fish Goddess Isis.

The Ancient Egyptian practice of Christianity also included some specific liturgical vestments that are still used by some Christian priests today... such as the Christian "Dalmatic" style of ceremonial robe. This word comes from "Dalmatia" on the Adriatic coast and is another indication true Christianity experienced a period of development in the Balkans before coming to Ancient Egypt.

The Israelites, during their well-known sojourn in Goshen or northeastern Egypt about 1700-1300 BC, apparently picked up this Egyptian belief in a world saviour and modified the Egyptian word *meseh* into the Hebrew word *messiah*, but still meaning "a rightfully anointed king." But the biblical Hebrews, while accepting the male Egyptian Messiah easily enough, felt compelled to change the sex of the supreme deity to conform with their male-dominant mindset. Earth Mother Isis became "our father" Jehovah as *Aten* eventually came to be called.

The Son and Saviour's "proper name" seems always to have been *Essa* or *Issa*, as used in the Koran, and this is still the Arabic/Aramaic for our word "Jesus", which is merely a Latin form of the same name.[36]

The prophets of the Old Testament are thought to have come out of "the wilderness," as the Bible calls it, which actually means any desert. The "Essene Community" was located in the wilderness around the Dead Sea in the last few centuries BC. These people were really *Essa*-enes, that is, hermit and ascetic believers in the world-saving *messiah*. One of the most famous prophets, Hosea (circa 750 BC), makes no bones about the *messiah's* originally Egyptian origins, from the Israelites' point of view. "Out of Egypt have I called my Son," wrote Hosea.

Obviously, however, so-called "prophecy" was not any sort of factor here. There was never any such thing as the so-called "Pre-existent Christ". This was merely a conception of desperate Christian theologians who had to explain away so much pre-Christian evidence of Jesus. Essenes like Hosea were actually historians of an already ancient religious tradition, although Israelite knowledge of it apparently did not reach back beyond Ancient Egyptian adoption of a much older creed.

This is why the Dead Sea Scrolls have caused so much controversy for orthodox Christianity and Judaism and why the complete translation of them was withheld for over half a century. The full translation was finally leaked on the Internet. The "Teacher of Righteousness," "Jesus," is mentioned in Dead Sea Scrolls that have been radiocarbon-dated to 250 BC.[37] This did not suit the purposes of either modern Christians or of modern Israel.

This name of "Essa" or "Issa" means, quite literally, the *issue* or *essence* of the Goddess Isis[38] and it is a muted and distorted whisper from prehistoric Neolithic times when the son-husband of the Great Fertility Goddess was believed to be "Her" consort.

There's biblical evidence this name, Iesu, which the Hebrews rendered "Y'shua" – or our modern "Joshua" or "Jesus" – was in usage by at least about 1400-1350 BC, or roughly around the time of Tutankhamun. But this evidence requires a clear explanation.

Left, Isis holding infant Horus as the "Madonna and child," Greco-Egyptian, 3rd Century BC. Right, familiar and later Christian Madonna and Child, 5th Century AD. Note (arrow) that even the Horns of Isis are replicated but as wheat sheaves, on this Madonna. The halo was originally the light essence of divinity in Isis.

Sigmund Freud, the discoverer of psychoanalysis, applied his methods to the Old Testament and fundamental Judaism. In *Moses and Monotheism* (1939), he concluded that biblical Moses had either been the Egyptian "heretical Pharaoh" known as Akenaten or else had been a prominent priest of Aten.

The biblical name "Moses" was just the well-known Egyptian suffix *mosis* – as in Thoth*mosis*, for example. The word meant roughly "rightful heir" or "rightful child" in Ancient Egyptian. It was used in some XVIII Dynasty legal documents.[39] Thus, the biblical Hebrews of the Exodus regarded Moses as the rightful child of *Aten*, or even the rightful "king", even if most of the Egyptians had repudiated him and had chased him into exile.

The successor of biblical Moses was, of course, "Joshua ben Nun" (or "Joshua, son of the Fish"), just as the successors of Akenaten was known to have been Smenkhkare and Tutankhamun, both of them being also the theoretical sons of the Fish Goddess Isis. Therefore, Tutankhamun must also have been "Joshua" or "Issa" or "Jesus".

Freud personally knew Howard Carter, excavator of Tutankhamun's famous tomb,[40] and met him several times at various European scientific conferences. Freud and Carter also conducted a long correspondence. Freud knew Tutankhamun had tried to reconcile Egyptians by permitting and restoring worship of the traditional gods and goddesses, even though he himself apparently believed in *Aten* during all of his brief life.

Freud also knew Tutankhamun was murdered by dismemberment while being hung on a tree, an ancient Israelite form of punishment reserved for particularly odious criminals or particularly dangerous enemies. The Talmud mentions Jesus – or more often, "a certain person" – over 20 times. According to the Talmud, Jesus had been a false prophet or "evil magician" who styled himself "king" and who was executed for trying to lead Israel astray. In the story of Moses and the Exodus, the Old Testament introduces Joshua as the successor to Moses.

Freud the psychiatrist suspected immediately that this Joshua, the Israelites' biblical conqueror of Canaan, had been a compensating psychological projection on the part of the Hebrews. The Hebrews, probably under orders from the deposed and exiled Akenaten, executed Tutankhamun as a traitor and apostate to *Aten*-worship. But, guilt-ridden at having killed a Pharaoh and Messiah, the priests then psychologically transformed their real victim into their mythic champion.

Freud's conclusions were given reasonable support because archaeology from the 1930s to the 1950s – and still, for that matter – has failed to find any evidence of Joshua's military conquest of Canaan, or *any* Hebrew military conquest of Canaan. Dr. Ze'ev Herzog, a prominent Israeli archaeologist that we have quoted before, caused a minor political crisis in Israel in 1998. He wrote in the pages of Israel's upscale *Ha'aretz* magazine that the victories of Joshua are a myth that is not supported by archaeology in the so-called "Holy Land". In fact, there's no evidence whatsoever of any specifically identifiable Hebrew presence in Palestine until about 850 BC.

There's no real mystery about where the biblical Israelites were from the time of the Exodus about 1350 BC until the first signs of them in Palestine about 850 BC, a period of roughly five hundred years. We have already dealt with this. And, by the way, there's equally no mystery about where the tomb of Moses is located.[41]

But, aside from all that, it is clear enough that Joshua didn't exist in his Old Testament role. However, his name "Y'shua" or "Jesus" was equated in time with Tutankhamun. Both biblical Joshua and Tutankhamun lived about 1350-1330 BC

So, the name "Issa", "Y'shua", "Joshua" or "Jesus" had been applied to the Messiah as early as about 1350 BC. In the present canonical Greek Orthodox version of the Bible, for example, there is no such person as "Joshua ben Nun" in the Old Testament. In the standard Greek version of the Old Testament, straightforward "Jesus ben Nun" – Jesus, son of the Fish – supposedly conquered Canaan for the Israelites.[42] Latin-speaking Romans and Palestinians of John the Baptist's time would have written the name as "Iesus" or "Jesus", but they still would have pronounced it something like "Yesus".

So, by this roundabout proof based on the work of Sigmund Freud, we know that the Egyptian Meseh or Messiah was familiarly known as "Jesus", "Y'shua", "Iesu", "Essa", "Issa" and so on, at least as early as 1350 BC, the time of Tutankhamun. It is also well known that the Celtic Church had especially close ties with Egypt and believed in a teacher of righteousness before the Christian Era began, and so now we also know who the Celtic Church's "Yesu" was.

This ancient and Egyptian Christian belief in "Jesus", son of Isis, was appropriated and distorted by Hebrews living in Palestine during the confused time of Roman take-over from the Greeks. This change in the political domination of the Mediterranean world followed the Roman victory over Anthony and Cleopatra in 31 BC at the Battle of Actium off the western coast of Greece. The Jews soon discovered Roman rule was much harsher than the easy-going Ptolemaic Greek rule of Anthony and

Cleopatra. The Romans had no patience with fundamentalist Hebrew religious beliefs that continually inspired Jewish zealots to undertake armed revolts against Caesar Augustus and his successors. The Roman response was a strong military presence, quick crucifixion of militant dissidents and even the eventual expulsion of Jews from Judea.

Greeks and their Roman successors have been presented in Judeo-Christian literature as immoral and decadent oppressors of righteously God-fearing monotheistic Jews who lived according to the strict morality of The Law of Moses. Well, that's one way of looking at it.

But another way of looking at it is that both the Greeks and Romans sought to create what Alexander the Great had termed a *Cosmopolis*, a "World City," a place where diverse people from different countries could live together with a degree of social and sexual equality – given the conceptions of that era, that is.[43] And it was a place where an open interchange of religious, intellectual, cultural, literary and scientific ideas could flourish. This concept is similar to modern ideals of tolerant "Multiculturalism" and our recognition of the so-called "Global Village."

The great Library of Alexandria, founded by Alexander's successor in Egypt, Ptolemy II, was a tangible manifestation of Alexander's dream. And the teeming, sophisticated and "cosmopolitan" city of Alexandria was itself the living proof of a "world city" where scholars from all over the known world, representing most known cultures and religious ideas, studied and taught freely.

The Jews wanted no part of this so-called "Cosmopolis" – not unless, that is, their own religious Law, which was the only possible right one in the eyes of their God, was imposed upon everyone. They fought first the Greeks and then the Romans with staunch determination to avoid any acceptance of, or assimilation within, any such world community. On a very basic level, they refused to intermarry with non-Jews, and they generally still do. The Greeks and Romans viewed this behaviour as a blatant form of what we would now term "racism."[44] Because they were the self-proclaimed "Chosen People," the inference was that Jews considered themselves superior to the rest of humanity. Where did this unbending religious intolerance and cultural chauvinism come from?

The belief in Isis and her Good Shepherd son and consort, the so-called "Messiah", had already made considerable inroads in Palestine before the Battle of Actium. This was completely understandable because both Palestine and Egypt belonged to Marc Anthony under the division of formerly Greek territory approved by the Roman Senate.

In fact, it is interesting to note, in view of subsequent Christian so-called "history," that Marc Anthony "gave" Palestine to his lover,

Cleopatra, in 44 BC. Cleopatra, then personally ruled Palestine until the victory of Octavian, better known to New Testament readers as Augustus Caesar. It was Cleopatra, not Anthony, who established Herod the Great as Jewish puppet king over part of Palestine.

This leads to an extremely interesting possibility that is, admittedly, just a speculation. The famous and beautiful Cleopatra who captivated both Julius Caesar and Marc Anthony was actually the seventh in a succession of Cleopatras. She was, in the belief of Egyptians at least, a direct descendant from the ancient Great Goddess Isis.

Egypt had a semi-matriarchal system. A male aspirant to the Egyptian throne could become Pharaoh – literally "the light," but by usage "king" – only if he married the current descendant of Isis. He then automatically also became the "Meseh" or "Messiah." This often meant that a brother married a sister, the supposed matrilinear descendant of Isis, in order that royalty and wealth would remain "in the family." But occasionally usurpers became Pharaoh by marrying an "Isis-descended" princess.

At least one of Cleopatra VII's brothers married her to become Pharaoh of Egypt and he was apparently either accidentally or purposefully drowned in the Nile. She appears to have married a second brother, too, and he seems to have been assassinated. All this happened before Julius Caesar arrived on the Alexandrian scene. He was the uninvited Roman "protector" of the grain-rich formerly Greek-ruled territory of Egypt that was so avidly coveted by Rome.

Caesar also married Cleopatra in order to solidify his position as Pharaoh. At least, he married her by Egyptian rites. However, he wisely didn't advertise this fact to the SPQR, the official and ponderously ubiquitous abbreviation for Senatus Populusque Romanorum or "the Senate and People of the Romans." Nonetheless, in Egyptian eyes, Caesar was Pharaoh...for a short time, anyway. After the assassination of Julius Caesar, his dashing cavalry commander, Marc Anthony, also promptly succumbed to Cleopatra's charms, married her, and so became the last Pharaoh of "Ancient" Egypt.

As we know, with Octavian's victory at Actium and his immediate invasion of Egypt, Marc Anthony fell on his sword and Cleopatra clasped a poisonous snake, an asp, to her bosom. Cleopatra's son by Julius Caesar, Caesarion, was summarily killed by Octavian. Caesarion was Caesar's legal heir and this made Augustus Caesar's own legal position more than just a little iffy. Being a Roman from a patriarchal culture, Octavian paid little attention to Cleopatra's daughters.

There were at least two daughters of Cleopatra VII and they were of crucial importance within the Egyptian matriarchal scheme of things because they were – supposedly, that is – direct descendants of Isis through their mother. Anyone who married them would have become the legitimate Egyptian Messiah. One daughter, thought to have been the eldest, was called Cleopatra Selene and is known to have married King Juba I of Mauretania. She is therefore accounted for.

But one daughter is not accounted for and this brings us to a matter all Christian historians and theologians have been very careful to avoid.

According to the Jewish-Roman historian Flavius Josephus in his *Antiquities of the Jews* (Book XVIII), John the Baptist from Egypt attracted crowds of 50,000 people in Jerusalem and Judea at some date after AD 21 but before AD 52, the exact duration of John's ministry is uncertain. John offered the Ancient Egyptian rite of Baptism in running water, or "living" water, as a prerequisite for the eternal life of the soul. This was before the days of mass media and therefore John must have had some obvious claim to fame among those people who fondly remembered the tolerant rule of Egypt and Palestine under Cleopatra.

First of all, it is important to realise that, in theory at least, only an Egyptian Pharaoh-Messiah could offer and conduct the rite of Baptism. The Pharaoh and Messiah was also the Chief Priest of Ptolemaic Egyptian life. And, although his secular title was "Pharaoh" and his spiritual title was "the Messiah", his more popular or "familial" name would have been something like "Iessu" or "Issa" or "Essa" – that is, "the essence or *issue* of Isis".

This may sound complicated, but it is roughly analogous to the custom that the "Prince of Wales" is traditionally "Heir Apparent" to the British throne and the present one is popularly known by his family-given name of "Charles". All three are the same person.

Was the figure we know as John the Baptist *a* legitimate Messiah of Egypt – *the* legitimate Messiah at the dawn of the "Christian" era?

Was he the longed-for Messiah of those Palestinians who were either of Egyptian extraction themselves or who were Jewish sympathizers of Cleopatra's former regime? Given the harshness of Octavian's (Augustus Caesar's) policy in both Palestine and in Egypt, there almost must have been some sort of "Palestinian-Egyptian Liberation Organization" in John the Baptist's lifetime. To stress how close in time Cleopatra was to the start of the "Christian Era," we should realise that at least a few Palestinians alive in John the Baptist's day could have retained a living memory of Cleopatra. She had been dead only fifty-one years in AD 21.

It is not at all unlikely that at least some Jews in Palestine would have also gravitated to this Egyptian Messiah in spite of his Egyptian origin, or may be even because of it. There was a sort of "Messiah madness" infecting the Jews of the day and, referring to the advent of the Messiah, the prophet Hosea had said it clearly enough: "Out of Egypt I have called my Son". Such Jews would have expected the Messiah to rally the "Palestinian-Egyptian Liberation Organization" and kick the hated Romans out of both countries.

Several things should be emphasised here, as they've been deftly side-stepped by Jewish and Christian writers. First, Palestine at the time of the Roman take-over from the Greeks was *not* predominantly "Jewish." The impression fostered in Judeo-Christian literature is that Palestine of the time was almost wholly a Jewish territory.

Biblical Hebrews did represent a sizeable minority of the "Holy Land's" population, but not the majority of it. This is clear from Roman taxation records. Also, when the Romans expelled the Jews from Judea in AD 70, well, the place wasn't in any way desolated or depopulated. All sorts of people lived in Palestine: Jews, Greeks, Egyptians and native Palestinians who worshipped all sorts of gods and goddesses. There is undoubtedly a much greater proportion of Jews in the territory of "Palestine" today than there ever was at any time in the past.

The "Messiah madness" that affected the Jews of the time has been attributed in Judeo-Christian literature solely to the Jewish expectation of the Messiah's advent that had been "prophesied" in the Old Testament. But this is also a distortion of reality and one that has been achieved by the simple expedient of ignoring everyone except Jews who inhabited Palestine and by ignoring everything that was not Jewish-related in Palestine. But the truth of the matter is that so long as the Ptolemaic Greeks ruled Palestine *there had always been a Messiah as a "saviour" who could offer baptism and "life" to the people.*

The "Messiah madness" of the first century was due to the *lack* of a Messiah, not due mostly to ancient biblical prophecies of one to come at some undefined time in the future.

Remember that Palestine had traditionally belonged to Egypt and was considered an Egyptian "sphere of influence." Marc Anthony's rule of Palestine and Egypt had been confirmed by the SPQR and he had "given" Palestine to Cleopatra – it was already hers and Egypt's by tradition. But since the time Marc Anthony and Cleopatra were defeated in 31 BC, and since Egypt had been occupied a year later in 30 BC, many Palestinian people had been bereft of their Messiah. If there was "Messiah madness" in Palestine after the time of Augustus Caesar's reign, it was because there had been no Egyptian Messiah for about 40 years and yet one was suddenly rumoured to be alive, well and active.

This excitement would have gripped the many Egyptians in Palestine most directly. But it would also have fascinated some Jews because of their own Old Testament "prophecies."

Greeks and pagan Palestinians would also have been curious about this rumoured Messiah because Roman rule was oppressive. The Messiah, in some peoples' opinion, would end Roman domination.

To have been the legitimate Egyptian Messiah meant that John would most likely have been born to a daughter or granddaughter of Cleopatra and also be married to his own sister. Cleopatra VII died in 30 BC and one of her daughters, Cleopatra Arsinoë, is thought to have been about 10 years old at the time. She would have been about 40 years old when John could have been born at about the time of the New Testament's nativity story. We are specifically informed in the New Testament that "Jesus" and John were born within six months of each other.

According to the New Testament, John's mother was named Elizabeth and she was "stricken in years" so that her husband was amazed to think that she could have a child. Forty was a fairly old age back then, but did not necessarily compromise a woman's fertility. Elizabeth could certainly have conceived a child at that age, or even more than one, and could also have borne them successfully.

Most books supplying "names for girls" say that the name Elizabeth means something like "Oath of God". It does not, at least, not in Hebrew. It means El ("god" or "goddess")-isa ("Isis")-beth/bat ("girl" or "house"). So, we have "House of the Goddess Isis" as Elizabeth's real name in Hebrew. "Oath of God" is not just ridiculous, it is serious disinformation. Perhaps this misdirection has been intended to obscure and disguise any possible connection between Jesus and Cleopatra.

The meaning of "House of the Goddess Isis" is fairly clear anyway, but becomes even a little clearer with an insight into Egyptian usage. And any daughter of Cleopatra VII, Queen of Egypt, even deposed and dead, would not have forgotten her own Egyptian origins.

In Egyptian, even any ordinary married woman was regarded as the "house" of her husband. The Queen of Egypt was "the house of Pharaoh". A descendant of Isis would certainly, therefore, have been the "house" or "dwelling place" of the Goddess. It would not have been so odd if a daughter (or grand-daughter?) of Cleopatra happened to reside in Palestine and called herself "Elisabeth" (i.e. "Elishabat" in the local Hebrew-Aramaic pronunciation). Palestine had just recently belonged to Egypt and Cleopatra, after all, and Cleopatra had even resided there for a time. It is even possible that Cleopatra Arsinoë had actually been born in Palestine if, as seems probable from her assumed age, she was the daughter of either of Cleopatra's two early husbands or Julius Caesar.

And as far as danger from the Romans was concerned, they occupied Egypt just as thoroughly and brutally as they occupied Palestine. Egypt was no safer than Palestine for the matriarchal heir of Cleopatra.

I have always found it a bit curious that two of the most dominant personalities of the early "Christian Era," the near-contemporaries Cleopatra and Jesus, are almost never mentioned in the same breath or sentence by historians. But here we have a definite indication that John the Baptist may have been related to Cleopatra. We have some reason to conjecture that John could have been the legitimate Egyptian Messiah and we have several very good reasons to think that the Messiah had always been called Jesus from at least 1350 BC.

The figure we know as Mary Magdalene, therefore, may well also have been John the Baptist's sister and wife. We know nothing much about her except that, according to the Gospel of Philip from the Nag Hammadi texts discovered in 1945, she was the Messiah's "special and beloved companion" and that he often kissed her on the lips.[45]

Perhaps it only has to be added that Cleopatra Arsinoë is thought to have died in Ephesus in modern Turkey at the age of 67... just like the Virgin Mary. It is recorded that Cleopatra Arsinoë ended her days as a priestess in the Ephesus Temple of Artemis. Artemis was the local "Turkish" name and identity of the Great Goddess.

Due to the popularity of John the Baptist, the Egyptian religion of the Messiah was already threatening the dominance of Judaism in some areas of Roman-ruled Palestine. Less than three generations after the Battle of Actium, for example, Paul went to preach "Christiantity" in Ephesus and found "Christians" already well established there. But in Ephesus "the Christ" was the Egyptian Messiah named John who had offered the Ancient Egyptian rite of baptism as the prerequisite for eternal life. John the Baptist, by the way, is the only major personality of the New Testament to be mentioned in any historical source outside of the New Testament itself. John is favourably described by Flavius Josephus in *Antiquities of the Jews* (Book XVIII).

Something had to be done about the threat to Judaism posed by Egyptian Christianity. And something was, indeed, done. The originally Ptolemaic-Egyptian religion of "Christianity" or "Messiah-worship" was given a specifically Judaic twist by Hebrews living in Palestine in order to disguise its legitimate Egyptian content and especially to disguise any possible connection with Isis. This historical distortion and imposition became so-called "orthodox Judeo-Christianity."[46]

This distortion occurred simply because Saul, a rabbinical student under the great Rabbi, Gamaliel, grandson of Hillel, suddenly "converted" to Christianity and became "Paul."

And, as Paul – later St. Paul – he wrote almost all of the original New Testament which modern scholars technically call "Marcion's Canon". Hyam Maccoby, a rather famous modern Jewish scholar at the Leo Baeck Talmudic Institute in London, England, has admitted and demonstrated Saul/Paul's hijacking of Christianity in his book *The Mythmaker: Paul and the Invention of Christianity* (1986).

Paul rather obviously used the truly historical career of John the Baptist as the basic structure of the New Testament story because he could hardly do anything else. John's activities were quite well known to literally thousands of people living in Palestine in Paul's time. John's existence and activities had also been acknowledged by one of the most respected historians of the time, and a Jewish one at that. But then, using the age-old "proper name" of the Messiah, Paul invented a fictitious "true saviour" named Jesus – John's "other" name. This Jesus came from a purely Jewish background and had no connections with Egypt at all, except for Hosea's awkward prophecy.

Paul played it even safer by writing that John and Jesus had been born only six months apart and to mothers who were actually related. It was thus fairly easy to confuse the real career of John with the fictional addition of Jesus – and then to meld one with the other. The ruse worked simply because very few people in either Palestine or Rome were literate and Paul was an extremely prolific and equally gifted writer.

He wrote almost all there was to read about "the Christ," including almost certainly the Gospel of John – there's an internal "almost proof" of Paul's authorship[47] – and possibly also the Gospel of Luke. In addition, Paul wrote the majority of Epistles in the New Testament. Subsequent Early Christian priests and bishops, having little recourse except to rely upon Paul's writing, preached Paul's version of the Christian story and it became orthodox at the Council of Nicea in AD 325.

So we see that the religion of the Holy Grail is really the same as the religion of true and original Christianity, reverence for the Great Goddess and her Good Shepherd husband-son consort. And we see that this earliest Western religion came from the Atlantic Coast of Europe, or even from somewhere out in the Atlantic Ocean itself. It did not originate in the Middle East and, in fact, only reached the Middle East belatedly via Ancient Egypt. There are papyrus records – quoted and sometimes illustrated in the various works of Osman, Kenyon, Badawy, Redford and Fakhry – indicating that Ankhsenpa-Aten, the wife of Tutankhamun, came from the fortified Egyptian border town of Mediggo, the

"Magdala" of the New Testament. The Ancient Egyptian word *mery*, meaning "beloved of the sea", was an epithet applied to Isis and is used, in existing papyri, to refer to Tutankhamun's wife (Ankhsenpa-Aten) and to Tutankhamun's step-mother, Nefertiti.

Therefore, even the orthodox New Testament preserves the ancient notion that *a Mary* had to be both the mother and the wife of Jesus. And this Mary, of course, is really the Great Goddess Isis.

We now come to something that must be dealt with at least superficially in order to satisfy the increasingly strident demands of racial politics in North America and even the world. Was Jesus "Black"… that is to say, "Negro"… as African-American historians have claimed with ever-increasing vehemence since Marcus Garvey's assertions?

As early as 1924, the Italian anthropologist Alessandro Biasutti concluded from his forensic study of several dozen pre-dynastic (natural, before 3200 BC) and dynastic (artificially mummified, after 3200 BC) Ancient Egyptian mummies that racially the Ancient Egyptian population had been a mix. It had been about equal thirds "Caucasian," Saan and Negroids. A slight preponderance of Caucasians was marked in pre-dynastic times, but gradually changed by the Eighteenth Dynasty (roughly the 1400-1300 BC era) to become a bit more than one-third Negroid. Biasutti's observations entirely agree with the very latest archaeological and geographic data from the 1970s and 1990s.

If we choose to regard Tutankhamun as a highly refined "Jesus figure" because of the Christian artifacts that Howard Carter discovered in his tomb in late 1922, then we also have to admit that Tutankhamun's facial features do display definite Negroid physical characteristics.

These could hardly have come from his putative "father" (Akenaten) and his putative "mother" or step-mother, Nefertiti. Akenaten had definite Caucasian characteristics, but with anomalies that have caused some archaeologists to think that he suffered from Froelich's syndrome, Marfan's syndrome – or both. These metabolic conditions could explain his own intolerance and also the monotheistic fanaticism of biblical Moses – assuming, as Sigmund Freud concluded, that they were almost undoubtedly the same person. Negroid characteristics in Tutankhamun's facial and skeletal features could also not have come from his putative "mother", Nefertiti, the wife of Akenaten. Her bust is the prize of the Berlin Museum and clearly shows a particularly exquisite example of a purely Caucasian, not a Negroid, type of beauty.

These facts reinforce the idea that Tutankhamun wasn't the actual son of Akenaten and Nefertiti, but was possibly the son of Amenhotep III (Akenaten's father) and his original wife, Sitamun. This idea is given some support by the fact that Akenaten and Nefertiti were often depicted with their six obvious daughters, but never with an obvious boy child as well. Therefore, Tutankhamun's definite Negroid features would seem to have come from Amenhotep III and Sitamun (or some other princess).

It is known, however, that Tutankhamun married the youngest daughter of Akenaten and Nefertiti, a girl called Ankhsenpa-Aten, and this would have been politically necessary, or at least desirable, in order to legitimise his reign after the deposition of Akenaten. It is also thought that Tutankhamun died too young to have a child by Ankhsenpa-Aten and this may be of interest to students of Masonic and Grail lore. The Masonic code phrase "Son of the Widow Lady" refers to a "spiritual" son of the actual son that Ankhsenpa-Aten never had a chance to bear.

Therefore, if we regard Tutankhamun as the original "Jesus figure," then he was at least partly and definitely Negro, if not purely "Black."

And what about the first century Messiah, John the Baptist? If he were, indeed, a descendant of Cleopatra VII, then he would have been at least "Blacker" than your average Egyptian or Palestinian. Roman historians like Plutarch and Suetonius make the point that Cleopatra was notably "dusky" and this tradition persisted up until Shakespeare's plays. John the Baptist, as the real New Testament Messiah, was very probably just as dusky as Cleopatra if not pure Negro.

Then, we are faced with the fact that there are several hundred "Shrines of the Black Madonna" scattered throughout Caucasian "Christian" Europe. One naturally wonders why – unless there had been an ancient and enduring belief that the mother of the first century Messiah had been "dusky".

Thus, the Judeo-Christian Tradition distorted real religious history by obscuring the Egyptian origin of recognisably modern Christianity. And it not only promoted a false perspective of Palestine's secular and ethnic history. It also changed the Messiah from being a racially mixed saviour for all people into a purely Caucasian Son of a purely Caucasian God.[48] This change of racial affiliation was dictated by the Judaic Talmud's so-called "Hamitic Curse" (circa 400 BC) which began the Judeo-Christian doctrine that Negroes were "inferior". This was a doctrine that subsequently justified slavery on the basis of race, a uniquely Judeo-Christian cultural legacy that resulted in immense human misery.[49]

Readers may be interested to know that very little has been written in this chapter about original and early Christianity that wasn't previously said in *The Templar Revelation* (Touchstone Books, Simon and Schuster,

London, 1997) by the well-known British authors Lynn Picknett and Clive Prince.

One can only read so much, however, and I didn't read *The Templar Revelation* until December 2003. It is interesting to me that two sets of authors came to almost exactly the same conclusions by following the same trail of available primary data. The objective facts really admit of no other conclusions about early Christianity.

Notes to Chapter 3.

[1] Many newspaper stories of the times neglect to mention the presence of Arthur "Pecky" Callender but he was highly important to the subsequent exploration of Tutankhamun's tomb. Carter had employed him to create the security grid that secured the otherwise open door to the crypt after the 3300-year-old entrance was first discovered and breached on November 1922.

[2] *Tutankhamun: The Exodus Conspiracy*, pages 55-68.

[3] *Tutankhamun: The Exodus Conspiracy*, pages 75-77.

[4] This and some other newspaper quotes in the text have been taken from a reading of some 163 newspaper articles of the era. I cannot vouch that all the quotes are accurate.

[5] *Tutankhamun: The Exodus Conspiracy*, page 71.

[6] See Note 4 above.

[7] See Note 4 above.

[8] See Ahmed Osman's *Out of Egypt* (1998).

[9] See the illustration in Ahmed Osman's *Out of Egypt* (1998).

[10] See illustration in Ahmed Osman's *Out of Egypt* (1998) and Michael Baigent's *The Temple and the Lodge*, (1989).

[11] *Tutankhamun: The Exodus Conspiracy*, page 155. But the direct quote in the text is from the *Times* of London, December 1, 1922.

[12] The *Times* of London. December 1, 1922.

[13] Date of "The Balfour Declaration": November 2, 1917.

[14] *The grand piano came by camel: Arthur C. Mace, the neglected Egyptologist*, Christopher C. Lee, page 139-140.

[15] See Ahmed Osman's *Out of Egypt*.

[16] See Ahmed Osman's *Out of Egypt*

[17] See Ahmed Osman's *Out of Egypt*

[18] Some sources list Khamose as the founder of the Eighteenth Dynasty, the father of Amose I?

[19] This fact supports the general idea that the Hi-bi-ru were constituents of the Hyksos horde that had settled around the former Hyksos capital.

[20] See *Stranger in the Valley of the Kings* (1987) and *Out of Egypt* (1998).

[21] Sometimes spelled "Ay". The Egyptian adoption of Hyksos-Hittite chariots and their roughly contemporary adoption of the composite bow about 1500 BC allowed them rough parity with the Hyksos invaders. This, combined with their greater local numbers, allowed them to force the Hyksos from Egypt between about 1550 BC and about 1350 BC

[22] *Tutankhamun: The Exodus Conspiracy*, pages 17-21.

[23] Ahmed Osman, *Out of Egypt*, pages 193-203.

[24] *Out of Egypt*, pages 193-195.

[25] Also mentioned in the Talmud.

[26] The Bible says that Moses stayed in the territory of "the Midianites" (or eastern, modern Jordan). But no one presently knows how far southward the "territory of the Midianiates" may have extended in biblical times of circa 1400 BC

[27] The "territory of the Midianites" may well have extended southward along the coast of the Red Sea to Saba (the "Sheba" of the Bible).

[28] There are many surprising repercussions of this reconstructed Exodus.

When Akenaten finally attained undisputed power, he transferred his capital from the traditional Thebes to a new city three hundred miles further south, "Tell El Armarna". So far, we have dealt only with Akenaten's northern followers concentrated in biblical "Goshen". But what about the followers he must have acquired around Tell El Armarna and even further south in Egypt under his fanatical rule? These people could not have participated in the biblical Exodus and yet they were "Jews" – that is, they adhered to Akenaten's "Mosaic Laws". But they would have been just as unwelcome as Akenaten's northern adherents in the reconstituted Egypt that followed the deposition and exile of Akenaten and (it seems) the death of Nefertiti. The most likely answer is that these southern "Jews" fled and were harried southward along the Nile. But at modern Khartoum in the Sudan, the Nile splits into the "White Nile" and the "Blue Nile". The White Nile continues to flow from almost due southward, coming out of Lake Victoria. The Blue Nile flows from the east and the highlands of Ethiopia, coming most directly out of Lake Tana. Therefore, there is completely logical reason why "Jews" would have been established at an early time in Ethiopia (now called the "Falasha") and even further south in Central Africa (the Limba tribe of modern Uganda). There is no real mystery here and no justification for the rather wild claims of being the "true and original Jews" on the part of some Afro-American writers. Then, too, if (as seems most likely) the Exilic "Israelites" actually trekked to Hijaz and Yemen, there are also important repercussions. It is known that there was a lively trade across the Indian Ocean between India and Yemen as early as 4000 BC. Therefore, there is no logical barrier to "Jewish" traders and small Jewish communities being established as far east as India and even Indo-China by, say, 1000 BC. But this means that "Jews" in India and modern Indo-China do not have anything to do with the supposedly "Lost Tribes of Israel", although this has been the theme of a highly-promoted television documentary produced by Simca

Jacobovici called *In Search of the Lost Tribes*. There is no archaeological evidence for any significant Hebrew settlement in northern Palestine that could have been these "Lost Tribes". But these mythical tribes were necessary to the myth of David's and Solomon's supposed great Jewish kingdom in the Holy Land. If it existed as described in the Bible, where was any remnant of its presumably large Hebrew population? The biblical myth of the "Lost Tribes of Israel" solved that problem. This remnant population had "disappeared", taken into captivity by the Assyrians about 860 BC. Needless to say, there is no independent record of the Assyrians capturing any "Lost Tribes" of Hebrews. But, as we will see, this myth of the "Lost Tribes of Israel" survived to influence notions of North American ethnography! See Chapters 4, 5 and 6.

[29] Dr. Marija Gimbutas believes that the bull-worship of some Middle Eastern cultures reflected the fallopian tubes of females, which do, in fact, resemble the shape of bulls' horns. This symbolism is especially prevalent at Catal Huyuk and Hassilar in Turkey and on the island of Crete during Minoan times.

[30] The meaning of "cornouaille" ("Cornwall") in French is a "congregation of horned animals", but more properly a "congregation of *polled* horned animals". That is, *domesticated* horned animals.

[31] See map in Pitman and Ryan's *In Search of Noah's Flood*.

[32] In *Le Renard Pâle* (1965), Marcel Griaule and Germaine Dieterlen established that a belief in Isis has been brought to the Nile delta by 6000 BC because of the known migration routes of the Dogon tribe of Mali. Griaule and Dieterlen also established that a belief in the son of Isis and Osiris as a "world saviour", at first called "Nomo", had been brought into Ancient Egypt at the same time.

[33] See bibliography.

[34] See *Civilization of the Goddess*, Dr. Marija Gimbutas, 1991.

[35] See Note 31 above.

[36] See Ahmed Osman's *Out of Egypt* (1998).

[37] See Ahmed Osman's *Out of Egypt* (1998), back cover.

[38] Readers are invited to look assiduously into the etymology of the common English word "issue".

[39] See both Ahmed Osman's *Out of Egypt* and Sigmund Freud's *Moses and Monotheism*.

[40] Freud's wife, Anna, was present at the "official" opening of Tukankhamun's tomb on Friday, February 16, 1923 (not Saturday, February 17th, as often reported in the press of the times).

[41] As a matter of fact, there are two presently revered tombs of Moses. One is at Jabal Musa (the Mountain of Moses) near Petra in modern Jordan and another is near Islamabad in modern Pakistan.

[42] There is no "Joshua ben Nun" in the present standard Greek-language version of the Old Testament.

[43] For example, Hypatia, a female professor of mathematics, was the head of the department at Alexandria until she was tortured to death by a Judeo-Christian mob in AD 391.

[44] Sigmund Freud referred to Greco-Roman "Anti-Semitism" in his *Moses and Monotheism*, 1939.

[45] It is interesting that the Nag Hammadi texts were judged as being "heretical" by the Vatican in 1969 – especially in view of the fact that these texts had been buried in Egyptian sand for some 1,570 years before their discovery and had been subjected to *no* editing whatsoever. The same cannot be said of the Vatican-approved Gospels.

[46] This is known today as the New Testament.

[47] See Chapter 24 of John. John (again) uses the phrase "beloved disciple" to refer to himself and yet the word "beloved" comes from the Ancient Egyptian word *mery*. How could John have known this unless he was also Paul? For Paul informs us in *I Corinthians* that he learned about Jesus "in Arabia" [i.e. the Dead Sea area then controlled by the Nabatean Arabs and thus "in Arabia"] and he says "I conferred not with flesh." This means he must have consulted, not with living disciples, but with the written records possessed by the Essenes of the Dead Sea region. These, as we know, referred to the Egyptian Messiah who was called some form of "Jesus" or "Joshua" as early as 1350 BC. The word *mery*, meaning "beloved" occurs in these records that must have been written in an archaic form of Hebrew or even in Egyptian. Only Paul, among all the disciples, was sufficiently educated to read such records. He must have known archaic Hebrew to have been accepted as a rabbinical student under teacher Gamaliel. Paul also spoke Greek and Latin because he claimed Roman citizenship. But all of John 24 is what Hebrew scholars would characterise as an extended *pesher*. That is, a "joke" or more literally "the interpretation of a dream." In this case, if read *very carefully* as a pesher, the butt of the joke is *fish* – that is to say, the fish goddess Isis. Paul says, in effect, that although the Judeo-Christian net he wove was flimsy in most respects, it was still sufficient to catch men and to bring them to Jehovah rather than have them escape to Isis and Egyptian Messiah-worship. Indeed, in Chapter 24, we find the fish are burned on the beach and the smoke ascends as a burnt offering to the Lord. Paul's Chapter 24 is probably why there is so much *fish* and *fishermen* symbolism in the New Testament. The preaching of Paul, plus that of other early Christian ministers based on his work, is likely why, to this day, all the Romance languages derived from Latin have the same words for *to fish* and *to sin*.

[48] Herodotus, circa 450 BC., was intelligent enough to realise that "Gods" were made by men in their own image. "I note," he wrote, "that the gods of the Ethiopians are always snub-nosed and black" as opposed to the gods of his own Hellenistic world that were generally white with longer noses.

[49] See *The Jewish Onslaught* by Professor Tony Martin of Wesleyan College.

Appendix to Chapter 3:

On October 10, 2000, my full-page article *In Search of the Lost Monarch* was published in the *Vancouver Sun*'s Insight section. This piece was about the Queen of Sheba and its immediately topical news peg was the upcoming expedition of the University of Calgary to the Queen's traditional capital of Ma'rib, now in modern Yemen.

In this article, I pointed out that Ethiopian traditions of the Queen of Sheba were fairly definitive. For example, her name was remembered as Makeba. It was, on the contrary, the Israelite kings David and Solomon whose existence seemed to be more problematical.

Based on evidence, I also stated the Israelite "Promised Land" could not have been in Palestine, but was somewhere on the Red Sea coast of Western Arabia. In this, I followed Kamal Salibi's linguistic research (more recently verified by Jewish linguist Chaim Rabin). The article put me in the bad graces of most major English Canadian newspapers, many of which are owned by the Jewish Asper family of Winnipeg.

Dr. Bernard Leeman was apparently already working along the same research lines, although my article may have encouraged him that this highly controversial direction of research was worth pursuing.

In any event, Dr. Leeman wrote to me in June 2005 about his book *Queen of Sheba and Biblical Scholarship* (2005, Queensland Academic Press, Australia). He kindly mentioned me in his Acknowledgements (page 5). On Sept. 5th, Dr. Leeman also gave me permission to reprint a short promo of his book as Appendix to Chapter 3 of *Swords at Sunset*.

Basically, this work vindicates the historical reconstruction of the real "Exodus destination" offered in Chapter 3 of *Swords at Sunset*. It was mainly this Chapter that "offended" a Dundurn Press staffer and caused Dundurn to repudiate *Swords at Sunset* and cancel its scheduled publication in May 2004. However, any *real* offence is all mine.

The Old Testament did not merely make an innocent mistake in placing the "Promised Land" in Palestine. Nor were the Zionists following naive religious loyalty to the Old Testament when they began to agitate for the creation of the modern State of Israel. The Zionist movement began about 1850 to 1870 and its notable personality was Theodore Herzl who organized the first Zionist Conference in 1896.

But some Jewish scholars knew very well that the real "traditional Jewish homeland" was in Western Arabia and not in Palestine. The major problem for the Zionists was, however, that Western Arabia was firmly under the control of the Saudi Royalty, was an ally of Britain which had fought with the legendary Lawrence of Arabia against the Turks and which was definitely not available for settlement and takeover.

Nonetheless, *someone* among leading Zionists knew where the truly historical Jewish homeland had been. The great danger of the Zionist deception was simply that an earlier version of the Old Testament (at least the Pentateuch, Kings I and II and perhaps Psalms) could be discovered at any time beneath the sands of Western Arabia. Two prominent Jewish orientalists, the Austrian Edouard Glaser and the Frenchman Joseph Ha lévy, were therefore dispatched to Western Arabia in order to steal or "confiscate" as many inscriptions as they could carry back to Europe. Thankfully for the Zionists of the time, nothing 'bombshell biblical" was discovered among the 1500-odd inscriptions that Glaser and Halévy were able to recover.

But it still remains possible, or even probable, that an earlier version of the Old Testament may yet be recovered from Western Arabia or Yemen.

The Semites knew writing from about 1400 BC and indeed Western Arabia and the Queen of Sheba's old realm of Saba (scholars prefer "Sabaea") are full of inscriptions. It's only a matter of time before an embarassingly early version of at least *some* of the Old Testament turns up from that area. Indeed, given the long period of time in which the Semites knew writing, it is a bit suspicious that the oldest version of the present Old Testament dates only from about 530 BC. This is because it must have been rewritten and canonized in its present form (ascribed to Ezra) after the "Babylonian Captivity" and its major purpose was to transplant the corpus of Jewish history from Western Arabia to Palestine.

Back then, about 500 B.C., Palestine could also be controlled by Jews using the allied power of the Persian army under Artaxerxes I. This is the purposefully misplaced story of "Esther" and Mordecai, which should have been one of the final books of the Old Testament. Ahasuerus has been firmly identified as Artaxerxes I (reigned 464-425 BC) by biblical scholars. Since 1948, with the modern State of Israel, the only real difference after 2500 years of this struggle is that Aglo-American military force has been substituted for ancient Persians. The Palestinians are no happier now than they were back in the days of Artaxerxes.

Palestine, unlike Western Arabia, *could* be negotiated and settled by 19th and 20th century Zionists because Lord Rothchild and other Jewish financiers had a great deal of power in Britain and they saw to it that Palestine became a British Mandated Territory after World War I.

By the way, several "unnecessary" military operations were fought during World War I in order to *ensure* that Palestine was occupied by Britain before any conclusion of the War. Anzac troups bore the brunt of these unnecessary casualties. Dr. Bernard Leeman's book *Queen of Sheba and Biblical Scholarship* is well worth buying or ordering direct from the Queensland Academic Press.

Read the following very brief synopsis of this book with its map.

The map alone is worth many thousands of words.

QUEEN OF SHEBA AND BIBLICAL SCHOLARSHIP

BERNARD LEEMAN

Professional archaeology in the Holy Land dates from the 1920s and has been characterized by Jewish and Christian attempts to substantiate the Biblical record.

While evidence has been unearthed that supports the account of the post-Babylonian captivity, renown archaeologists such as Kenyon, Pritchard, Thompson, Glock, Hertzog, Silberman, and Finkelstein have concluded that the *Old Testament* is either a fantasy or highly exaggerated.

Joshua's invasion of Canaan has been reinterpreted as a peaceful migration and no traces have been found of the massive public works allegedly contracted in Jerusalem by Solomon or in Samaria by Omri.

If these monarchs existed, they'd have been little more than petty village headmen with imaginative publicists.

This so-called *minimalist* outlook is fiercely challenged by others who believe the evidence to support the *Old Testament* has literally yet to be uncovered.

This book examines evidence connected with the life of Queen of Sheba, including Sabaean inscriptions on the Ethiopian plateau, aspects of the Ancient West Arabian language, and geographical references in Ge'ez *Kebra Nagast* to offer a third alternative.

It argues that the *Old Testament* is an accurate account but its events prior to 586 BCE took place not in Palestine but in *West Arabia*, and to a lesser extent in Ethiopia and Eritrea.

It suggests that scholars are unwilling to consider such a strong possibility because, if true, it would not only completely undermine the raison d'être of the State of Israel but also force a total reassessment of Biblical, Arabian, and North East African history.

By accepting African traditions in providing a solution to the bitter division in Biblical scholarship, this book ranks with Martin Bernal's *Black Athena* in its degree of controversy and presenting evidence that most scholars should address.

About the Author

Bernard Leeman holds Bachelor and Doctorate degrees in African History from London and Bremen Universities and a Masters in Applied Linguistics from Australia. He began his academic career teaching at Asmara University, Eritrea. In 2001 he was Visiting Fellow at Oxford University, and from 2002 to 2004 taught at London University's School of Oriental and African Studies.

Map: Israelite Promised Land shown in Western Arabia, not Palestine

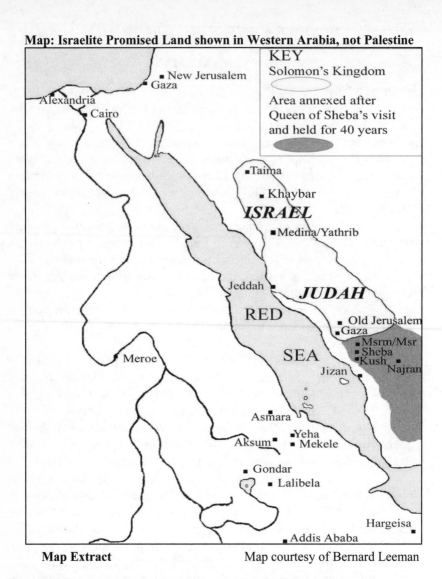

Map Extract   Map courtesy of Bernard Leeman

The marked area is the region that contains the "Hebrew-isms" recorded by Chaim Rabin in Ancient West Arabian, the Old Testament place names noted by Kamal Salibi, iron deposits, and an ancient Ark culture. It also straddles the lucrative incense, gold, precious stones, and luxury goods trade routes from Sabaea (Sheba). This area was temporarily abandoned by Egyptian and Assyrian imperial control ca. 1000-920 BCE, the same years as the zenith of the Israelite states under David and Solomon. – Bernard Leeman

4

The Last of the Mohicans

Readers will recall that during the Arts & Entertainment filming from October 31 to November 2, 1998, definite evidence came to light that the community around Lake Memphremagog had been associated with Henry Sinclair. Like so many things connected with the tale of the Grail, this news got to us in an ironic and paradoxical fashion.

We were then at Gérard Leduc's house in Mansonville, Quebec within figurative spitting distance of the lake. The cottage owner had been at Lake Memphremagog the previous week closing up her cottage for the winter. Taking a last walk around the lake's shore not far from her cottage, she noticed a boulder that she had always seen but had taken for granted. However, since she had just been reading *Holy Grail Across the Atlantic*, the markings on the boulder didn't seem so much like natural weathering anymore. She *looked* at the boulder for the first time, as Sherlock Holmes might have put it. And she saw for the first time what seemed to be a rendition of Henry Sinclair's coat-of-arms that had been illustrated in *Holy Grail Across the Atlantic* (page 123) taken from an old heraldry book called the *Armorial de Gelre*.

But the cottage owner didn't call us right then because she had also read on the back cover that I lived in Toronto, as she did herself. Therefore, she drove home for the last time that summer after buttoning up her cottage for the season. She called my Toronto publisher within a couple of days, only to be told that we were at Lake Memphremagog filming a documentary! She told Tony Hawke of Dundurn Press about the boulder with its Sinclair coat-of-arms. Using his brains and his discretion, because he quickly realised that the boulder could possibly add to the documentary, Tony Hawke first called us in Mansonville and, when he got our okay, then gave Gérard's phone number to the cottager.

Joëlle took the call that miserable afternoon while Gérard and I were doing endless re-takes in the sleet and rain for Joshua Alper's cameras. When we finally arrived at Gérard's house with the cosy fire, to find Joëlle plotting artifacts on road maps of the Niagara region, we were too numb, stiff and pre-pneumonia-like to go out into the early darkness to look for a boulder on the other side of the lake. The boulder was only about five miles or eight kilometres away from Gérard's heated floors as crows are alleged to fly, but at least twenty times that distance around the shore of the long lake by secondary roads.

Nonetheless, as unofficial "expedition secretary" Joëlle returned the cottager's call on my behalf later that evening saying that we would try to locate the boulder in the morning before we ourselves left for Toronto and home. Joëlle also thanked "Elizabeth," as I will refer to her henceforth because she doesn't want her name publicised. She is too well known in the Memphremagog area, many local people know where her cottage is and they are trustworthy. But wider publication of her name might attract both modern-day artefact hunters and modern-day vandals who might damage the boulder.

And naturally, a foot of snow fell that very night. It would be difficult, if not impossible, to distinguish just one snow-covered lakeside boulder from millions of others. Thousands, anyway.

The word "discovery" means a new revelation, but neither the definition nor the significance of that word is carved in stone, no pun intended. The true nature of a discovery can be surprisingly changeable, and often has been.

For example, most biographies of Columbus state that he thought, and insisted to his dying day, that in 1492 he had "discovered" part of the Great Khan's realm in Asia. He was quoted as frequently insisting that "Cuba" was just the local way of saying "Kubla". Conventional history insists that the true nature of Columbus's discovery wasn't known until forty-one years later in 1533. At that time, Amerigo Vespucci (1454-1512), who had been dead for twenty-one years, was *quoted* as realising that the newly revealed land was a new continent, a "New World", and supposedly gave his name to "America".

Unconventional historians, however, point out that the word *Merika* or even *A-Merika* ("toward Merica") referred to a bright star in the western skies, the planet Venus as the evening star.[1] Unconventional historians also remind us that Columbus himself admitted that he had a map of his "discovery" in advance. This map is mentioned in Columbus's Log. In his entry for October 1, 1492, after returning to his *Santa Maria* flagship from a conference with his Pinzón co-captains of the ships *Nina* and the *Pinta*, Columbus wrote that they all agreed: "to change course in accordance with our map and the over-flights of land-seeking birds."[2] The fleet sighted land eleven days later. Diaz and Magellan also had maps showing their "discoveries" in advance. I have quoted their navigators in several books,[3] such as the Portuguese pilot, Pigafetta, who referred to Magellan's chart showing the "Strait of Magellan" before the fleet even left Iberia. Unconventional historians challenge us to wonder where these maps came from, while conventional

118

academics simply ignore all of the references to them.

But such "pre-Columbus" maps of the Americas have now been recovered by modern researchers and they show that lands across the Atlantic from Europe were known to exist at least as early as AD 1398,[4] or even as early as AD 1360,[5] and were mentioned by the Arabic cartographer Abulfeda in AD 1250. These maps, which seem to be so similar that they might have been copied from one original, *also clearly show that this transatlantic land was not Asia*. These maps are generally called "Portolan Charts" and a good analysis of them can be found in Charles Hapgood's *Maps of the Ancient Sea-Kings*.

Did Columbus insist he had reached Asia in order to conceal a heretical haven from those fanatical Roman Catholics, Ferdinand and Isabella of Spain? It seems so when the evidence is examined and not ignored. This was the contention of the famous post-war Nazi hunter, Simon Wiesenthal, in his 1983 book, *Sails of Hope: The Secret Mission of Christopher Columbus*. It was also the argument of my own book, *The Columbus Conspiracy* (Hounslow Press, Toronto, 1991).

And again, a supposed dramatic discovery may not exist at all, in spite of much recent media hoopla. According to some scientists with impressive credentials, the spate of new DNA and Y-chromosome studies relating to Jewish origins and the Middle East, studies that have enjoyed such immense recent media coverage, do not represent legitimate scientific "discoveries" at all. According to anthropologists Drs. Eric Trinkhaus, Milton Wolpoff and Loring Brace, geneticist Dr. Alan Templeton and a number of other experts, many recent DNA and Y-chromosome "studies" are merely statistical juggling intended to distort the facts, not to clarify them. The general contention of all these studies is there is no Neanderthal genetic influence in humans alive today.

There was no interbreeding, no genetic mixing, between Neanderthals and Cro-Magnons.

These studies have flooded the popular North American media since June 1997 – by coincidence, just when Dr. Eric Trinkhaus' massive book *The Neandertals*[6] (hardcover, 1996) was about to be released in mass market paperback by Random House. Perhaps the media blitz has been due to the fact that Trinkhaus, who is the world's acknowledged living authority on Neanderthals, had concluded his definitive work with the words (page 451): "Only people from parts of Eastern Europe and the Middle East can boast Neanderthals in their direct ancestry."[7]

Indeed, the media saturation of "no Neanderthal" propaganda dissuaded Random House, just as it was intended to, from releasing *The*

Neandertals in an inexpensive and widely available mass market paperback edition.

It seems fairly obvious to me and to others with some anthropological training, that these Neanderthal DNA and "Abraham" Y-chromosome so-called studies are merely statistical manipulations to support Jewish and Israeli geopolitical, religious and financial interests. As the old saying goes: "First come lies, then damned lies and then statistics." These highly-touted, politically correct and too-convenient statistical "discoveries" may turn out to be "non-discoveries" as scientific critics of the deluge of recent DNA and Y-chromosome studies are starting to be heard more often in popular media and scientific journals.

As we shall see, this controversy about whether or not Neanderthals genetically influenced modern Western humanity turns out to be the crux of what the Holy Grail is really all about, not to mention the fundamental cause of contemporary crisis in the Middle East.

Iron spearhead

So, in this cautious spirit of accepting the word "discovery," Elizabeth was finally sitting in our High Park apartment on July 28, 2000. We had spent almost the entire summer of 1999 in the Niagara region and had then honeymooned in France in the autumn, while Elizabeth had spent her 1999 summer at her cottage on Lake Memphremagog. We had never actually been able to meet, but we had exchanged letters and seen some of her photos of the boulder. But this Toronto resident with a cottage on Lake Memphremagog was now sitting in our living room with an artefact that could be carried in her purse and photos of the boulder that could be computer enhanced.

Elizabeth revealed two "discoveries" that may change North American history. Lake Memphremagog, about 65 miles or 100 kilometres, south-east of Montreal, is a long narrow lake about 27 miles long and four miles wide (45 kilometres long and 7 kilometres wide) that straddles the Quebec-Vermont border in the foothills of the beautiful Green Mountains.

In the 1970s, Elizabeth's father had discovered, beneath their cottage on Lake Memphremagog, an iron object that seemed to be an iron spearhead (in 2000, Joëlle Lauriol digitally scanned a photo of the spearhead shown below). This curiosity was given to then-teenage Elizabeth because she had been interested in archaeology from an even earlier age. Sensitised by this apparent iron spearhead, Elizabeth kept looking for other unusual things when the family, and later she alone, visited the cottage and the shoreline woods in the neighbourhood. This was how some 30 years later Elizabeth had finally noticed the inscribed boulder a few hundred yards from her cottage on the shore of the lake.

Elizabeth knew about this Sinclair coat-of-arms and Henry Sinclair's transatlantic voyage because of reading my two books *Holy Grail Across the Atlantic* (1988) and *Grail Knights of North America* (1998) where I related Frederick Pohl's superb historical detective work in some detail. Pohl had first reproduced Henry Sinclair's coat-of-arms in his book *Prince Henry Sinclair*. Quoting an obscure medieval document known as "The Zeno Narrative" thought to have been composed about AD 1400 by a Venetian navigator in Sinclair's service, Pohl presented geographic evidence that the settlement Apparent iron spearhead Sinclair is said to have established in "Estotiland" had been in Nova Scotia. Actually, a University of Michigan geologist, William Herbert Hobbs, had previously argued the same thing in the January 1951 issue of the prestigious *Scientific Monthly*.[8] But Frederick Pohl had brought this formerly obscure episode of history to more general knowledge in a popular book and he also supplied a great deal of additional information on Henry Sinclair.

Unlike Columbus, Henry Sinclair and his Venetian navigator, Antonio Zeno, did not mistake the new land for the realm of the Great Khan. The narrative of this transatlantic voyage states explicitly that "Estotiland" was part of a vast *nuovo mundo* – a "New World" – and also provided a map. And so – so much for Amerigo Vespucci's realisation, or "discovery."

Why did Henry Sinclair cross the Atlantic? The answer, I argued in *Holy Grail Across the Atlantic*, could most probably be found in his relationship to the mysterious, romantic and outlawed Order of the Knights Templar. This famous and infamous body of elite knights was formed in Jerusalem in AD 1114 (some sources say AD 1118) for the stated purpose of "guarding the Holy Grail". We have covered this "greatest story ever told" up to the time of Henry Sinclair's voyage of AD 1398 and his decision to establish a settlement in the new lands.

Henry Sinclair had called his new discovery "Estotiland". And, of course, it is an intriguing speculation whether or not some of the Templar treasure, as well as alleged descendants of the Holy Blood, may have been taken across the Atlantic along with refugee Templar descendants as guardians.[9]

After she had found and photographed the curious boulder with its apparent depiction of the Sinclair coat-of-arms, Elizabeth called me in Toronto and we arranged to meet. When we finally got together on July

28, 2000, my new wife Joëlle Lauriol noticed what she thought was another illustration opposite the coat-of-arms on the boulder.

Apparently carved, these features seemed to be a fairly accurate map of the North American Atlantic coast from Yucatan to Nova Scotia, although the "north-eastern" coast was progressively obscured by a growth of lichen on the existing photos of the boulder.

The iron spearhead seems an indisputable "hard artefact" in both the literal and figurative senses of the phrase. And, of course, Europeans commonly used iron spear-heads only up to about AD 1450-1600 when most traditional projection-type weapons were superseded by firearms. Colonials didn't normally make spearheads either – while pre-contact North American Indians were not supposed to have worked iron at all.

However, the features on the boulder are in a different category. Nearly as "hard" (granite) in one sense, the interpretation of them is in the eye of the beholder. Were these features purposefully carved in stone, or are they only the suggestive work of nature? Joëlle spent hours scanning a modern map and the Sinclair coat-of-arms in order to offer these comparisons.

The Memphremagog dam, gargoyle, spearhead and boulder engraving seem to be late medieval or early Renaissance in date, and tally with the era of Sinclair's recorded voyage and settlement. These artifacts indicate an established European community in the Memphremagog region that mocks Canada's official history. Will Elizabeth's "discoveries" change American and Canadian history, or are these Memphremagog artifacts destined to be regarded as "non-discoveries."

The Lake Memphremagog boulder, complete with its growth of lichen obscuring the top or north-eastern portion of the apparent map. The Atlantic coastline is to the lower left and the Sinclair coat-of-arms is to the right. See detail below.

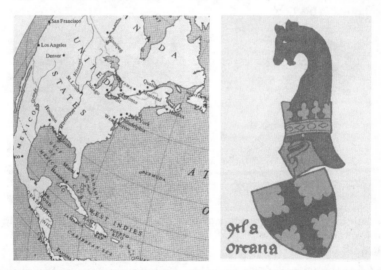

Boulder features reproduced with a modern orthographic map (left) and the Sinclair coat-of-arms (right).

Modern orthographic map projection (left) compared with the boulder coastline (right). The boulder map seems to have been based on a map, like the Piri Re'is map of AD 1519, using an orthographic or "azimuthal equidistant" type of projection. Several other Medieval period maps were based on this type of projection, which was supposedly not invented until the 19th Century. Some experts, like Dr. Charles Hapgood of the University of New Hampshire and Capt. Arlington Mallory of the U.S. Navy's map department, believe that such maps, called "Portolans," were based on source maps made by some unknown ancient seafaring culture with sophisticated mathematical ability. Copies were handed down within certain families for hundreds or thousands of years. Columbus had a map of the New World and the West Indies, probably similar to the Piri Re'is Map and this modern one, when he set sail from Palos, Spain, August 3, 1492. This map is mentioned in his Log.

Sinclair coat-of-arms reproduced from the "Armorial de Gelre" heraldry book circa AD 1375 (left), and Boulder image of the Sinclair coat-of-arms, (right).

Elizabeth's "discoveries" would be a bit easier to shrug off were it not for two other artifacts across Lake Memphremagog only about four and a half miles away (about 9 kilometres) in Quebec's Potton Township.

An astonishing stone-carved "gargoyle" was found, in 1985, in a stream bed only a kilometre from the stream's mouth on Lake Memphremagog's western shore. In 1998, two Toronto art historians said the gargoyle resembled the style of Celtic-Scandinavian sculpture of 1400-1500, as evidenced in the monastery of Léry in France (Morbihan Département). They said the Memphremagog gargoyle especially resembled the style of the so-called "Apprentice Pillar" at Rosslyn Chapel in Scotland. Rosslyn was the domain of Henry Sinclair.[10]

In 1997, wooden (hemlock) surveyors' stakes found in association with the ruins of a dam were C-14 dated between 1400-1550. Previously, most residents and all experts had accepted the dam as a colonial relic of the early 1800s. But the dam's C-14 date is even before the explorers, let alone European colonists, were believed to have come into the area. Only a community needs a dam for a mill, and Indians of the region are not known to have constructed stone dams and mills. Moreover, the gargoyle, found a kilometre away, has a closely matching date of origin.

Above, Joelle Lauriol at Memphremagog dam ruins. Below, the intriguing Memphremagog "gargoyle."

The gargoyle was displayed in May 1997 at a regional archeological exhibition in Mansonville, Quebec called "Arkeopotton" organised by Gérard Leduc. And both the dam and gargoyle were featured in a television documentary for the Arts & Entertainment network filmed in November 1998.

Aside from the dam and the gargoyle, which have been at least somewhat publicised, there are two other Lake Memphremagog finds that are so far known only to a few investigators.

There is an iron-reinforced elm dugout canoe that has been in the Colby-Curtis Museum in Stanstead, Quebec since its discovery ten years ago by a scuba diver some thirty feet down in Lake Memphremagog. The former museum curator would never allow carbon dating of the wood, possibly because he feared that the canoe might be "pre-contact" in age, like the ruined dam. However, there is now a new curator at the Colby-Curtis Museum and she allowed samples to be taken for C-14 dating in late March 2001.

Interested researchers led by Gérard Leduc contributed money for the C-14 testing. Because of the backlog of tests at Isotech Labs at the University of Toronto, however, results became known only in October 2001. In this case, the iron reinforced canoe dated to the AD 1850s.

In addition to this canoe, a thirty-foot-long, apparently plank-built, sunken barge was discovered in Lake Memphremagog during the summer of 2000 by another scuba diver, Jacques Boisvert of the town of Magog, Quebec. It had carried a load of fire-baked bricks and is also probably genuinely colonial.

On the other hand, fired clay bricks were invented about 1500 BC by the Indus Cultures and spread to Europe by 500 BC with the Etruscans, and so the barge and its cargo could also date from late medieval times. We just won't know until some of the barge and a few of its bricks are recovered for analysis.

Therefore, in addition to the dam and gargoyle and Elizabeth's spearhead and boulder, there are other potentially pre-colonial European artifacts from Lake Memphremagog and the surrounding area.

Elizabeth's discoveries would also be much easier to dismiss were it not for the cluster of apparently European sites and stonework along the not-too-far-away Connecticut River in Vermont, New Hampshire and Massachusetts. According to the New England Antiquities Research Association (NEARA), the Early Sites Research Association (ESRA) and Harvard University's prestigious Gungywamp Society, there are over three hundred non-Indian archaeological sites in this heart of New England. Conventional academics have always done their best to ignore these sites.

These non-Indian sites along the Connecticut River date from approximately the year of 3000 BC until about AD 500, according to C-14 dates so far obtained, and so they are much older than the late medieval artifacts concentrated around Lake Memphremagog. Most of the few experts who have examined them feel that these New England sites are "proto-Celtic" in origin. Some writers have maintained that north-eastern North America was the "Tir á nOg", "Iargalon" "Avalon", and "Brendan's Isle" of progressive and continuing Celtic legend from pre-Gaelic to Brythonic linguistic times and on into the Christian medieval era.

Canadian epigrapher and linguist, Dr. David H. Kelley, enjoys a truly international reputation because of his contribution to the "breaking" of the Mayan glyphs. Kelley argued in the prestigious pages of the *Review of Archaeology*, September 1991, that "proto-Celts" and "proto-Scandinavians" had penetrated as far west as southern Ontario near Peterborough by about 800-1200 BC. The famous Canadian writer, Farley Mowat, argued in his 1998 book *The Farfarers* that Celts from Scotland and Ireland were trading and settling in the St. Lawrence estuary between about 400 BC and AD 1300.

Bill Fitzgerald, an archaeologist trained at Sir Wilfred Laurier University in Guelph, Ontario who was working with the Bruce County Museum, told me an interesting bit of archaeological gossip during one of our many phone conversations in the summer of Year 2000. The well known Canadian archaeologist, Dr. James Pendergast, had begun to suspect toward the end of his career that some unknown Europeans had been active along the St. Lawrence as far west as the rapids near Cornwall, Ontario during the AD 1400s.

The Zeno Narrative" describes a fairly large expedition across the Atlantic, and infers that several hundred people, described as "soldiers", stayed behind to populate the city that Sinclair founded in Estotiland. A populous colony would inevitably have explored its new territory, and there is some evidence that pre-Columbian Europeans penetrated inland along the St. John and Connecticut Rivers in the two centuries before Cabot's supposed voyage in 1497. Several late medieval coins have been discovered in Nova Scotia, New Brunswick, New Hampshire and Maine dating from the 1200s and 1300s.[11]

Why would a secondary settlement have been established around Lake Memphremagog? Today, the region is something of a backwater of both Quebec and New England.

But it would have been of strategic importance for a limited number of fourteenth and fifteenth Century Europeans who were confined to travel along major rivers. They had to travel along rivers wide enough to provide protection by crossbows because Europeans did not then possess reliable firearms. Lake Memphremagog is located on the watershed of three major rivers. It controls access to the St. John, the Connecticut and the St. Lawrence Rivers.

Using the Connecticut River, the largest river in New England, access into most of New England could be controlled south to Long Island Sound from Lake Memphremagog. The lake provided access to the St. Lawrence for explorations either to the Great Lakes or to the Atlantic. The lake also controlled access to the St. John River through modern Maine and New Brunswick and on to the Bay of Fundy and Nova Scotia.

One *could* argue that Lake Memphremagog actually controlled, or nearly so, even a fourth major river system. Lakes Champlain and Lake George, the source of the Hudson River flowing southward to modern New York City – the route of today's New York State Barge Canal – are just 25 miles (40 kilometres) west of Lake Memphremagog. Moreover, Lakes Memphremagog and Champlain are connected by the Missisquoi River which flows less than five miles (8 kilometres) from the ruined dam in Potton Township.

Did Europeans, perhaps from Sinclair's AD 1398 settlement in Estotiland, travel inland to establish an outpost on Lake Memphremagog in order to control this junction of major Northeast river routes?

As a very much younger man in pursuit of the final location of Sinclair's colony I knew from Frederick Pohl's *The Lost Discovery* (1954) that Sinclair's initial settlement or "city" had been in Nova Scotia because his expedition had happened to make a landfall there. But I doubted even then that the majority of the settlers would have stayed on the Nova Scotia coast for long. It was too vulnerable a location if other European mariners got the same idea of crossing the Atlantic. Then, too, an entire continent beckoned to be explored.

By 1967, I had already pinpointed Lake Memphremagog as being the most likely eventual site of Sinclair's European colony during the 1400s. In fact, I applied for a Canadian Centennial Project grant to explore the region with archaeologists in 1967. There remains something uncanny about this 1967 Centennial Project grant application because at that time I did not even know that Henry Sinclair had been associated with the

Templars and the Holy Grail. Neither did Frederick Pohl, my primary source, ever so much as mention any Templar connections with Sinclair. And Pohl never breathed a word about the so-called "Holy Grail". I don't think that Frederick Pohl, or anyone else in 1950s North America when Pohl's *The Lost Discovery* was published, would have viewed the Holy Grail as anything but quaint medieval myth.

Nor had I yet heard about the ruined castle in the middle of Nova Scotia, although I was to demonstrate to the Nova Scotia Ministry of Culture, Recreation and Fitness between 1982 and 1984 that the ruins were most probably the remains of Henry Sinclair's initial settlement or "city".

For some reason I do not now remember clearly, and probably couldn't put my finger on even then, I just *knew* that the majority of Sinclair's people must have colonised the region around Lake Memphremagog. This was long before the discovery of the spearhead, the boulder, the gargoyle or the dam – or at least long before any of them came to my attention – but the country just looked, to me, as though it had been "lived in" by Europeans long ago.

My Centennial Project of 1967 was rejected as being "far fetched" by the historians and archaeologists to whom it was submitted for assessment. However, I travelled frequently to Lake Memphremagog anyway and asked cottage owners, cottage tenants and local sportsmen to keep an eye out for unusual artifacts or "ruined walls" around the lake.

I also developed contacts over the years with trained investigators who either lived around the lake in 1967 or who later settled there. Among these were Jacques Boisvert of Magog, a scuba diver in search of "Memphre," the often reported lake monster, ex-RCMP investigator and cottage owner, Gordon Hardy,[12] and later Dr. Gérard Leduc, a Concordia University biologist who developed archaeological interests when he retired to Potton Township in the Lake Memphremagog area.

As a retired biologist, Gérard Leduc was also initially somewhat interested in the hundreds of reports of "Memphre" the lake monster, but then he became even more interested in traces of an ancient stone-working and metal working culture around the lake.

Gérard founded the Potton Heritage Association Inc., which first displayed the gargoyle publicly in May 1997 in Mansonville. Gérard arranged for C-14 dating of the dam in the face of much opposition from Quebec archaeologists.

In fairness to Dr. Gérard Leduc, I should say here that he has another theory about these Lake Memphremagog artifacts. Gérard has stated that he believes that there was a race of "White Aboriginals" in addition to the better known "Red Indians" of North America. These people were, Gérard thinks, possibly related to the Caucasian genetic stock represented by Kennewick Man whose bones have caused much recent controversy because they exhibited marked Caucasoid or Caucasian features.

I related in the first chapter how the repatriation of Kennewick Man's skeleton actually caused something of a public and media outcry, even in this politically correct day and age.[13]

Gérard speculates that these White Aboriginal People may have come originally from Atlantis about 10,000 years ago or more. They were, he thinks, responsible for the Memphremagog-area artifacts and ruins, most of the "Celtic" ruins along the Connecticut River and for much of the "Moundbuilding" further south in the U.S. along the Ohio and Mississippi Rivers. I tried to present Gérard's viewpoint, fairly and objectively, in *Grail Knights of North America.* [14]

I have no objection to the notion of White Aboriginal People in North America and I also argued a detailed case for them in *Grail Knights of North America.* And, as we shall see, I don't even quibble that they may have been refugees from "Atlantis" when it sank in the tectonic cataclysms that caused the end of the last "Ice Age" about 11,500 BC.[15]

However… it would be very difficult to distinguish between the works and artifacts of these putative White Aboriginal People and the remains left by historically attested Celts and others, like Vikings and Sinclair's people. Also, these White Aboriginal People may have inter-married with these later European visitors and so any lines of original distinction between them would have become blurred even more.

Therefore, with regard to these specific Lake Memphremagog artifacts and ruins, I feel that it is easier and more intellectually sound to attribute them to a known European population of the late medieval period. I would prefer to do that than to attribute these particular ruins and artifacts to a still hypothetical population of Caucasian aboriginal people in North America.

If Elizabeth's boulder is ever generally accepted as a map and Sinclair's coat-of-arms, then the question is settled regarding these particular Memphremagog artifacts and evidence of medieval pre-colonial Europeans *in this area*. Other and older ruins around Lake Memphramagog, and also the "Moundbuilder" ruins and artifacts in the United States, dated to the era from about 750 BC to about AD 750, are not, of course, explained by Sinclair's expedition and colony.

Indeed, the Memphremagog area was so favourable for late medieval Europeans that it is even possible that the majority of Sinclair's Nova

Scotia settlers might have relocated to Lake Memphremagog once it was discovered by Estotiland scouts.

The Nova Scotia site of Sinclair's initial settlement, thought by Frederick Pohl to have been at today's Guysborough Harbour in the lee of Cape Canso, was vulnerable to accidental or purposeful discovery by ships searching for heretics on behalf of the Inquisition.

The reason is that Cape Canso is the largest and most prominent cape on the Atlantic Coast of Nova Scotia and would have been an obvious landmark for European explorers, just as it attracted Henry Sinclair himself in 1398. This cape would have been a landmark for other medieval mariners all during the 1400s. Cape Canso even remained a landfall for Champlain, for example, sailing two hundred and six years after Sinclair in 1604.

But nestled inland up in the Green Mountain foothills, the Lake Memphremagog region would have remained unknown for a much longer time to marauding European mariners.

If the Memphremagog area did become the "capital" of Sinclair's refugee colony, this would explain the existence of a pre-Columbus and pre-Cabot dam. Only a settled and fair-sized European population would need a dam.

A sizeable European settlement deriving from Sinclair's initial Nova Scotia "city" would also explain the features on Elizabeth's boulder – it's features were symbolic of the refugees' loyalties and their domain. The map on the boulder demonstrates that much of the North American coast was known to these European settlers, either because of a map they possessed, or because of their own coastal explorations. It is known, in fact, that Henry Sinclair did have a map. This map accompanies "The Zeno Narrative" and is known to cartographers as "The Zeno Map of the North".

Conventionally, it is attributed to Antonio Zeno, Henry Sinclair's Venetian navigator. But Antonio Zeno could not have drawn it because it is based on a conical projection that was unknown in the 1400s. This map is like the mysterious Portolans that guided Diaz, Columbus and Magellan on their voyages of "discovery". Henry Sinclair and Antonio Zeno apparently had their Portolan-like map before they set sail, and so their Estotoland settlers could certainly have had a copy of it too.

These Green Mountain foothills had yet another advantage in addition to concealment. They were rich in metals. Although most of the deposits were worked out in early colonial times, many abandoned mines in the area attest to former pre-colonial attempts to exploit Vermont's copper and gold. In Quebec's Potton Township, within a few miles (kilometres) of the dam and gargoyle, and just across the lake from Elizabeth's spearhead and boulder, there is an old copper mine that was discovered by the first "history book" colonial settlers.

According to a local historian of the Memphremagog region, Katherine Mackenzie, author of *Indian Ways to Stagecoach Days* (Pidwidgeon Press, Ayer's Cliff, Quebec, 1996), the area to the west of Lake Memphremagog was known to the early history book settlers of the 1820s as "the country of the lost nation."

Two other independent frontier legends also refer to pre-colonial Europeans in this Green Mountain region. The Green Mountains foothills were the original homeland of James Fenimore Cooper's "Mohicans", those White Indians of which Chingachgook was the last great chief. Cooper informs us repeatedly in *The Deerslayer*[16] and *The Last of the Mohicans* that "Chingachgook" meant *"Great Serpent"*. Or, as Joëlle Lauriol immediately perceived as we were driving toward the Green Mountains on one of our many trips between 1997 and 2000, Cooper may as well have written "Pendragon" or even the Ancient Egyptian "Meseh". Precisely the same meaning was intended.

A little research did uncover the fact that Great Serpents did, indeed, mark the boundaries between the Mohicans and other tribes, such as the Algonquins. Monster hunters like Jacques Boisvert of Magog in Quebec, and lake monster buffs like ex-RCMP officer Gordon Hardy of Sargent's Bay on Lake Memphremagog, are quick to insist that these "Giant Serpents" did exist and still exist. They were worshipped by the Indians, they say.

Their contention is borne out, to some degree anyway, by the research of Dr. Rémy Savard, an anthropologist with the James Bay Development Corporation. According to Savard, these "Great Serpents" were known by the general name of *Mantouche*. When white missionaries eventually asked the North-eastern Indians *what they worshipped as God*, the Indians scratched their heads a bit, not generally having the concept of *a God* but believing in a number of gods and goddesses. But finally, they mostly answered "Mantouche", which was good enough for the missionaries. This gave both Whites and Native People the bogus word *Manitou* as the Native Indian word for *"God"*.[17]

But the Mantouche(s) were never *gods* or *the God*. They were just Giant Serpents, although they were respected.

Although the Potton Township gargoyle was described as a "lion headed gargoyle" in Gérard's Arkeopotton archaeological exhibition

132

held in Mansonville, Quebec in May 1997, Jacques Boisvert gave his opinion that it had been intended as a sculpture of Memphre the lake monster. There are people, like Jacques Boisvert and Gordon Hardy, who believe in these lake monsters as actual biological entities. Joe Zarzynski believes in "Champ", the very similar monster of Lake Champlain.[18] Plenty of people believe in "Nessie", the monster of Loch Ness. Who's to say they are wrong?

However... with regard to the Americas, at least, the only known aquatic snake that approaches anywhere near the size to fill the bill for Memphre, Champ or Nessie is the so-called "anaconda" (*Eunectes murinus*) of South America. I have spent many uncomfortable hours and even days on sincere and "scientific" expeditions to find evidence of Champ and Memphre. I even mounted my own open-minded expedition to look for "Mussie", the monster of Ontario's Muskrat Lake – see *More Than a Myth* (Hounslow Press, Toronto, 1989). But I've never found even a single scale. So, I've come to think that these Giant Serpents are symbolic entities rather than biological ones.

I've come to the conclusion that nothing remotely like an anaconda could survive a Northern Boreal Zone winter.

I now tend to think that these Giant Serpents were originally Mohican representations of their chiefs in the Grail-related tradition of a Pendragon or a Meseh – that is, an approved consort of the Fertility Goddess. Her divine wisdom, which the chieftain acquired by being her consort, was often symbolised by a snake – like the serpent of the Garden of Eden. Sometimes, this serpent was depicted as an elongated fish-like thing, recalling Isis, like the Scottish "horse-eel" that is supposed to be Nessie. Sometimes wisdom was symbolised by a real ordinary snake, or a pair of snakes, still the symbol of a physician's wisdom, the caduceus.

The Mohicans sometimes made Giant Serpent representations, like the Potton gargoyle, to mark their territory. These sculptures awed and intimidated other tribes. The Giant Serpents therefore went from Grail-related tokens of loyalty and authority among Mohicans into neighbouring Indian legend, then transferred into colonial folklore and now persist as bait for monster hunters. At least, that's my take on the Potton gargoyle and the regional lake monsters. But I wouldn't be too surprised if Memphre, say, was found washed up on a Lake Memphremagog beach next week and proved to be a giant serpent!

Aside from this matter of lake monsters, the other independent piece of frontier legend that is fascinating to research is the tradition of "money-digging". In American colonial times, the Green Mountains of Vermont were the centre of a money-digging industry. As late as the 1790s in post-colonial and early republican times, according to a

Vermont newspaper, at least five hundred people were still engaged in excavating metal dust and even coined money left by the "Ancients." I have already covered this in some detail in *Grail Knights of North America*, but we must discuss it again when we come to deal with Joseph Smith and the Book of Mormon.

There is also some evidence, including several early maps, and curious remarks in Cartier's and Champlain's journals, suggesting that these earliest history book explorers knew of an inland European settlement and were trying to establish contact with it.[19]

If there was a European community in the Memphremagog region from about AD 1400-1550, what happened to it?

Because the dam, carbon-dated to about AD 1400-1550, appears never to have been completed, and because the gargoyle was tumbled into the stream bed, this European community may well have come to a violent end just a generation or so before the first known history book explorers arrived. This date corresponds to the first phase of Iroquois expansion, which was in progress when the French were settling at Quebec City (1607), the Dutch were settling in New York State (1609) and when the Pilgrims arrived in Massachusetts (1620).

These early European colonists all recorded that their Indian neighbours were in tumult and migration because of some remote conquering tribe in the interior to the west. This turned out to be the Iroquois Confederacy of Upper New York State, thought to have been established by the real, not poetical, Hiawatha sometime between AD 1470 and AD 1570.

The European community around Lake Memphremagog was directly in the path of Mohawk Iroquois expansion between AD 1550-1619. And, possibly not possessing any firearms, or not many compared to the early known European colonists, this community was defeated and its few survivors were dispersed.

The Dutch and English in Vermont and upper New York State, listening to Indian legends of their recent destruction as a nation, learned about these all but vanished "Mohicans". The very earliest Dutch settlers on the Upper Hudson River near Albany, established possibly as early as 1607-1609 as residents of Renssalaerwyck, recorded the Mohicans as living nearby in five villages.

At almost the same time, 1609, Champlain went on to Lake Champlain to participate with Ottawa and Huron allies in a raid on the Iroquois. Champlain noticed that although the surrounding region looked like rich hunting grounds, the area around the lake seemed uninhabited. Champlain was told by his Indian companions that "fifty years ago" the inhabitants had been attacked by the Iroquois and that the survivors had moved south.[20] From these two pieces of information, if we can trust them, the Mohicans of the Green Mountains in the vicinity of Lake Memphremagog were attacked about AD 1560 to AD 1570 or so. They could not flee northward to the St. Lawrence because it was firmly held by the Ottawas, Hurons and Algonquins. They could, however, have kept to the highlands of the Green Mountains, Catskills and Adirondacks to reach the Upper Hudson River near Albany. That was where the Albany Dutch placed the five Mohican villages at some time around 1610-1620.

According to the Dutch, these Mohicans were preferred trading partners as they seemed both more Caucasian and also more Christian than other Indians in the region. Their five villages were each arranged in the shape of a cross. About 1610-1620, Dutch traders in Albany began to make trinkets in the form of Mohican motifs for use in trade. They were usually small items of jewellery rendered in pewter, which was cheap, to be bartered for much more valuable furs. These trinkets travelled widely as they were bartered among various Indian tribes. This one was found on Chief's Island in the middle of Lake Scugog about 50 miles, (80 kilometres), west of Peterborough. The astounding thing about this Albany Dutch trinket intended for the Mohican trade is that it is a double-barred cross, the symbol of the House of Anjou.[21]

(Double-barred Cross of Anjou or "Cross of Lorraine" trade trinket supposedly manufactured by the Dutch in Albany around AD 1620. This specimen was found on Chief's Island in Lake Scugog in 1928. Lake Scugog is about 70 miles (110 kilometers) west of Peterborough and about 90 kilometers north-east of Toronto

To document this association between the Holy Grail and the Cross of Anjou, we can start with a quote from the most famous Grail Romance, *Parzival* by Wolfram von Eschenbach. In an introductory explanation of the discovery of the Grail story, he writes:

> Kyot (i.e. Guiot of Provence, troubadour), the wise master, set out to trace this tale in Latin books, to see where there had ever been a people dedicated to purity and worthy of caring for the Grail. He read the chronicles of the lands, in Britain and elsewhere, in France and in Ireland, and in Anjou he found the tale.

Here is an illustration of the Arms of the House of Anjou. Perhaps it should surprise no one that the double-barred Cross of Anjou, sometimes known in modern times as the "Cross of Lorraine", was the symbol of the Free French and the Resistance (and now of Easter Seals). Originally, it was a Merovingian symbol.

Fourteenth Century Hungarian coin depicting the Arms of the House of Anjou and the Cross of Lorraine.

Perhaps it will now be conceded by at least some readers that the Green Mountains around Lake Memphremagog once harboured a community of Grail Refugees that had expanded inland from Sinclair's original Nova Scotia settlement.

These "Mohicans" were nearly wiped out of existence around the year AD 1560 to roughly AD 1570 by the first phase of Mohawk Iroquois expansion, just as James Fennimore Cooper told it in *The Deerslayer* and *The Last of the Mohicans*. But they survived, according to the Dutch in Albany, until about 1640 or so.

Recent newspaper articles ("Who are the Melungeons? Appalachia's genetic mystery", *Toronto Star*, July 19, 1998) and even recent scientific interest in the so-called "Melungeons" may refer to some of these Mohican refugees who managed to survive the first phase of Iroquois expansion by hiding in the Appalachian Mountains.

Melungeons are mountain folk, white people, who greeted the very earliest known European explorers in the late 1500s and early 1600s.

Further north in the Quebec's "Shick-Shock" extension of the Appalachians that become the Green Mountains around Lake Memphremagog, these mountain folk were called "Maltais" – Maltese. Quebec's Minister of Culture (1998-2000), Agnes Maltais, was interested in this part of Quebec's lost history as a girl.

Her present position in the government is a testament to her continuing interest and determination in real Quebec history. The Parti Quebecois, if no other expression of Canadian government, is interested in this evidence of unknown European settlement of Quebec before John Cabot.

However, something further is at least inferred by the Memphremagog artifacts. If there was a sizeable population of Europeans around this lake in the 1400s and 1500s, then they would surely have explored inland. Joëlle and I came to believe that traces of their explorations are remembered by the place-name "Saguenay" and its variants, which occur all through the St. Lawrence and Great Lakes Basin as far west as Michigan.

Joëlle suggested this "Saguenay" could be a corruption of the hypothetical French word *Sanguiniers* – *"Bloodline People"* – and was applied to areas these Grail believers explored or settled.

The Mohicans seem to have been almost exterminated by the second phase of Iroquois expansion, which can be put between the years 1645 and 1690 – the same expansion that saw the massacre of Lachine in 1689.

Thereafter, when James Fennimore Cooper was writing about the New York frontier of about 1700, the great chief and "Great Serpent" Chingachgook was for all practical purposes the last of the Mohicans.

Notes to Chapter 4.

1 See Robert Lomas and Christopher Knight, *The Hiram Key*, pages 148-155. But I also discuss this in *Grail Knights of North America*, pages 35-93.

2 *The Log of Christopher Columbus*, Robert Fuson (Ed.), International Marine Publishing Company, Camden (Maine), 1987.

3 *Holy Grail Across the Atlantic* (1988) pages 96-108, *The Columbus Conspiracy* (1991) pages 135-157 and *Grail Knights of North America* (1988) pages 50-60.

4 "The Zeno Map of the North" is one such map that shows land westward from Europe that was not Asia and it is dated (now) to AD 1398-1398, the time of the Sinclair voyage.

5 The so-called "Franciscan Map" is dated to AD 1360, but I have never dealt with it because I am not yet convinced of its authenticity.

6 Most unfortunately, Dr. Trinkaus chose to use the new and revised German spelling system that leaves the "h" out of Neanderthals. Therefore, Trinkaus's book is called *The Neandertals*.

The problem is that the Germans themselves (and everybody else) has ignored the new system with respect to the word "Neanderthals". The revised system is not satisfactory in that it doesn't truly reflect the subtleties of German pronunciation. There *is* a slightly aspirated "h" in the usual German pronunciation of Neanderthals.

7 *The Neandertals,* page 451.

8 Hobbs, William Herbert. "The Fourteenth-Century Discovery of America by Antonio Zeno" *Scientific Monthly*, Vol. 72 (January, 1951), pages 24-31.

9 Since 1988 and the publication of *Holy Grail Across the Atlantic*, I have been bothered by supposedly high-ranking Masons and ordinary treasure hunters about the most likely location for this supposed "Templar Treasure". I have identified three separate geographic sites where all or part of such a treasure (if it ever existed) most likely might have been hidden (in my estimation). Maybe I should publish some facsimile treasure maps!

10 *Grail Knights of North America*, page 300.

11 See Michael Salvatore Trento's *The Search for Lost America: The Mysteries of the Stone Ruins.* Trento documents several finds of Roman and medieval European coins in New England, including a twelfth century English penny from Maine.

12 Mentioned in *Holy Grail Across the Atlantic*, page 3 of Acknowledgements because Gordon Hardy assisted in trying to obtain aerial photos of New Ross from military archives.

13 Elaine Dewar's *Bones: Discovering the first Americans* gives a full exposition of the Kinnewick story.

14 See *Grail Knights of North America*, pages 300-302.

15 Gérard Leduc has long been of the opinion that refugees from Atlantis came to North America as "White Indians" when Atlantic supposedly sank about 11,500 BC. I admit to having been sceptical about this idea between 1991 and 2003, but it now makes more sense to me about explaining *some* (not all) artifacts that are being recovered in North America.

But refugees from Atlantis fled to the European side of the Atlantic too. As more and more artifacts are being recovered from ever-earlier periods, it is starting to make sense that the European Atlantic Coast Neolithic and the megalithic traditions were cultural gifts of these Atlantean refugees. There is also mounting evidence that the art and concept of *alphabetic writing* came to Western Europe from somewhere out in the Atlantic about 10,000 BC. The evidence for this is fascinating but well beyond the scope of this book.

16 James Fenimore Cooper's *The Deerslayer* is a curious novel in some respects. It takes place on Lake Oneida, the source of the Susquehanna River and therefore not far west of Lakes Memphremagog and Champlain. Much of the plot revolves around an old man and his two daughters who inexplicably

live on a barge that endlessly cruises on the lake. This allows them, with their primitive firearms, to escape massacre by the Iroquois. Cooper never explains satisfactorily exactly how the barge and its white occupants got onto the lake in the first place.

17 Private correspondence with Dr. Rémy Savard, 1975.

18 I participated in several of Joe Zarzynski's 1976-1978 expeditions to try to get evidence of "Champ". At the same time, I worked for Dr. Robert Rines of the Boston-based Academy of Applied Science attempting to locate North American lake monsters that might be easier to photograph than Nessie.

19 One interior wall of a chateau on the Loire was once painted with a map showing the Memphremagog stretch of the St. Lawrence River. This wall-map has been dated by some authorities to AD 1526 – *a decade before Cartier's supposed first voyage.* Unfortunately, this wall-map was subsequently disappeared. Joelle traced it as far as Lauzanne in Switzerland in 1997, but from there it apparently passed into the hands of a German collector in 1998.

Aside from this map, however, there are many references in Cartier's *original French account* of his first voyage that refer to barns, tended vineyards, purposefully domesticated roses and even horses seen ashore in the stretch of the St. Lawrence between the Straits of Belle Isle and the region of Lake Memphremagog. Then, too, Cartier refers to a big ship from La Rochelle that he encountered near modern Baie Comeau. The sailors aboard this ship spoke French. Cartier was told that it was the flagship of the fleet of the "king" of the region.

20 This well-known account is recorded in *The Journal of Samuel de Champlain* (6 Vols. And map folio) incrementally published by the Champlain Society up to 1936 (Edited by H.P. Biggar) and reprinted by the University of Toronto Press, 1971. This edition is in the original French with a facing English translation.

21 Illustrated on page 377 of *Grail Knights of North America*. But I made a mistake in the accompanying text of that book that I would like to correct here. The text states that Lake Scugog is about "fifty miles" or ninety kilometres *east* of Peterborough (page 376). In reality, Lake Scugog is about that distance *west* of the town of Peterborough.

5

History by the Pound

On the night of September 21, 1823, according to the sworn testimony of Joseph Smith, the angel Moroni first appeared in Smith's darkened room in dazzling light "as bright as noon" and told him about a record of a forgotten people that was inscribed on "golden plates". But the time was not yet ripe for revelation, Moroni said. After three more years of annual visitations to Smith, Moroni finally led him to the location of the gold plates on September 22, 1827. They were in a stone-lined crypt on the side of Hill Cumorah nor far from the towns of Manchester, Palmyra and Elmira, New York in the general area of Rochester.

Although Smith could read, or was just learning to read at this time, he could not yet write. But he was able to "translate" the inscribed plates with the aid of two "seer stones" called Urim and Thummim that were mounted in silver frames and were found along with the plates themselves. While Joseph Smith thus read the record and dictated it, other people wrote it down. Smith's first scribe was Martin Harris, a New York State farmer who lived near Elmira. Later on, Smith's wife Emma wrote some of the account.

Smith commissioned a Palmyra, New York carpenter, Willard Chase, to make a wooden case for the plates and Smith kept this case under his pillow at night. Obviously, from this we can infer the original plates were not very large and the collection wasn't very thick. It seems that these plates actually existed. Several people gave sworn testimony that they had seen them from a distance.

No one was allowed to see these plates closely or make a detailed examination of them, however. Smith regarded the plates as a holy record and he feared that if anyone but himself, the chosen Prophet, looked at them closely enough to read, he or she might be struck down by the Lord.

Joseph Smith's wife, Emma, said that they made a "metallic rustling sound" under their cloth covering when she dusted the kitchen table. And Emma was no cowed wife, either, although she was a loyal and devoted one. In 1840, or eight years after the Mormon Church was founded by Smith, Emma was still attending the Presbyterian Church. She never tried to examine Joseph's "golden tablets", but not out of obedience to her husband.

As a good Presbyterian and orthodox Christian, she was never quite certain about how this revelation of the "golden tablets" should be regarded. Was apparition Moroni a minion of the Lord or the Devil? Emma therefore apparently ignored the plates as much as possible while they lay covered on the kitchen table – except when she noticed that "metallic rustling sound."

It appears that the first record, the one transcribed entirely by Martin Harris, was fairly brief. It was 116 pages long in Harris's somewhat large scrawling handwriting and it took almost two years to complete.[1] This record was lost or stolen and Smith was forced to do the work all over again. But the original plates had disappeared. Joseph Smith claimed that he then worked from other plates, a longer account that he kept in two large trunks. These trunks were certainly heavy because they required two strong men each to lift and carry. They were probably filled with rocks.

Joseph Smith much more probably worked from his memory of the first 116 pages, but this time he gave his imagination free rein. The final version of the Book of Mormon, as published in 1830, is a 561-page text of some 275,000 words. It required just eleven months to dictate. By any standards, the Book of Mormon is an intellectual and literary tour-de-force dictated by an illiterate but highly intelligent and incredibly creative man. Although Smith elaborated this "second translation" into what has been called "a Moundbuilder epic" he never deviated from the theme of those first 116 pages. Martin Harris had transcribed most of both versions. Emma Smith had transcribed some of the second version but she had heard and read the first version many times. Neither Martin nor Emma ever commented on any discrepancies.

In *Grail Knights of North America*, I gave a somewhat more detailed account of the "coming forth" (as Mormons put it) of the Book of Mormon. This was to support my own speculation that these plates may actually have been discovered sometime between 1823 and 1826 in Pennsylvania along the Susquehanna River. I thought it possible that they were part of a hoard of "coined money" that Joseph Smith, as a professional "treasure seer," had found while he was employed at a salary of ten dollars per month by Josiah Stowel of Harmony, Pennsylvania.

In 1827, Josiah Stowel testified in a Bainbridge, New York court that Smith had discovered this treasure on his behalf. My suspicion was that Smith might have claimed a New York State origin for these plates so that Stowel could not later claim ownership of them himself. I couldn't think of any better reason for the angel Moroni's three years of stalling.

Grail Knights of North America was illustrated with photographs of three artifacts – an inscribed tombstone, a sculpture and a rock inscription – from that same stretch of the Susquehannah River in the vicinity of Harmony, Pennsylvania. All three had definite Templar or Masonic associations. I therefore thought it at least possible that Joseph Smith had discovered the golden plates of the Book of Mormon in the same place where he had actually found a cache of coined money for Josiah Stowel.

We must digress here to mention that "money digging" was a recognised and at least semi-reputable occupation on the American frontier of the early 1800s. The *Green Mountain Patriot* weekly newspaper in Vermont wrote in May, 1801:

> "We could name, if we pleased, at least five hundred respectable men who do, in the simplicity and sincerity of their hearts, believe that immense treasures lie concealed upon our Green Mountains, many of whom have been for a number of years industriously and perseveringly engaged in digging it up."[2]

In 1767, a popular stage play of the times entitled *Disappointment; or, the Force of Credulity* opened in Philadelphia, Pennsylvania. It was about money digging. A false magician named "Rattletrap" conned people into looking for buried money, claiming that he could find it as a seer. On the American frontier of the 1800s, money digging was inevitably associated with folk magic and the ability to locate buried treasure by psychic means with the help of dowsing rods, pendulums and "seer stones". Joseph Smith himself was an adept "seer" and, as we have seen, was hired by Josiah Stowel to find "coined money" along the Susquehanna River. And, according to Josiah Stowel who banked this money, he did.

The reader may choose to ridicule this frontier money digging mania. I cannot dismiss it so easily because "five hundred men" could not have been "industriously and perseveringly engaged in digging it up" if it wasn't there in the first place. Money digging must have had the occasional payoff or else it would not have justified itself. In *Grail Knights of North America*, I described one Potton Township site in the Green Mountains foothills that seems to have been a series of artificial settling ponds down a mountainside stream. It looks like an automatic metal panning system more than anything else – for copper, gold or silver – big nuggets would settle in the upper ponds, smaller nuggets in the middle ponds and dust would accumulate in the ponds at the bottom of the mountain. All one had to do was collect the metal every so often, melt the dust and nuggets, strike the metal into coins, and cache the treasure for later shipment back to Europe. But if the miners were Europeans who were eventually massacred by Indians, there might have been quite a few caches remaining for frontier money diggers to find.

The Book of Mormon and the life of Joseph Smith are inevitably bound up with the so-called "Ancients" who could have left this money, Smith's own professional "seership" and frontier money digging. This has sometimes been embarrassing for Mormons, but these subjects were accepted aspects of American frontier life in Joseph Smith's day. Smith would never have found his "golden plates" if he had not been previously sensitised to the occasional *fact* of buried treasure and if he had not been a professional seer who was, on occasion, gainfully employed by professional money diggers like Josiah Stowel.

Our major interest, however, is in the content of the Book of Mormon, not its origin, however fascinating and puzzling its provenance may be.

It is the story of a people called by Joseph Smith the "Nephites". According to Smith, they were Israelite refugees from Jerusalem who sailed to the New World about 600 BC. They helped the Indians to develop their material and spiritual culture and also intermarried with them. Joseph Smith called these mixed people "Lamanites". But gradually conflict developed between the Nephites and the Lamanites. There was one group of mixed people, however, whom Smith called "Anti-Lehi-Nephi" people, also sometimes called the "People of Ammon", who remained determinedly neutral.

Finally, there was all out war between the Nephites and the Lamanites and violent conflict continued sporadically for centuries. The "People of Ammon", however, were so non-violent and neutral that they would not even protect themselves when the Lamanites sometimes attacked them. They were protected, at least insofar as that was possible, by the Nephites.

In the year AD 384, this war culminated in the great and terrible "Battle of Hill Cumorah" in which the Nephites were massacred and all but exterminated. In AD 400, the sole survivor of the Nephites, Moroni, who had been hiding in the mountains for sixteen years while writing a history of his people, returned to Hill Cumorah and buried the golden plates that fifteen hundred years later he, as an angel, revealed to Joseph Smith.

For those who are interested, "Mormon" was the father of Moroni, the general who commanded the Nephite forces at the final great Battle of Hill Cumorah.

Some Americans of the time were tolerant of, fascinated with or convinced by the Book of Mormon because they were already obsessed with the "Moundbuilders".

When the first colonists crossed the Allegheny Mountains, mountains that had been named after a vanished tribe of white men, according to their "Late Woodland Culture" Indian guides, they encountered the mounds by the hundreds and even thousands. Sometimes, these mounds were just isolated hills of earth, but in some places there were concentrations of them that seemed almost like the ruins of cities. And these "cities" didn't only have mounds. Sometimes they consisted of earth embankments in circles, octagons, squares and other geometric shapes.

The colonists thought that these shapes were too exact for the Woodland Indians ever to have made. And, in fact, the Woodland Indians, when asked, said that they didn't know who had built these mounds. They had just "always" been there. There were literally thousands of mounds along the Ohio, Illinois and Mississippi Rivers. There were some mounds along the lower Missouri, too, and also along the tributaries of all these major rivers. Obviously, at one time, there must have been a large population working to build all these mounds and embankments. That meant that at one time there must also have been intensive agriculture that had fed all these busy Moundbuilders. But the modest agriculture of the Northeast Woodland tribes known to the white settlers seemed altogether inadequate to account for the number of mounds.

Some novelists of the 1800s suggested that agricultural problems associated with mound building might have been alleviated by draft animals, but not horses. Most writers even then knew that horses had long been extinct in the Americas until reintroduced by the Spanish. Mastodons and mammoths were the favourite draft animals of the many Moundbuilder novels. This may seem farfetched for people today, but the idea was inspired by the then recently discovered (1821) "Elephant Mound" in Wisconsin. Modern experts maintain that this mound depicts a bear, but it looks more like an elephant to me.

An obscure group of Spanish castaways had to cross north east North America in AD 1596 and they reported "elephants" as part of the north east fauna. Then there's the well-known Mayan stele that shows an elephant with a mahout in the view of some, a toucan with a funny hat in the opinion of others. Maybe a few mammoths and mastodons lingered from "Ice Age" times into the Moundbuilder era.

Now, the only dramatically lost civilised population known to Americans of the frontier era were the biblical "Lost Tribes of Israel". We know today that there is absolutely no archaeological evidence for the historical existence of these supposedly "Lost Tribes" but they were necessary to the process of transplanting the core of Hebrew history from Yemen to Palestine.

Something had to explain what had happened to the presumably large population of David and Solomon's kingdom that had supposedly existed only three hundred years previously in Palestine. There was certainly no large Hebrew population in Palestine as of 600 BC and no folk memory of one either. Since it was known, however, that the Assyrians had attacked Palestine about 730 BC it was convenient to attribute the complete disappearance of the necessary "Lost Tribes" to them.

So, we see that Judeo-Christian biblical myths have even affected ideas of North American ethnography. Early American ministers like Cotton Mather – and there were many others – preached that the "Moundbuilders" had been the "Lost Tribes of Israel". In *Grail Knights of North America*, I discussed this Moundbuilders-as-the-Lost Tribes notion at some length,[3] contrasted with the modern dogma that the Moundbuilders were merely the ancestors of historically known Indian tribes. The current politically correct perspective is well presented in Robert Silverberg's *The Moundbuilders: Archaeology of a Myth* (1968).

However, the current politically correct view of the Moundbuilders is obviously just as flawed as the frontier certainty that they had been the "Lost Tribes of Israel". An almost daily accumulating deluge of data indicates that at least *some* of the Moundbuilders had been a ruling elite of Celtic and Teutonic people who migrated across the Atlantic about 1000 BC or even before that. The society they created, or helped to create, lasted from about 750 BC to about AD 750 or a little later. It is usually called the "Adena-Hopewell Culture".

By the year 2003, this idea of early Celtic, Celtiberian and Teutonic influence on the Adena-Hopewell Culture has very nearly been proved beyond any reasonable doubt. Firstly, epigraphers like Drs. Barry Fell of Harvard and David Kelley of the University of Calgary have shown that Celtic Ogham inscriptions and Teutonic Tiffinagh inscriptions positively clutter Adena-Hopewell sites. Secondly, books by maverick archaeologists have presented dozens of photographs of inscriptions, plus Celtic-looking dolmens, menhirs and dry-wall constructions identical to revered sites in the British Isles and France – Michael Salvatore Trento's

Search for Lost America is a good example among dozens of others. But thirdly, cutting edge science has now added its support.

Now it is known that the so-called "X Lineage Sequence" of DNA occurs among samples taken from hundreds of schoolchildren born of Celtic and Scandinavian families in Europe. But this same "X Lineage" also occurs among samples taken from the remaining few nearly direct descendants of some north-eastern North American Indians, especially the "Mohegan", Algonquin and Iroquois groups – those people generally thought to have inherited the legacy of Adena-Hopewell Culture most strongly.[4]

Therefore it seems that everyone has been correct and incorrect except for the conventional academic experts. They have been simply irrelevant. People like Barry Fell, David Kelley, Michael Salvatore Trento, Hjalmar J. Holand and Frederick Pohl were correct in thinking that the non-native influence was mainly Celtic and Teutonic in origin, but they probably over-estimated its importance to Adena-Hopewell Culture as a whole. Frontier Americans were right that there had been some "civilised" people in ancient North America, whom they called "Moundbuilders", except that these people had had nothing whatever to do with the spurious "Lost Tribes of Israel".

So, there were some Americans of Joseph Smith's day who were biblically predisposed to accept the Book of Mormon more or less at face value. But most Americans of the 1830 era regarded the Book of Mormon as a grotesque blasphemy. It claimed that the Nephites were both Jewish and Christians because Jesus had appeared as an apparition to the Nephites in AD 33 and they had all immediately accepted him in the spirit of the New Testament. But the "Christian" content of the Book of Mormon is actually close to nil. Jesus makes only his one appearance and is otherwise irrelevant. Modern members of the "Church of Jesus Christ of the Latter-day Saints", or "Mormons" as they are much more commonly called, claim to be Christians. But their values – in particular their long and controversial tradition of polygamy or "multiple marriage" – marks them as being much closer to biblical Hebrews.

The Book of Mormon was not only dismissed as blasphemy in 1830, but was also disregarded by most people as being ridiculous. Smith had written of a semi-civilised Indian population of millions. There were armies composed of tens of thousands of armoured men armed with just as many swords, axes and metal-tipped spears and arrows. Some of these items should have been found. And *some* few such artifacts *had* been discovered, as we have seen and shall see, but not nearly enough to equip the huge Nephite armies described by Joseph Smith.

But thirteen years after the Book of Mormon was published in 1830, William Hickling Prescott's multi-volume *History of the Conquest of Mexico and Peru* began to be published (1843-1847). This massive historical work was well received by the scholars and the reading public of the day. Prescott's work substantiated the large and semi-civilised native populations that had been described by Joseph Smith more than a decade earlier.

The advanced Mexican, Central American and Andes civilisations were completely unknown and unsuspected by the great majority of ordinary North Americans. Prescott's "Mayas of Yucatan" therefore gave much-needed contemporary credibility to Smith and the Book of Mormon. During the years between 1830 and 1843, up until the publication of Prescott's work, "the Prophet Smith" was regarded as a charlatan by the majority of people who had any knowledge of him. But Prescott's work surprisingly supported at least *some* of Smith's outlandish assertions. The Mormon Church was quick to appreciate this.

Joëlle had been taught at the missionary school in Provo, Utah that most of the history of the Book of Mormon had taken place in "Yucatan" and Central America. Joseph Smith's "Eastern Sea" was the Atlantic Ocean and his "Western Sea" was the Pacific.

But, nonetheless, the Niagara Frontier makes more sense than Central and South America as a general location for the history recounted in the Book of Mormon. After all, the "golden tablets", from which the Book of Mormon was allegedly "translated", had supposedly been discovered at Hill Cumorah near Rochester in Upper New York State. This is a long way from Yucatan, but barely over a hundred miles from the Niagara Frontier. Joseph Smith had never been anywhere near Yucatan and the Book of Mormon was published a full decade *before* Prescott's massive work.

After she learned of my research in 1997 and had looked at it objectively over the course of several months, Joëlle tended to agree that Joseph Smith's "Eastern Sea" had been Lake Ontario, and his "Western Sea" must therefore have been Lake Erie.

Joëlle also found references in the Book of Mormon that it required a day and a half to walk across this peninsula between the two lakes. It is almost exactly thirty miles – fifty kilometres – from Vineland, Ontario on the shore of Lake Ontario to the shore of Lake Erie. This distance takes about a day and a half to walk, for people who can walk that far, that is. Although this correlation of actual Niagara geography with Joseph Smith's text didn't prove anything, it encouraged Joëlle that other correlations might be discovered. She therefore began to re-read the Book of Mormon's 561 pages and 275,000 words of text. The results are startling when applied to north-eastern North America in general and to the Niagara region in particular. We will see the results of Joëlle's labours soon.

My contention is that Joseph Smith actually found a record inscribed on *golden looking* plates, probably copper or brass. It had been written by one of the last descendants of Henry Sinclair's colonists who had initially been established in Nova Scotia in AD 1398. This colony, or at least part of the population, had moved to the Lake Memphremagog area by about AD 1450 or so. A second daughter colony had been founded above Niagara Falls in order to permit navigation into the far west via the so-called "Upper Great Lakes". One of the last survivors of these later daughter colonies had written the account that Joseph Smith discovered.

I further assumed that the record had been written in a Scandinavian-Scottish-English dialect of around AD 1500. I found an example of this in the *Chronicis Scotiae* for the year AD 1500. I could get the gist of it and I figured that Joseph Smith could have got it too.[5]

By the time I finished *Grail Knights of North America* and it was on the press in late 1998, I had concluded that the Lake Memphremagog colonists had probably been the so-called "Mohicans". They seemed to have been decimated by the first phase of Mohawk expansion, the easternmost tribe of the Iroquois Confederacy, about AD 1570 and been pretty well exterminated by the second phase of Iroquois expansion ending in 1690.

I had thought that the Niagara settlement had probably suffered the same fate at about the same time, but at the hands of the Seneca, or westernmost, tribe of the Iroquois Confederacy. In *Grail Knights of North America*, I had already suggested that the Niagara Frontier settlement had been on the southern shore of Lake Erie, possibly near Lake Chautauqua and the present Jamestown.[6]

Even I knew that the Book of Mormon's geography fitted the Niagara region in a very general way. The Mormon Church had also sent me an expensive and very professionally produced brochure about the annual Hill Cumorah Pageant. Hill Cumorah was a bit closer to the Niagara Frontier than to the Green Mountains foothills around Lake Memphremagog, so I assumed that Joseph Smith's record had been written by a survivor of the Niagara community. I suspected that the Book of Mormon might allow me to write a somewhat more detailed history of the Niagara Frontier settlement.

But as Joëlle's detailed investigation of the book's text progressed, it became clear that some of my assumptions had been wrong. The Book of Mormon seemed to be an actual history of the Grail Refugees, all right, but whoever had written it had had a detailed knowledge of their entire North American adventure. This, indeed, had added to Joseph Smith's already formidable problems. Not only did he have to cope with a barely readable dialect, and especially for him because he was just learning to read, but he had to digest what must have been, to him, puzzling complications of the story. Yet, these very same complications themselves strongly suggest that the Book of Mormon is basically an actual history of the Grail Refugees as attested by the artifacts so far discovered.

We also had to interpret the Book of Mormon because Smith "translated" it under some assumptions of his own. Smith represented the Judeo-Christian biblical fundamentalism of his time. The Bible was about the only book he knew "chapter and verse". Everybody did. There's a phrase in the Book of Mormon, "the tragedy of Jerusalem", and Smith naturally took this to mean the New Testament Crucifixion, roughly AD 33 or so. Smith knew that Nebuchadnezzar of Babylonia attacked Jerusalem about 590 BC, so he made his Nephites leave Jerusalem about ten years before the calamity around 600 BC.

I simply forgot about the Nephites' supposed escape from Jerusalem in 600 BC, dismissing this episode as a necessary, in Smith's view, introduction to the book. I also assumed that the "tragedy of Jerusalem" referred to the fall of Jerusalem to the Saracens in AD 1187 and not to the biblical Crucifixion.

It had been this "tragedy of Jerusalem" and not the earlier New Testament one that had transformed the Grail Believers from a major religion symbolised by the most prestigious throne in Europe into miserable, hunted Grail Refugees.

When this was done, the few dates in the Book of Mormon actually coincided with the known dates of Grail-related artifacts and the text supplies a quite plausible chronology for the Grail Refugees' entire adventure in North America.

By this assumed chronology, then, the final battle of Hill Cumorah took place not in AD 384 but in AD 1571. Moroni took the record back to Hill Cumorah sixteen years later, not in AD 400 but in AD 1587. By this chronology, the Grail Refugees' history in North America as a cohesive people – that is, still preserving a European identity – numbered 173 years from Sinclair's Nova Scotia landing in AD 1398 until their destruction and dispersal by the Iroquois about AD 1571. That is to say, there were about eight to ten generations of culturally European "Grail

Refugees (with much Native admixture), counting twenty years as a generation.

The original Templars who came into Scotland about AD 1314 were sworn to celibacy, but it is hard to say how far this went in practice. In any event, the Templar order was disbanded in AD 1312, or two years before the Templars actually formed Robert the Bruce's right flank at Bannockburn in June, 1314. These ex-Templars could have taken women or "wives" in Scotland and many of them probably did. By the time of the Sinclair voyage in AD 1398, these ex-Templars had been in Scotland for eighty-four years and there could have been only very few of the original Templars remaining alive, if any. By Sinclair's "soldiers", we are talking about the *descendants* of these original Templars, and second or third generation descendants at that.

But they were descendants of men who had once been the most revered knights in Christendom and it is unlikely they would have forgotten their heritage. Genealogy was *the* cornerstone of feudal European society. Their fathers and grandfathers had been the elite guardians of the Holy Grail. Making knights was a privilege of the feudal nobility, not the Church, and it can hardly be doubted that ex-Templar descendants would have been made knights if they demonstrated a warrior's attributes.

Some may have sworn themselves to celibacy and chastity in the Cathar and troubadour tradition. Magda Bogin in her *The Women Troubadours* notes that while male troubadour poetry extolled the usual non-sexual "courtly love", female troubadour poetry, as might be expected, was much more frankly sexual and earthy. So, it may be that most of Sinclair's soldiers were not married, or else the soldiers had casual relationships they left behind in Scotland.

Sinclair came to Nova Scotia with about five hundred "soldiers" in AD 1398. The presence of women is inferred, but only just barely, in "The Zeno Narrative". It is clear that only a few women were participants in the expedition. It is equally clear, however, that a viable "city" could not be established without women. So, there must have been at least a few women originally, and more European women may have been brought from Orkney and Scotland in a few subsequent voyages to Estotiland. Let's say that only five percent (5%) of the Sinclair's "soldiers" had wives, twenty-five married "soldiers" or married couples. These would most likely have been the chieftains, officers and leaders and, maybe, members of the Holy Bloodline itself.

These few facts tempt me to do some speculative number crunching.

We will assume an average male life expectancy of about fifty years –
Henry Sinclair died at the age of fifty-five – but a female reproductive
life of forty years. We will also assume that each married couple could
produce an average of eight children, of which only four would survive
to reach reproductive age because of the high medieval rate of infant
mortality. Counting the Nova Scotia settlers of AD 1398 as the "first
generation", we would get a total of about 12,800 people *of mainly or
purely European ancestry* by the "ninth generation", the median between
eight and ten generations. I would welcome any independent actuarial
calculations from readers.

Some of this population would have remained in Nova Scotia, some
would have concentrated around Lake Memphremagog in the Green
Mountains and some would have settled themselves in the Niagara
community. By the early 1500s, some people must also have manned far-
flung garrisons in order to keep an eye on the Spanish in Florida, the
English in Newfoundland and on Chesapeake Bay and the French on the
St. Lawrence.

My original suspicion back in 1967 was that most of the Estotiland
colonists would have left their exposed location on the coast of Nova
Scotia. By 1983, I knew that they had relocated first to the inland castle
at New Ross, Nova Scotia. And by 1997, artifacts had confirmed that
some of them had relocated further inland to the area around Lake
Memphremagog in the foothills of the Green Mountains. The castle ruin
at New Ross would eventually have served as only a lookout post on the
Atlantic for a relatively small garrison.

But once Niagara Falls was discovered, the Niagara settlement could
have become just as important as Lake Memphremagog. Let's say that of
this total of 12,800 "Nephites", two thousand stayed in Nova Scotia
settlements, five thousand settled around Lake Memphremagog in the
Green Mountains and five thousand somewhat later moved on to
populate the Niagara community. That leaves eight hundred to garrison
lookout posts along major river routes and to populate smaller centres.

In *Grail Knights of North America* I also suggested that there had
been a sort of mid-way settlement between Lake Memphremagog and
Niagara on the Lake on the Mountain overlooking Adolphus Reach at the
mouth of the Bay of Quinte.[7] For some years I had been starting to
suspect that there must have been a "Grail Related" settlement
somewhere in the area where Lake Ontario becomes the St. Lawrence
River. This would mean the general region between Kingston and Picton
in Ontario. Several readers have written to report curious ruins in this
area. My guess would be that for defensive reasons a settlement or
lookout post at the source of the St. Lawrence would most probably have

151

been on one of the large islands there (Wolfe Island, Amhearst Island or Howe Island), but it could also have been in Prince Edward County. In fact, there could have been several little settlements in this general location. It was the strategic link between Grail Refugees on the Great Lakes and their Nova Scotia beachhead. It was a crucial point in their line of supply from Europe.

And in what follows we must never forget *the* fundamental fact. The Grail Refugees' new domain was, and is, the greatest inland waterway in the world. Indian canoes were sufficient to explore it initially, but not to exploit its resources in a medieval way or to defend it according to medieval precepts of warfare. Men must have been assigned to build boats, or even small ships, that could both carry more cargo than birch bark canoes and could also be used as military platforms against birch bark canoes. Fishing must also have been almost as central to their economy as agriculture. Sinclair's domain of Orkney was famed all over Northern Europe as a place of boat builders, fishermen and sailors.

My previous number crunching wasn't just a numbers game. Known demographic ratios indicate that in medieval communities fifteen non-combatants were needed to put one warrior in the field. These people included wives and children, agriculturists, artisans like armourers, bakers and millers, the community's leaders, elders and administrators, and so on. The same would hold true not only for warriors in the field, but for men free to construct dams and defensive walls, carve gargoyles, build moated homesteads, build and crew ships, and so forth.

Therefore, at this ratio, we have less than one thousand European men at any given time free to garrison distant outposts and to build some of the large artifacts that we find. In Nova Scotia there's the ruined castle at New Ross and perhaps one other site near Noel Shore. In the Green Mountains there is the community dam, the "settling pond site" and at least three other sites near Potton Township alone. In Niagara there are those moated homesteads along the line of the Welland Feeder Canal, plus fortifications mentioned in Bert Wheeler's newspaper clippings. There are also the mountaintop sites in Pennsylvania and the evidence of old mines that yielded "coined money" to Josiah Stowel and others. There are also probably other sites that have not been discovered yet.

Actually, there were much less than a thousand European men available for this work at any given time because this figure of 12,800 represents the ninth, or last, generation of "Nephites."

For most of those 189 years, there were less than five hundred European men available for all these tasks – say, seventy-five or so in Nova Scotia, two hundred each in the Green Mountains and Niagara and the rest distributed along river route lookout posts.

Thus we see how vulnerable these Europeans really were among the aboriginal population of northeast North America north of the Ohio River and east of the Mississippi. This population has been estimated at about two million people in early colonial times. But these late medieval Europeans did not have the qualitative advantage that firearms gave early colonials.

As for the unmarried soldiers of the original Nova Scotia settlement, most of them would have intermarried with Indian women and their descendants would probably have forgotten their European ancestor by the third or fourth generation. These are Joseph Smith's Lamanites. The European genetic contribution may still be discernible because of the "X Lineage Sequence" of DNA, but the culture would have remained mainly aboriginal.

One further matter must be dealt with and they are Joseph Smith's "Anti-Lehi-Nephi" people who, according to the Book of Mormon, remained steadfastly neutral between the Nephites and the Lamanites. They would not even defend themselves and lived as a sheltered population under the protection of the Nephites.

The curious thing is that there was a tribe of Indians just like this, the so-called "Neutral Indians" of the Niagara Peninsula in the immediate area around Hamilton, Ontario.

They lived in about twenty villages so far located, mapped and partly excavated. Bill Fitzgerald has been interested in these Neutral Indians, has excavated several sites while at Sir Wilfred Laurier University in Guelph, Ontario and has found blue glass trade beads dating from the early 1500s in some Neutral villages.

Presently, these beads are attributed either to Basques trading up the St. Lawrence as early as about AD 1530 or to the Spanish in the Gulf of Mexico.

Either way, the beads are supposed to have travelled to Hamilton by tribe-to-tribe trade. The beads themselves are thought to have been made in either southern France or northern Spain.

Nonetheless, some students of Canadian archaeology have become suspicious of these blue glass trade beads.

Why did no many of them end up around Hamilton, Ontario?

Why are they not more randomly distributed throughout the entire Southeast and Northeast of North America?

The logical answer is that there was a plentiful local supply of these blue glass trade beads around Hamilton, Ontario.

But that would infer an unknown European population somewhere on the Niagara Escarpment.

The problem is that the Neutral Indians were not really well known in Joseph Smith's time.

They are mentioned in the *Jesuit Relations* and in French-language accounts of Huronia, but it is hardly likely that Joseph Smith – who was just learning to read American English, remember – could have consulted these mostly French-language sources.

How did he include these Indians so accurately in the Book of Mormon? This is another indication that the "golden plates" were a record of the Grail Refugees and pinpointed the Niagara region as the "Peninsula."

It should be emphasised yet again that the Neutral Indians were localised around Hamilton.

Altogether, I think that 12,800 "Europeans" is a very reasonable estimate of the population of the "European" Grail Refugees by the time of the "Battle of Hill Cumorah" and the "Last of the Mohicans" about AD 1571.

There are ways of getting artifacts other than digging for them in the sun. I had already concluded from the topographical maps and little gummed coloured discs that the Niagara Community had been laid out along the line of the present so-called "Welland Feeder Canal."

This ditch runs from Wainfleet Marsh to Dunnville, Ontario at the mouth of the Grand River. The "doughnut lakes" or putative "moated homesteads" were roughly arranged parallel to, but north of, this feeder canal.

Being naturally lazy, I knew that if I was right, well, some residents of the area must have already discovered some artifacts.

And, doubting that any expert would have bothered ever to look at them, no matter how often they might have been asked previously, I imagined that some artifacts were still in attics, basements and dresser drawers of the Niagara area. All I had to do was advertise for them. This beat digging any day, especially hot ones.

I had some friends and fans at the St. Catharines *Standard* daily newspaper, the biggest daily near my major area of interest. I called them up and told them the truth.

I was (politely) an "amateur historian" – or really a middle aged tomb raider and grave robber – who was looking for a story about possible artifacts in the newspaper's distribution area. I had this crazy theory that Europeans had been in the region long before the known colonials.

Reporter Don Fraser of the St. Catharines *Standard* was extremely interested and wrote a big photo-feature story in the Saturday, April 28, 2001 issue of the newspaper.

Don had listened to my theory carefully, too, and he wrote that I expected to get some reports of curious artifacts from around the village of Wainfleet, Ontario. Fraser mentioned the town of Wainfleet on the first page of the article in the fourth paragraph.

Don had warned me, however, that due to the dictates of "responsible journalism," he would have to interview some accredited, conventional experts about my theory.

He managed to locate Chris Andersen, a regional archaeologist with the Ontario Ministry of Tourism who gave the opinion that my theory was "archaeology beyond the fringe".

Don Fraser also got hold of Bill Severin of the Niagara Historical Museum who said: "I know of no reputable source or evidence that would support that thesis." I never claimed to anyone that I was even remotely reputable, only that I was probably right.

I would like to mention here that I am a bit disappointed in the St. Catharines *Standard* newspaper. The reporters did a fine job and produced an interesting and balanced story to which many people responded. But the newspaper's management showed less good will.

When *Swords at Sunset* was about to be published, I thought it would be neat to reproduce the entire story so that the artifacts that *The Standard's* readers had reported could be illustrated. I thought that the readers themselves would appreciate the results of their own years of interest that had helped to conserve old relics.

But *The Standard* was interested in charging a good deal of money as opposed to serving the readers' obvious interest, and I couldn't afford to pay the price of reproducing the April 28, 2001 article (which was based on my own work!).

I offered this chapter as an except for *The Standard* in exchange for permission to reprint the article, but this offer was refused.

It is possible – and I strongly suspect – that word had already got around concerning the growing Jewish opposition to *Swords at Sunset* that culminated on April 28, 2004 with Dundurn Press's refusal to publish the book – see Dan Rowe's "Dundurn drops controversial book" in the April 29, 2004, online edition of *Quill and Quire*. Fortunately, Manor House Publishing Inc. of Ancaster, Ontario, fearlessly stepped into the fray and thoughtfully agreed to publish the book you're reading

Here are some of the artifacts reported to me by readers of the St. Catharines *Standard* newspaper because of the April 28, 2001 story:

May 3, 2001

This silver and gold medallion was discovered in the late 1970s by the parents of Dennis Farkas of Wainfleet, Ontario. It was found under the roots of an overturned apple tree in an old orchard.

According to a Freemason historian residing near Rosslyn Chapel in Scotland, this is a Templar-Freemasonic medallion made during the time of Pope Alexander VI about AD 1496. It represents the Vatican's "Keys of the Kingdom" reversed, as they appear on Pope Alexander VI's banner.

There are some indications that Alexander VI was a "heretical pope" in that he authorised French and Italian explorations of the New World when he himself had set the "Line of Demarcation" in AD 1494 that supposedly divided the whole world between fiercely Roman Catholic Spain and Portugal.   Image scanned by Marty Meyers.

Both sides of a 5-inch diameter (133 mm.) inscribed brass plate found in Grimsby, Ontario. The inscription is in Hebrew, Latin and Greek characters. Note the pentagon on one side, symbol of the planet Venus, and by extension of biblical Mary Magdalene (see *The Holy Place* by Henry Lincoln for a detailed explanation). The "all seeing eye" is on the other side. This was the second inscribed plate that was obtained from roughly the same area, but the inscription on the other plate is too defaced to even see any of the characters.

The rust stain on the "all seeing eye" side of the plate (right) was caused by a rusted "sword blade" that was reportedly found laying on top of the plate when it was discovered. This blade crumbled into rust flakes and all the pieces were eventually lost. But the stain itself tells us something. The blade was about 35 mm. wide, too narrow for a "Viking" sword or a "hand and a half wheel pommel sword" ("Claymore") of the Scottish medieval period. It is, however, a blade width typical of the early sixteenth century or about AD 1500 to AD 1530. Photo by Michael Bradley, digital imaging by Joëlle Lauriol.

In actual fact, five artifacts were shaken out of the local woodwork by this article in *The Standard*. They are all still being investigated and analysed, including the two that are a convenient size to be illustrated here. I have sent high-resolution, computer-enhanced photos to Oxford, Cambridge – and, yes, the Sorbonne – as well as to "The Cloisters" in New York City. Where possible, actual samples have also been passed around to various experts in sequence and I would like to thank Federal Express for their promp and always courteous assistance.

Everyone is still waiting for the final verdict, the combined and collected opinions of world class experts.

There was a coin that initially excited us – until it was (more or less) proved to be a souvenir of the 1901 Pan American Exposition hosted by Buffalo, New York.

The present city of Buffalo was founded in 1803 and was supposedly named after one of the last woodland bison east of the Mississippi that was killed in the area. However, the site is a strategic one, the first quiet water of any expanse above Niagara Falls, and there can be little doubt that it was inhabited by, at least, the French much earlier than 1803. For example, Detroit (i.e. *Détroit*, "The Straits") was founded by Antoine de la Motte Cadillac in 1701 – a hundred and two years before the official establishment of Buffalo – but had been a French outpost for over forty years by then. However, the site of Buffalo, like Detroit, may have also been inhabited by Europeans who lived there even before the history book French.

Beau flot (pronounced "flo") *de l'eau* would mean, more or less, "beautiful flow (or expanse) of (slightly moving) water", which perfectly describes the site of Buffalo. But also the French word for an ox is *buffle* and therefore a *buffle a l'eau* would mean roughly "an ox (or bison) in the water". These hypothetical names may have lingered to be corrupted into "Buffalo".

There was movement afoot about the time of the 1901 Pan American Exposition to stress the antiquity of Buffalo. Entrepreneurs did strike souvenir coins in mock-antique style during this Exposition. However old the city of Buffalo may be, and whatever its French name really was, it seems that the specific coin that came to us because of the newspaper story was one of 10,000 souvenir coins made for the Exposition.

Readers will see from this discussion of the name of Buffalo that almost no artifact can be identified with absolute certainty, no matter what anyone says. If a maverick or "fringe" archaeologist says that an inscription is Celtic Ogham, well, it *could* be just weathering on rock. An accredited academic expert may says confidently that the first European to see Niagara Falls was the "French Father Louis Hennepin in December 1678" as Bill Severin was quoted in the above newspaper story. But he will almost certainly be wrong because many Europeans whose names are unknown to us very probably saw the falls previously.

The fourth artifact is part of the blade of what looks like an iron or "Austenitic steel" battleaxe also discovered not far from Wainfleet along with ten arrowheads nearby. It was found in 1936 while someone was digging a foundation for a streamside boathouse. Parts of it have been sent to the Ethnology Museum at Cambridge University. I viewed these artifacts in the bottom of a footlocker in a rural basement near Wellandport. But I asked to see the pasture where they had been discovered. I was led along a growth of willows and elders flanking a channel of Beaver Creek where the scattered artifacts had been found.

In my imagination, anyway, I could visualise the pursuit along the stream by Indians of someone desperately clinging onto a near-useless battleaxe. The European had finally fallen in a hail of Indian arrows. Artifacts in footlockers are very nearly valueless because they were not recovered *in situ*. By the simple expedient of refusing to go and look at artifacts as soon as they are reported, conventional archaeologists guarantee that they will hardly ever find any embarrassing artifacts *in situ*. Then they can be safely ignored. But farmers and boathouse-builders sometimes keep the artifacts in footlockers.

And when embarrassing artifacts *are* sometimes found in undisturbed strata of Canadian Indian sites, they may be thrown away on the spot. Gérard Leduc told me about an iron nail that had turned up in Montreal-area Iroquois strata of a village indicating an age of about AD 1400. Gérard recounted that the university supervisor of the dig picked up the nail, looked at it carefully and then threw it into the nearby lake! "These things cause too much trouble," he said.

The fifth artifact uncovered because of this newspaper article was a stone-carved spindle whorl of typical "Viking" pattern, but it would be hard to distinguish between a "Viking" artifact and a "Scottish-Scandinavian" one. It's like six of one and half-dozen of the other. It was found in 1972, also not far from Wellandport, Ontario.

It is symptomatic of our politically correct era that every one of these artifacts was reported to authorities like the Royal Ontario Museum. There was not much official interest in them, and the experts obviously didn't know what they were. Dennis Farkas has an old letter from the ROM saying that his medallion was a "religious medal", which it is, but there was no indication of its provenance or age.

The five artifacts, together with the ones we had excavated and those mentioned in Bert Wheeler's Niagara Frontier newspaper clippings, brought the grand total of "European" artifacts to more than one thousand separate articles or items that should not have been found in the Niagara Frontier region. This tally includes "brass plates" and "breastplates", copper kettles and over a hundred human skeletons found with their hands tied behind their backs *with braided fibre cord*.

After Marco Polo (AD 1254-1324) returned home to Venice in the winter of AD 1295 after having spent seventeen years in China, mostly in the employ of Kubla Khan, he quickly earned the nickname *"Missire*

Millione", or "Master Million". This was because of the exaggerations that people supposed that he told about the wonders of China.

One of Marco Polo's jobs under Kubla Khan had been customs inspector on several of China's rivers and so he saw the Grand Canal. This canal, begun about AD 500, was greatly expanded by Kubla Khan until it connected virtually every major river system in China when Marco Polo was collecting tariff fees along it. In order to go over higher-elevation watersheds between river systems, the Chinese had invented the "pound canal" and Marco Polo brought a description of this technology back to Europe.

A "pound canal" consists of long ditches, or "impoundments" of water with an embankment at either end. Each stretch of water is level, of course, but is at a slightly different elevation – a matter of two to four feet – and by having a series of these "pounds" or "ponds" boats could gradually climb up and down a watershed.

The Chinese invented, but didn't ordinarily use, the so-called "pound locks" of later eighteenth century European canals. Examples of traditional hand-operated pound locks with wooden floodgates can be seen on Canada's Rideau Canal. The Chinese found that pound locks were wasteful of water and, since water always runs downhill, the "summit level" of a canal had to be a vast reservoir in order to provide water all through a navigation season.

The Chinese much preferred to stick with lock-less impoundments. Boats could be dragged over mudslides on the embankments at either end. That way, the only water loss was through evaporation and the long "ponds" could also be stocked with fish. These fish would stay put, not being able to escape through a floodgate, and they would keep the impoundment clear of vegetation and also be a source of food for the canal-side population.

There was another social advantage to this system. Barge crews were so tired out by the hauling that they didn't drink so much when they had negotiated an embankment. By contrast, a tavern was established at almost every lock along England's many Industrial Revolution canals. Many of these English locks had colourful names, but my favourite is "Totterdown" on the Grand Union Canal, which demonstrates the social advantages of the Chinese system. Drinking and swearing like "a bargee" has come into the English language because of these lock-side taverns.[8] Marco Polo may never have seen a pound lock along China's Grand Canal because they were fairly rare. But he brought the technology of the simple pound canal back to Europe in AD 1295. By the time of the dispersal of the Templars in AD 1312, the Templars had already constructed some pound canals in order to increase navigation, and thus their tariff income, on the rivers of southern France (mainly the Garonne system) and northern Italy (the Po River and its tributaries).

I first saw the Welland Feeder Canal in 1995 in the charming company of Zoë Nickerson, the statuesque red headed girlfriend of Bob Hall who worked as a special effects technician in the film industry. Zoë made several day-trips with me to the Niagara Escarpment during 1995 and 1997 because Bob was sometimes then working literally night and day on film shoots. Aside from being fascinated with history – Zoë was from Nova Scotia and had read *Holy Grail Across the Atlantic* – she sometimes got lonely not seeing Bob for weeks on end.

Zoë and I arrived near Wainfleet one day, and I looked for the first time at a stretch of the "Welland Feeder Canal," as it was marked on our map. I suspected immediately that I was actually looking at a Late Medieval pound canal that had been dredged out and used when the Welland Canal was built. Near Wainfleet that day, I thought that I was looking at some rounded and artificial-looking "hills" running down to the water that had once been an embankment closing off a segment, or "pound" (or "pond"), at a certain level.

The first Welland Canal, completed in 1833, from St. Catharines on Lake Ontario to Port Colborne on Lake Erie, was Canada's belated answer to America's Erie Canal that had been completed eight years earlier. Canadian captains could get into the Erie Canal at American Lake Ontario ports like Rochester and then they could use the canal to navigate their ships onto the Upper Lakes.

A great deal of Canadian tonnage therefore used this all-American route and some Canadian Lake Ontario ports began to suffer the economic consequences. Therefore, there was an immediate outcry for an all-Canadian route from Lake Ontario to Lake Erie. The Welland Canal crosses the Niagara Escarpment more or less parallel with the line of the natural Niagara River but about ten miles, or roughly eighteen kilometres, to the west.

Canada got a lucky break in 1958 when the upgraded and larger St. Lawrence Seaway was built. The new Seaway, intended for ocean freighters, had to have a larger channel and larger locks than earlier canals.

The Seaway was simply too large to follow the old Erie Canal's route through large American cities that had been built up closely around it. Therefore, the St. Lawrence Seaway chose the route of the Welland Canal because the affected Canadian cities had not grown so large as American ones and the Seaway caused less social disruption.

The Welland Feeder Canal supplied water for the summit level of the original Welland Canal of 1833. It runs in a dead straight line from Wainfleet Marsh to the town of Dunnville on the Grand River some thirty miles, or fifty kilometres, to the Northwest.

This in itself made no sense to me because the summit level, in this case, is the level of Lake Erie.

Any ditch, and a much shorter one, could have been dug from Lake Erie to the marsh in order to serve a couple of the original locks that were, indeed, a bit higher than the level of Lake Erie because they had to go over some local higher ground along the route. Why dig a feeder canal that long?

I suspected that this ditch had been there long before the original Welland Canal had been constructed. The Welland surveyors had decided, I suspected, that it was easier to dredge this canal of its weeds and to dig through its embankments than to excavate a completely new feeder canal about ten miles (16 kilometres) long.

If this was true, then there might have been some record of it in surveyors' reports and diaries of the 1830s.

Bert Wheeler began looking for such references after our meeting in December 1998 in Niagara Falls, Ontario.

In April 1999, Wheeler called me to say that he had found a reference to the feeder canal's existence before 1833.

But this reference later seemed too ambiguous for us, and we have not since been able to find any colonial record that supports my notion.

Joëlle's "doughnut lakes", however, do generally parallel the line of the Welland Feeder Canal on its north side between it and the courses of Beaver Creek and the Welland River.

These "doughnut lakes" also seem once to have been connected to both waterways by natural streams and short ditches.

This can be seen on any large-scale topographical map of the Niagara region. Because of limitations in the number of illustrations allowed for this book, I have not reproduced such maps here. They are obtainable at Government Printing Offices.

Don Eckler thought back in 1998 that these "doughnut lakes" had once been moated homesteads arranged along the line of the Welland Feeder Canal and thus constituted the axis of the Niagara community of Grail Believers.

This seemed obvious from our maps with all those little coloured gummed discs. It is intriguing, therefore, that the Book of Mormon seems to refer to them. The relevant references are all in *Alma 48* and *49*.

The "he" in these passages refers to a general of the Nephites called "Moroni I" who lived about "Year 85" of the Nephites' occupation of the Niagara Peninsula. If our basic chronological assumption is anywhere near correct, this works out to about AD 1511 or so:

> Yea, he had been strengthening the armies of the Nephites, and erecting small forts, or places of resort; throwing up banks of earth round about to enclose his armies, and also building walls of stone to encircle them about, round about their cities and the borders of their lands; yea, all around about the land.
>
> *Alma 48:8*

> But behold, how great was their [i.e. the Lamanites'] disappointment; for behold, the Nephites had dug up a ridge of earth round about them, which was so high that the Lamanites could not cast their stones and their arrows at them that they might take effect, neither could they come upon them save it was by their place of entrance.
>
> *Alma 49: 4*

> Now behold, the Lamanites could not get into their forts of security by any other way save by the entrance, because of the highness of the bank which had been thrown up and depth of the ditch which had been dug round about, save it were by the entrance.
>
> *Alma 49:18*

The only thing that isn't said *explicitly* is that the deep ditches around the "small forts" (that could accommodate armies!) were filled with water, but that is at least inferred. It is also inferred that there were many of these forts because they were "all around about the land" but that any given individual fortification was "small". The only way in was by an "entrance" across the ditch and this must be because the ditches were filled with water. I had assumed that all the "doughnut lakes" that were no longer true circles had been gradually eroded into more of a "closed horseshoe" configuration. But perhaps these tongues of land leading to the central island had been purposefully left as a narrow causeway. In other cases, a wooden bridge or causeway had once been constructed. Such wooden bridges would have rotted away.

We doggedly surveyed the line of the Welland Feeder Canal and these "doughnut lakes" between 1998 and 2003, working always on private property for reasons of legality, but we did not find any single dramatic artifact that absolutely proved late medieval occupation. For example, even a piece of fine Austenitic chain mail (see Chapter 1) could have been brought in early French colonial times. This sort of mail was still worn up until about AD 1670 and it would have proved more useful to early explorers of North America than it would have been in Europe itself. One could even imagine a short-term and localised revival of this example of military fashion.

It is not really so surprising that we're able to find much that was suggestive, but nothing that was definitive. We were able to examine only a few dozen square metres of turf in the aggregate. We could only excavate during summer weekends because of the pressures of work, and not always on every weekend. We were looking for that figurative needle in a haystack.

The most promising place to excavate would be along the Welland Feeder Canal itself, of course, and especially at the "hills" beside it that I believe were once embankments. But most of this land is publicly owned and that precludes freelance archaeological excavations. But it was encouraging that two of the artifacts uncovered by *The Standard's* article actually came from Wainfleet, a place that I had specifically referred to in the article itself.

Further artifacts will come from the residents of this Niagara region, some of whose families have farmed there for decades. I would greatly appreciate it if anyone who knows of any interesting artifact would contact me or Joelle Lauriol at: P.O. Box 97035, 149 Roncesvalles Avenue, Toronto, Ontario, Canada, M6R 3L0.

Notes to Chapter 5.

1 I covered this in much greater detail in *Grail Knights of North America*, pages 353-358.

2 Quoted from Richard L. Bushman's *Joseph Smith and the Beginning of Mormonism*, University of Illinois Press, Urbana, 1984, page 5.

3 *Grail Knights of North America*, page 342.

4 See Norman Davies *The Isles: A History, Oxford University Press*, 1999, pages 3-20.

5 For an example of this dialect see *Grail Knights of North America*, page 280.

6 See *Grail Knights of North America*, page 391.

7 See *Grail Knights of North America*, pages 325-338.

8 This information about the growth of the European canal systems comes from R.T.C. Rolt's entertaining *Narrow Boat* and his scholarly *Inland Waterways of Britain*.

6

The Tragic Trail to Hill Cumorah

No one can reasonably contend, and I certainly do not, that the Book of Mormon is an exact record of the Grail Refugees' North American history. The original plates may have been such a detailed history, but if it was written in a Scottish-English-Scandinavian dialect that had been current about AD 1500, then Joseph Smith got only the bare gist of it – those first 116 pages. But these original plates disappeared after this "translation" was accomplished. Smith says that the angel Moroni took them back ("Testimony of the Prophet Joseph Smith" as the Introduction to the Book of Mormon, page 3).

Then, even that initial "translation" of 116 pages was lost and Smith dictated his "second translation", probably from recall and sheer imagination, as a 275,000-word elaboration of the much shorter original. He seems to have worked from his memory, which seems to have been exceptional in his case, but it wasn't perfect. The elaboration published as the Book of Mormon is a jumbled and confused record. Never the less, Smith had a good remembrance of numbers and there is therefore a reasonable *relative chronology* for most of the history presented. His memory for numbers also preserved the days of travel that were required to go from one place to another, and sometimes there are two figures: one for overland travel, one for travel along waterways by, presumably, Indian canoes. Thus, with a great deal of patience, it is possible to arrive at a relative geography.

"The Zeno Narrative" ends with Antonio Zeno's unwilling return to Orkney as captain of Sinclair's fleet. Sinclair stayed behind, "retaining only boats propelled by oars." to found his "city" with the "soldiers" who were to stay in the New World. Obviously, he would have had to build a small ship for his eventual return to Orkney, and European records state that he must have returned to his domains by the summer of AD 1400 because he was killed in August of that year in a skirmish.

Frederick Pohl in his book *Prince Henry Sinclair* has presented evidence that Sinclair's ship was built during the winter of AD 1398-1399 in Advocate Harbour, Nova Scotia and that his "stone canoe" was remembered in Mi'kmaq Indian legend. But the Sinclair expedition could also have spent the year AD 1399-1400 in the New World, leaving for Europe in May or June of AD 1400, and could have explored the Atlantic Coast southward of Nova Scotia. Apparently, it did.

On Prospect Hill near Westford, Massachusetts, a 465-foot elevation, there was for many years a "rock drawing" that was attributed to local Indians. Then in 1940, a man named William B. Goodwin looked at the drawing more carefully and saw that the figure was a depiction of a medieval knight. Later, Frederick Pohl and Frank Glynn, President of the Connecticut Archaeological Society, went to the site and made a careful drawing of what they then realised was an effigy figure. The knight's sword was broken, symbol of a knight's death. The climb to the top of the hill, in armour and the summer sun, had possibly proved too much for one of the knights in Sinclair's entourage. Pohl and Glynn were even able to make out the markings on the knight's shield, his coat-of-arms. The drawing was sent to Prof. T.C. "Tom" Lethbridge, Curator of Cambridge University's Ethnology Museum.

One of several drawings of the Westford Effigy that have appeared in several recent Grail-related books. This one is an original 1947 sketch by Frank Glynn.

Lethbridge identified the sword as a "hand and a half wheel pommel sword", or a Scottish "Claymore" of the late fourteenth century. The helmet was a type known as a "basinet" that was in vogue for only twenty-five years, from AD 1375 to AD 1400. The coat-of-arms was "the galley of Orkney" worn by the Gunn clan of Sutherland or the Gunne clan of Caithness. Ian Moncrieff in his *The Highland Clans* writes:

> Startling enough, the earliest surviving example of the Gunn chief's coat-of-arms appears to have been punch-marked by a medieval armourer-smith on a rock in Massachusetts. The heater shaped shield there, borne by what appears to be the effigy of a Fourteenth-Century knight, appears to show a distinctively Norse-Scottish character.[1]

It is known from other sources that the Gunn(e) clans were subject to Henry Sinclair and loyal to him. We therefore know that Sinclair's expedition either visited Massachusetts during the navigation season of AD 1399-1400, or that another voyage was made by trusted chieftains soon after the original expedition.

A "city" or settlement of five hundred soldiers would have had enough personnel to have almost immediately established secondary settlements and to explore their new domain. No history of Sinclair's "city" has survived – unless that history is incorporated in the garbled and elaborated work of Joseph Smith. And, according to Smith, the first settlers of the new great land of "Lehi-Nephi" almost immediately dispersed. This is likely enough on the basis of simple logic, and it is proved by the distribution of artifacts (see *Grail Knights of North America*). But Smith gives the additional information that departure from the original area of the Nova Scotia landfall was hastened by the abduction of twenty-four Indian women by the Europeans. This, too, is likely enough and it caused conflict with the local Indians.

I am very much indebted to Joëlle Lauriol who patiently compiled a relative chronology and also prepared maps of relative geography from the dates and distances given in the Book of Mormon. Because of her work, we can trace the history, explorations and settlements of these Grail Refugees in the New World with, at least, some greater probability of being generally correct.

Joseph Smith uses the appellation "land of Lehi-Nephi" to mean the entire Atlantic Coast from Nova Scotia south to Long Island Sound, the present states of Massachusetts, Rhode Island and Connecticut westward to New York State and City.

> ...And now, they knew not the course they should travel in the wilderness...and when they had wandered forty days they came to a hill which is north of the land of Shilom, and there they pitched their tents.
>
> *Mosiah 7: 4-5*

> And it came to pass that he built a tower near the temple; yea, a very high tower, even so high that he could stand upon the top thereof and overlook the land of Shilom, and also the land of Shemlon, which was possessed by the Lamanites; and he could even look over all the land round about. And it came to pass that he caused many buildings to be built in the land of Shilom; and he caused a great tower to be built on the hill north of the land of Shilom which had been a resort for the children of Nephi at the time they fled out of the land; and thus he did do with the riches which he obtained by the taxation of his people.
>
> *Mosiah 11: 12-13*

Standing in the middle of Newport, Rhode Island today is a sizeable artifact that has caused great controversy for more than three centuries. It is a squat round stone tower, standing on eight stonework legs, that is about thirty feet in diameter and about as tall. It is situated on a hill, its base five feet lower than the highest elevation in Newport and its "arrow slits" are randomly set in the sides to offer views of the surrounding water approaches. In architectural style, it is unquestionably fourteenth century Scandinavian, according to many authorities including Hjalmar J. Holand. Analysis of its dimensions has shown that it was built according to a unit of measure known as the Icelandic *fet*, consisting of 12.31 English inches. This unit was common throughout the medieval Norse-Scottish sphere of influence and survived until about 1920 in some rural regions as "Norsk" measure. Steel tape measures of the mid-1920s were sometimes manufactured in Sweden with dual Metric and "Norsk" units.

I have discussed the Newport Tower at fair length in both *Holy Grail Across the Atlantic*[9] and *Grail Knights of North America*[10] but there are many books and articles that have previously dealt with it. Our concern here is that the Book of Mormon seems to refer to it. If this is the case, then it was built in "Year 22" after the arrival of the Sinclair expedition of soldiers and Grail Refugees in AD 1398.

That is to say, the Newport Tower was built some time around AD 1420. This date would explain its architectural style and oddities very well. If the Newport Tower was built by Smith's Nephites, then this also locates the land of Shilom as being in the present region of Rhode Island, Massachusetts and Connecticut.

"He caused many buildings to be built" in the land of Shilom may refer to the ruins described on the Charles River by Edward Everett

Horton in 1898, which seem to be of medieval Scandinavian provenance and not of a much earlier "Celtic" age.

According to Joëlle's relative chronology, after the tower was built there were two years of relative peace between the Nephites and the Lamanites but then relations deteriorated again. In "Year 26", or two more years later, the Nephites abandoned the land of Shilom and trekked toward the Green Mountains and the Niagara Frontier.

This is interesting because the Newport Tower has an overhanging bevelled flange all around that was obviously intended to accept the roof of another and larger building that would have surrounded the tower. The sturdy tower (its walls are three feet thick) would then have become this larger structure's core. But it appears that this further planned construction was never even begun. On the other hand, the tower shows no signs of violent assault or fire. It seems merely to have been abandoned.

A "rownd stone towre" standing on a hill in the woods was mentioned as an "existing commodity" in the prospectus of Sir Edmund Plowden's proposed "Colony of New Albion" published in 1632, or seven years before Newport was founded. The tower is referred to on a map called "New England's Prospect" published in 1635, or four years before the colonial settlement of Newport, Rhode Island.

> And they fled eight days journey into the wilderness.
>
> *Mosiah 23: 3*
>
> And they came to a land, yea, even a very beautiful land, a land of pure water.
>
> *Mosiah 23:4*
>
> And they pitched their tents, and began to till the ground, and began to build buildings; yea, they were industrious, and did labour exceedingly.
>
> *Mosiah 23:5*
>
> And it came to pass that they began to prosper exceedingly in the land; and they called the land Helam. And it came to pass that they did multiply and prosper exceedingly in the land of Helam; and they built a city, which they called the city of Helam.
>
> *Mosiah 23:19-20*

From the land of Shilom in the immediate vicinity of the Newport Tower, the Green Mountains of Vermont are only about eight days journey northward up the broad Connecticut River, the largest river in southern New England. If scouts had gone ahead, the wide valley of the Barton River beckons off to the left (or west), toward the mountains, and leads straight to Lake Memphremagog. This was, indeed, a land of pure water. Numerous streams flow into Lake Memphremagog.

But also, brooks and fountains tumble down the mountains and, as I have related, metal-collecting settling ponds seem to have been constructed on some of them. It is tempting to take this trek of Nephites as the establishment of the Green Mountain community around the lake starting about AD 1424. Lake Memphremagog is about 24 miles in length, almost 40 kilometres. It would be a day's journey by canoe to paddle from one end to the other.

> And Alma and his people departed into the wilderness and when they had travelled all day, the pitched their tents in a valley, and they called the valley Alma, because he led their way in the wilderness.
>
> *Mosiah 24:20*

My understanding of this text is that Helam was at the southern end of Lake Memphremagog near the location of modern Newport, Vermont. Alma would have been at the northern end of the lake where the town of Magog, Quebec is today. Most of the artifacts and sites have so far been discovered on the west side of about the middle of the long, narrow lake in Quebec's Potton Township. But that's doubtless only because this area is more rural. The building of Newport and Magog must have covered many artifacts and sites, but there are probably more yet to be found if only someone looked for them.

> And it came to pass that they departed out of the valley, and took their journey into the wilderness. After they had been in the wilderness twelve days they arrived in the land of Zarahemla; and king Mosiah did also receive them with joy.
>
> *Mosiah 24:24-25*

My interpretation is that Zarahemla is the Niagara Frontier area. This twelve days of travel may seem a stretch to get from Lake Memphremagog to Niagara, but it depends on the route you travel.

I have canoed from within 10 miles of Lake Memphremagog to Lake Champlain in three days using the Missisquoi River. Taking the Richelieu River that flows into Baie Missisquoi at Rousse's Point, it requires another day to reach Sorel on the St. Lawrence above Montreal.

Then one is on the mighty St. Lawrence with eight days remaining to reach Zarahemla. Using the shoreline counter-currents on the St. Lawrence past Cornwall and through the Thousand Islands, the old *goelette* cargo boats used to average 75 miles a day going upstream. That's only three or four days to Lake Ontario at Wolfe Island between

Kingston, Ontario and Cape Vincent, New York. That's eight or nine days, leaving three or four days to reach Zarahemla on Lake Ontario.

Now, in these early days of the Nephites, it seems that Zarahemla extended far to the east of the Niagara Frontier along the southern shore of Lake Ontario, mainly because the Iroquois Confederacy had not yet come into being. It is difficult to be certain, of course, but the early eastern border of Zarahemla seems to have been somewhere around modern Rochester. Perhaps the landmark signifying the border was even fateful Hill Cumorah. *This* earlier border of Zarahemla would have been easy to reach in twelve days from Lake Memphremagog.

Only later, after the Treaty of "Year 350" with the Lamanites – or AD 1537 as calculated from the fall of Jerusalem to the Saracens in AD 1187 – did the land of Zarahemla come to mean *only* the Canadian side of the Niagara Frontier. But we are now in the first fifty years of the Nephites' expansion from Estotiland, about AD 1448 or so, and the futile treaty with the Lamanites, or Iroquois, is still 89 years in the future.

We now have the land of Shilom near the Newport Tower, Helam and Alma on Lake Memphremagog and Zarahemla on the Niagara Frontier somewhat triangulated. If it takes a total of twenty days to reach Zarahemla from Shilom via Helam and Alma by water, then it should take much longer to reach Zarahemla from Shilom by the overland route. This is because travellers would have to cross several mountain ranges in Pennsylvania and New York State – the Alleghenies, the Catskills and the Adirondacks – and would have much smaller streams and rivers to use as paths through the northeastern forest. And this is the case in the Book of Mormon.

We learn this because some people from Zarahemla later decided to visit or relocate back to the "land of Lehi-Nephi" on the Atlantic Coast in the region of Shilom:

And now, it came to pass that after king Mosiah had had continual peace for the space of three years, he was desirous to know concerning the people who went up to dwell in the land of Lehi-Nephi, or in the city of Lehi-Nephi; for his people had heard nothing from them from the time they had left the land of Zarahemla; therefore, they wearied him with their teasing.

And it came to pass that king Mosiah granted that sixteen of their strong men might go up to the land of Lehi-Nephi, to inquire concerning their brethren.

And it came to pass that on the morrow they started to go up, having with them one Ammon, he being a strong and mighty man, and a descendant of Zarahemla; and he was also their leader.

And now, they knew not the course they should travel in the wilderness to go up to the land of Lehi-Nephi; therefore they wandered many days in the wilderness, even forty days[11] did they wander.

And when they had wandered forty days they came to a hill, which is north of the land of Shilom, and there they pitched their tents.

Mosiah 7: 1-5

From all this we learn that it took twice as long to get from Shilom to Zarahemla by the overland mountainous route as it did to get from Shilom to Zarahemla by the longer but much easier waterways. Forty days as compared with twenty days. This is entirely in accord with the geographic reality of the Northeast.

Henry Wadsworth Longfellow (1807-1882) may have been an acceptable poet, but he was a terrible historian. In "The Song of Hiawatha", published in November of 1855, Longfellow presents an epic about an Ojibway brave who lived in the region of Lake Superior. The word and name "Hiawatha" is not even part of the Ojibway language. Longfellow credits Henry Rowe Schoolcraft, early American historian and explorer and Superintendent of Indian Affairs for the state of Michigan from 1836 to 1841, with the supposed Indian traditions incorporated in "The Song of Hiawatha".

In real life, Hiawatha was an Onondaga from the Finger Lakes region of New York State. He is usually credited with starting the Iroquois Confederacy by predicting an eclipse, a feat that impressed his tribal colleagues, but no one knows for certain when the Iroquois Confederacy was established. I have seen dates ranging from AD 1470 to about AD 1570.

In Iroquois tradition, as recounted in a number of books – and a fairly recent one is *The People of the Pines* by Loreen Pindera and Geoffrey York (Little, Brown, New York, 1991) – Hiawatha had a teacher named Deganawidah, as it is usually spelled. He resided on the Canadian side of Lake Ontario at "The Lake on the Mountain" at the entrance to the Bay of Quinte. Deganawidah taught Hiawatha what seems to have been a simple form of Christianity and "Golden Rule" ethics. Specifically, Deganawidah insisted that the Finger Lakes tribes should give up cannibalism. Deganawidah may also have informed Hiawatha about the imminent eclipse.

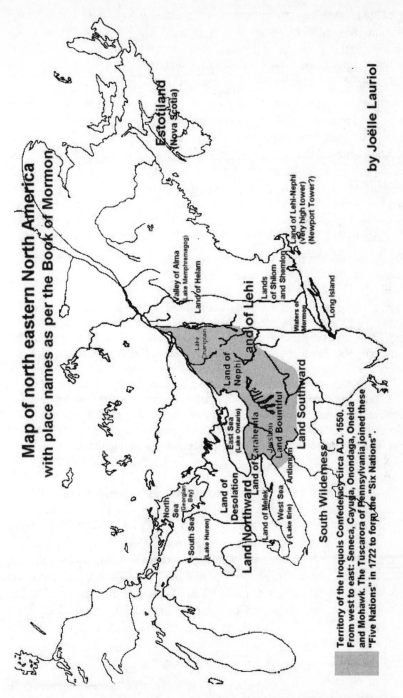

Map of north eastern North America with place names as per the Book of Mormon

by Joëlle Lauriol

Estotiland (Nova Scotia)

Land of Lehi-Nephi (Very high tower) (Newport Tower?)

Valley of Alma (Lake Memphremagog)

Land of Helam

Lands of Shilom and Shemlon

Waters of Mormon

Long Island

Lake Champlain

Land of Nephi

Land of Lehi

Land of Zarahemla

East Sea (Lake Ontario)

Land Bountiful

Land Southward

Jershon

Antionum

North Sea (Georgian Bay)

Land of Desolation

Land Northward

Land of Melek

West Sea (Lake Erie)

South Sea (Lake Huron)

South Wilderness

Territory of the Iroquois Confederacy circa A.D. 1550. From west to east: Seneca, Cayuga, Onondaga, Oneida and Mohawk. The Tuscarora of Pennsylvania joined these "Five Nations" in 1722 to form the "Six Nations".

Hiawatha returned to his tribe and converted the Onondagas, who had about twenty populous villages, to the new ethics. Previously independent, these twenty villages were welded into a loose confederacy based on non-cannibalism, the "Golden Rule" and mutual non-aggression. Thus presenting a united front to other independent villages, Hiawatha convinced four other distinct tribal groups to accept Deganawidah's precepts, especially mutual non-aggression.

These five tribes of the Finger Lakes region of New York State became the Iroquois Confederacy. From east to west they were: the Mohawks around Lake Champlain and the Hudson River, the Oneidas, the Onondagas in the area of Rochester, the Cayugas and finally the Senecas on the shores of eastern Lake Erie. They were also known as the Five Nations. The Confederacy's capital, insofar as it had one, was agreed to be the Onondaga village where Hiawatha had been born because the Onondagas also happened to be the geographically central tribe of the five.

The Book of Mormon seems to refer to the formation of the Iroquois Confederacy, but in a very general way:

> And it came to pass in the thirty and first year that they were divided into tribes, every man according to his family, kindred and friends; never the less, they had come to an agreement that they would not go to war one with another; but they were not united as to their laws, and their manner of government, for they were established according to the minds of those who were their chiefs and their leaders. But they did establish very strict laws that one tribe should not trespass against another, insomuch that in some degree they had peace in the land; nevertheless, their hearts were turned from the Lord their God, and they did stone the prophets and did cast them out from among them.
>
> *III Nephi 7:14*

In a complicated calculation of relative events, much too detailed to go into here, Joëlle figured out that this verse most probably recounts events that can be assigned the date of AD 1517 to AD 1519. The "thirty and first year" doesn't mean from the date of the Nephites' arrival, which we have associated with Henry Sinclair's voyage of AD 1398, but to a series of other events after the apparition of Jesus appeared to the Nephites. This date of AD 1517-1519 is as good a date as any for the establishment of the Iroquois Confederacy and seems more likely than some. The date of AD 1470 seems too early, while AD 1570 is almost certainly too late.

Who was Deganawidah?

Gérard Leduc told me that Concordia University had taken some core samples from the bottom of Adolphus Reach at the entrance to the Bay of Quinte on behalf of the Ontario Ministry of Natural Resources. This was during the late 1980s but Gérard, who had been a Professor of Biology at Concordia, could not remember the exact date when he recounted this story to me on September 20, 1997. We were both speaking at the "Earth Mysteries Conference" of maverick historians and Celtic-megalithic buffs that was being held in Peterborough, Ontario at the time.

According to Gérard, these core samples revealed another layer of lye-caused pollutants indicating a lye based soap using population far beneath the layer representing the known Loyalist settlers of the AD 1800 era. This layer was also beneath the traces indicating occasional French occupation of the area. The concentration of pollution correlated to a population of about twelve hundred unknown soap using Europeans who lived around Adolphus Reach during the 1500s. "The Lake on the Mountain" overlooks Adolphus Reach at the mouth of the Bay of Quinte.

Three separate correspondents from Glenora and Picton, Ontario – both towns are in the general area of the Bay of Quinte – wrote to me after the publication of *Grail Knights of North America*. All three insisted that there were medieval European ruins and artifacts in Prince Edward County and specifically at Adolphus Reach. Although not one of these three correspondents, the famous hockey star Bobby Hull had previously told me personally that there were ancient ruins near his cattle ranch not far from Picton.

Now, I will admit here that I simply have never had the time to investigate these claims, although one of my correspondents offered to host us for a week of surveying and excavation. However, in *Grail Knights of North America* I argued that a Grail Refugee settlement at the entrance to the Bay of Quinte was at least logical.[12]

First of all, the Bay of Quinte is an excellent harbour. It is almost exactly half way between Lake Memphremagog and the Niagara Frontier. Prince Edward County projects out into Lake Ontario more or less opposite Rochester and would make an excellent place to station two or three small ships that could control the lake against canoes. Then Gérard mentioned that the word "quinte" is an archaic Scottish word meaning a "shepherd's crook". The Bay of Quinte has a shepherd's crook shape.

In short, there are several excellent *theoretical* reasons why Deganawidah could have been a European. Whether he actually was or not is another matter, and a highly controversial one. The very idea enrages both conventional historians and Aboriginal spokespersons.

The reason is that the system of "checks and balances" operative in the Iroquois Confederacy somewhat reflects the political systems of modern representative democracies.

It is presently fashionable for Aboriginal leaders to claim that the Iroquois Confederacy contributed to the U.S. Constitution.

But Albert H. Hooker had asserted, back in 1934 and 1935 in a series of talks and lectures in the Buffalo area, that Hiawatha's grandfather had been a European and that the structure of the Iroquois Confederacy had been inspired by the political developments of the Icelandic Republic.

That is, the Iroquois had been inspired by Europeans and not the other way around. As we have mentioned already, Hooker thought that the "stone giants" of Iroquois legends related to armoured Europeans that had lived among them in their not-so-distant past.

The whole idea of a Grail Refugee community on Lake Erie was to enable them to navigate into the far west on the so-called "Upper Lakes". The St. Croix River at the western end of Lake Superior takes a traveller to the edge of the Prairies.

This desire became an urgent necessity in "Year 350" as calculated from the fall of Jerusalem in AD 1187 – or, AD 1537.

In that year, after two decades of warfare with the new and formidable Iroquois Confederacy, the Nephites managed to negotiate a treaty with the "Lamanites."

They were offered a respite from continual warfare, but they had to give up some land to get it. They yielded the territory they had occupied on the south shore of Lake Ontario.

> And the three hundred and forty and ninth year had passed away. And in the three hundred and fiftieth year we made a treaty with the Lamanites and the robbers of Gadianton, in which we did get the lands of our inheritance divided.
>
> And the Lamanites did give unto us the land northward, yea, even to the narrow passage which led to the land southward and we did give unto the Lamanites all the land southward.
>
> *Mormon 2:28-29*

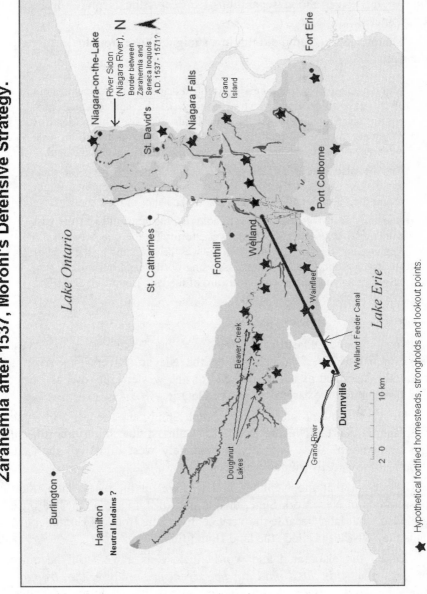

Zarahemla after 1537, Moroni's Defensive Strategy.

★ Hypothetical fortified homesteads, strongholds and lookout points.

After this treaty, therefore, the Nephites and the non-violent mixed people called the "People of Ammon" were confined to the land northward of the "River Sidon". This River Sidon is described twice in the Book of Mormon and the following passage is the clearest reference to the river and to the entire strategic situation facing the Nephites. Their general "Moroni" – this is probably our "Moroni I" again – fortified the line of the River Sidon separating, by treaty, the Nephites from the Lamanites.

And the land of Nephi did run in a straight course from the east sea to the west.

> And it came to pass that when Moroni had driven all the Lamanites out of the east wilderness, which was north of the land of their own possessions, he caused that the inhabitants who were in the land of Zerahemla and in the land round about should go forth into the east wilderness, even to the borders by the sea shore, and possess the land.
>
> And he also placed armies on the south, in the borders of their possessions, and caused them to erect fortifications that they might secure their armies and their people from the hands of their enemies.
>
> And thus he cut off all the strongholds of the Lamanites in the east wilderness, yea, and also on the west, fortifying the line between the Nephites and the Lamanites...from the west sea, running by the head of the River Sidon, the Nephites possessing all the land northward, yea, even all the land which was northward of the land Bountiful, according to their pleasure.
>
> *Alma 50:8-11*

Now, if Lake Ontario is the "east sea" and Lake Erie is the "west sea", then the River Sidon must be the Niagara River. This river is correctly described as taking its head on the western sea, or Lake Erie, and flowing into the eastern sea, Lake Ontario.

The geographic problem facing Joseph Smith, and the cause of some verbiage, is that the Niagara River flows almost due south-to-north. All the land "north" of it is really immediately west of it. All the land "south" of it is really immediately east of it.

It is clear that the Nephites had to give up their best land, their possessions in New York State, or that part of Zarahemla that had once included what later became the very centre of the Iroquois Confederacy. This they wistfully called "the land Bountiful".

Taking the elaborated and wordy history as a whole, it becomes obvious that *this land had to be given up because the Iroquois Confederacy developed on this territory* and, within about two decades, was powerful enough to dictate the terms of the treaty of "Year 350." And this, in turn, at least infers that the Iroquois had been influenced by European ideas of political organisation, personal arms and armour, fortification technology and even military strategy.

The "Lamanites" had descended from Joseph Smith's shipload of religious refugees who intermarried with Aboriginal women, just as most of Sinclair's five hundred knights of Estotiland had to marry Aboriginal women. There were too few European women to go around. Aside from the genetic influence of these knights who "went native," it is at least thought-provoking that Iroquois fortifications become much more "European-looking" after about AD 1530 with corner extensions of the village palisade to permit "enfilade fire" on anyone attempting to force the village's main entrance. Formerly, before about AD 1530, village palisades were haphazardly round or oval. This time around AD 1530 is also when Iroquois body armour first appears, bound-together slats of wood, and perhaps it was in imitation of European armour.

Learned volumes have been written about the sudden appearance of Iroquois "False Face" societies about AD 1530 and almost every large museum in North America has at least one example of a grotesque looking Iroquois mask. These masks were worn by members of supposed agricultural and magical secret societies. But might they not really be imitations of European helmets rendered in wood? Some European helmets were just as grotesque as Iroquois "False Face" masks. And might not the "secret societies" have been the Iroquois version of orders of knighthood?

The Nephite defensive strategy in the smaller Zarahemla behind the line of the River Sidon betrays the hand of a master European strategist. The Book of Mormon calls him "Moroni I" and it is entirely possible that Joseph Smith actually read this name correctly and remembered it. Perhaps this Templar-descended knight did have a southern French or Italian family name.

A close *study* of the map of "The Niagara Community" shows just how good a military strategist "Moroni I" was. He fortified the treaty border, the River Sidon. He removed any Lamanites who might have lived west of it by defeating them. He then, as we saw in the last chapter, built a system of *small*, fortified places along the course of the Welland River and its Beaver Creek tributary. These were located at an axis that was a right angle, ninety degrees, to the line of the River Sidon and *above the lip of the Niagara Escarpment.*

It is my notion that these fortifications must have been protected by water-filled moats, and not just dry ditches, because otherwise this community defence makes no sense. Why build "doughnut" lakes along the Welland River and Beaver Creek if they didn't use water from this system to fill their moats? I think that the Welland Feeder Canal was dug at this time, around AD 1537 to AD 1550 on the *south* side of the "doughnut lakes" and these lakes were connected to it by natural or artificial streams, creeks and channels.

What we see here is a highly sophisticated community and strategic defence plan that makes maximum use of a relatively small population, rather primitive agriculture and the available transportation technology. Farmsteads could be isolated to take advantage of the available arable land atop the Escarpment. At the same time, the farmsteads were interconnected by water so that their produce could be brought easily and in quantity to the community's concentration of population *and fighting men* along the waterway axis. But also, help could come to any farmstead fairly quickly by the boatload.

The Welland Feeder Canal runs thirty miles, or fifty kilometres, from Wainfleet Marsh to Dunnville, Ontario on the Grand River at Lake Erie. Why? In order to give the reduced territory of Zarahemla after the treaty of 1537 some room for expansion while maintaining the basic strategy, of course. Then, too, when the eventual Lamanite attack came – and I cannot imagine that "Moroni I" was deluded about *that* – much of the population could escape along the Welland Feeder Canal by barge to Dunnville and Lake Erie.

You can travel by water faster and much easier than by running overland until you're exhausted. And you can carry more provisions that would be necessary to victual ships. Using a canal, your people can be kept together under coherent leadership instead of being dispersed all over the countryside. The keys to this strategy are ships, and ships based on Lake Erie at Dunnville.

Therefore, in *Grail Knights of North America* I made a mistake because I had always lacked the courage to read the Book of Mormon myself. The ship building centre of the Nephites or Grail Refugees wasn't on the south shore of Lake Erie somewhere in the neighbourhood of Lake Chautauqua and modern Jamestown. It had been on the Canadian side of Lake Erie because the Nephites were confined to the Niagara Peninsula and northward by the treaty of AD 1537.

It has already been emphasised, but it will do no harm to stress it once more, that the Book of Mormon seldom gives definite dates that can be re-calculated from AD 1187. Much more frequently, the text will say something like "in the seventh year of the reign of the judges" such and such happened. And Joëlle had to figure out, sometimes by a train of ten or more such references, what solid date this could be associated with – and *then* re-calculate *that* figure from AD 1187.

The truly amazing thing is that the resultant dates do roughly correlate with the age of actual artifacts that have been discovered. But these dates cannot be taken as being certain. The date of the treaty is relatively "hard" in that it is given as a figure of "Year 350". This treaty of AD 1537 was itself a desperate concession to the Lamanites in order to buy time for the Nephites. Their general of the time, or "Moroni I", would have known that the handwriting was on the wall and there's no doubt, from the defence he contrived, that he could read it.

Since the Nephites had long occupied the Niagara Peninsula as part of the land they called Zarahemla, it is possible that they fortified it, built the moated farmsteads and the canal – and built ships – even before the treaty was negotiated and while negotiations were in progress. "Moroni I" *knew* that he could hold a well-defined line of the River Sidon – for a while, anyway – while he also knew that the Nephites lacked the forces to hold any larger exposed territory in New York State or any front longer than the Niagara River.

Only about half of this line needed to be strongly garrisoned anyway, even against overwhelmingly superior numbers of Lamanites from New York State. This half was the southern stretch of the Niagara River from Lake Erie to Niagara Falls. North of the Falls, the Lamanites could not cross the Niagara Gorge in any significant number. Only a few men were needed to keep an eye on that stretch of the river. A small ship or two would have been needed, stationed on the Zarahemla or "Canadian" side of the Niagara River's mouth, in order to oppose any fleet of canoes trying to outflank the border of the River Sidon.

The Welland Feeder Canal and the ships at Dunnville justified the entire Nephite strategy behind the treaty's provisions.

But before getting to the ships, we can digress to mention the people of reduced Zarahemla called the land to the north and west of them the "land of Desolation". Now, this is an odd name for the land of southern Ontario from the present town of Milton to, say, London, Ontario. This is presently the agricultural heartland of Ontario. It must have been a vast forest in pre-colonial times. How could anyone in the Niagara Peninsula have called the land to the Northwest the "land of Desolation"?

> And now, no part of the land was desolate, save it were for timber; but because of the greatness of the destruction of the people who had before inhabited the land it was called desolate.
>
> And there being but little timber upon the face of the land…And it came to pass as timber was exceedingly scarce in the land northward, they did send forth much by way of shipping.
>
> *Helaman 3: 6 and 10*

181

Almost every detailed and scholarly book-length work on the traditions of the Huron, or Wyandot, Indians at least mentions their legend of the great fire that devastated southern Ontario. It raged for years before burning itself out, and the Hurons insisted that the fire had destroyed the forest from about the Bruce Peninsula in the east to the Detroit River and Lake St. Clair in the west. This is all the land between Lake Huron in the north to Lake Erie in the south. It was a disaster for people, too, not for just trees and wildlife. Many Hurons were killed outright by the fire while many more starved because their cornfields were also consumed and there was no good hunting for many years.

It is difficult to say just how far back in the past this great fire had been, but the traditions of it were still vividly remembered around AD 1640 at the French mission of "St. Marie Among the Hurons" near the present Midland, Ontario. The people of Zarahemla reported a "land of Desolation" with no timber but also no fire, so perhaps the fire had just burned out shortly before they occupied the Niagara Peninsula. The land was a desolation of young secondary growth. This would be about five generations before the traditions related at St. Marie.

It is at least possible, therefore, that this large territory Northwest of Zarahemla on the Niagara Peninsula was still desolate recovering scrub land in AD 1537 when the Nephites found themselves confined there by the treaty.

The Book of Mormon specifically mentions that several ships were built on the western sea, or Lake Erie, and most were built in the years AD 1537, 1538 and 1539 *as far as Joëlle was able to figure from the relative chronology.* This is the year of the treaty and two years thereafter.

> And it came to pass that in the thirty and seventh year of the reign of the judges, there was a large company of men, even to the amount of five thousand and four hundred men, with their wives and their children, departed out of the land of Zarahemla into the land which was northward.

> And it came to pass that Hagoth, he being an exceedingly curious man, therefore he went forth and built him an exceedingly large ship, on the borders of the land Bountiful by the land of Desolation, and launched it forth into the west sea by the narrow neck that led to the land northward.

> And behold, there were many of the Nephites who did enter therein and did sail forth with much provisions and also many women and children;

and they took their course northward. And thus ended the thirty and seventh year.

And in the thirty and eighth year, this man built other ships. And the first ship did also return, and many more people did enter into it; and they also took much provisions, and set out again to the land northward.

And it came to pass that they were never heard of more. And we suppose that they were drowned in the depths of the sea. And it came to pass that one other ship did sail forth; and whither she did go we know not.

Alma 63: 4-8

I have already suggested elsewhere Joseph Smith probably misread the words *"a Goth"* as the name "Hagoth". Goths were southern Swedes who were famed as shipbuilders and mariners.

The reason for building these ships at this particular time is more than obvious. Zarahemla was doomed to be attacked in force sooner or later.

It is interesting that the figure of "five thousand and four hundred men" with their wives and children is not so very far from the number-crunching estimate of what the population of Nephites, or Grail Refugees, could reasonably have been.

I think that what is being said here is that, with all due respect for Joseph Smith's "translation," much of the remaining western Nephite population may have abandoned Zarahemla. I suggested in the final pages of *Grail Knights of North America* that these people may have formed much of the population of the later "Louisiana Purchase"

Surprisingly, Zarahemla was defended for some thirty-four years after the treaty of AD 1537 – if our chronology is correct, that is.

The Book of Mormon says that the treaty bought ten years of peace with the Lamanites, but after that there were twenty-four years of constant fighting.

Finally, the Nephites, now under the command of a new general named "Mormon" were overwhelmed.

The details are not given, but if Joseph Smith's account is at all accurate we can more or less reconstruct the fall of Zarahemla in AD 1571.

The Lamanites must have outflanked the line of the River Sidon by attacking across the extreme eastern end of Lake Erie. That is, they paddled in force "from Buffalo to Port Colborne," probably at night. They landed in Zarahemla and immediately cut the line of the Welland Feeder Canal near Wainfleet, Ontario.

The defenders along the River Sidon were outflanked and they were herded northward along the Niagara River toward Lake Ontario.

Some may have been herded across the river, probably at the south end of Grand Island.

A great running battle was fought though the present Township of Thorold where Ron Williamson discovered seven thousand flint arrowheads. This is where many odd relics from the War of 1812, which may not really be from the War of 1812, have been discovered.

Somehow, the Nephites crossed the mouth of the Niagara River. Possibly they had one or two small ships there to protect that flank against canoes.

They struggled ashore in New York State and began a desperate eastward retreat with Lake Ontario at their backs.

If they had a plan, or even hope, they may have been heading for the Green Mountain community.

They made it as far as Hill Cumorah.

> And it came to pass that they came to battle against us, and every soul was filled with terror because of the greatness of their numbers.
>
> And it came to pass that they did fall upon my people with the sword, and with the bow, and with the arrow, and with the axe, and with all manner of weapons of war.
>
> And it came to pass that my men were hewn down, yea... and I fell wounded in the midst; and they passed by me that they did not put an end to my life.
>
> And when they had gone through and hewn down all my people, save it were twenty and four of us (among whom was my son Moroni) and we having survived the dead of our people, did behold on the morrow, when the Lamanites had returned unto their own camps, from the top of the Hill Cumorah...my people who were hewn down being led in front by me...
>
> ...even all my people, save it were those twenty and four who were with me, and also a few that had escaped into the south countries, and a few who had deserted over unto the Lamanites, had fallen; and their flesh, and bones, and blood lay upon the face of the earth.
>
> *Mormon 6: 8-11, 15*

Fall of Zarahemla 1571

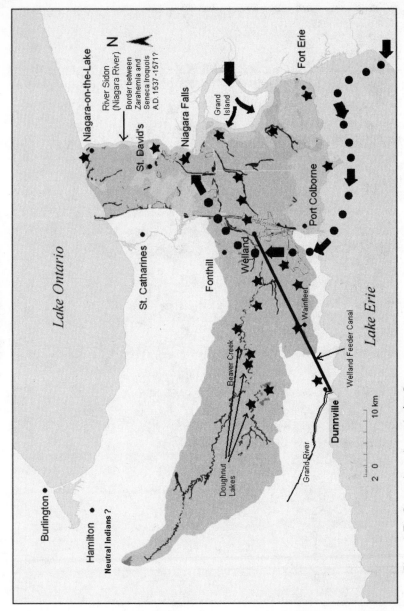

Phase 1, The Seneca Iroquois attack. ●

185

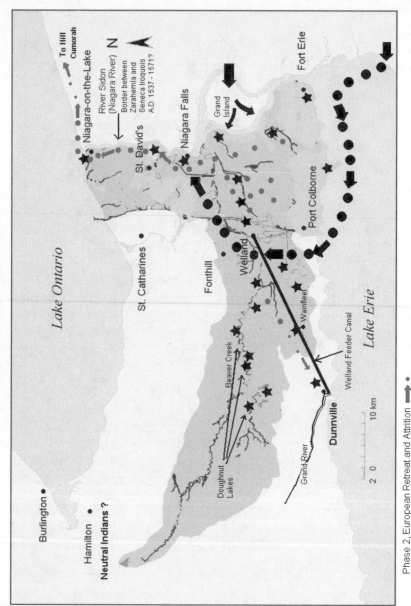

Fall of Zarahemla 1571

Phase 2, European Retreat and Attrition

Final Words:

And now, it came to pass that after the great and tremendous battle at Cumorah, behold, the Nephites who had escaped into the country southward were hunted by the Lamanites, until they were all destroyed.

And my father also was killed by them, and I even remain alone to write the sad tale of the destruction of my people. But, behold, they are

gone, and I fulfil the commandment of my father. And whether they
will slay me I know not.

Mormon 8: 2-3

These final words were written by Moroni, son of Mormon, who was
the Nephite general at the Battle of Hill Cumorah. Moroni hid in the
wilderness for sixteen years and completed the record of the Nephites
that he had already begun, as commanded by his father. He returned to
Hill Cumorah to bury the "golden plates" in a stone-lined crypt dug into
the side of the hill. The year was AD 1587 if our chronology is correct.

One early morning in mid-October 2003, Joëlle bounced out of the
shower to say: "You know, of course, that Cartier's voyage of 1535 was
the death warrant for the Nephites."

She elaborated as she dressed for work as a temporary receptionist at
the Canadian Institute of Chartered Accountants. "You see, once Cartier
appeared at Hochelaga in September 1535 asking around for people who
were dressed in woven cloth like himself, the Iroquois would have
computed the danger. If Europeans were coming in force, they would
trade and ally themselves with other Europeans in preference to relations
with the Indians. Cartier seems to have been looking for them. He
learned about the city of Seguna at Hochelaga, but it was too late in the
season to get there on the 1535 voyage. Therefore, the Nephites had to be
isolated from the French on the St. Lawrence immediately and, if
possible, exterminated before the French could establish a colony. That's
what the treaty of 1537 was all about."

"Hmmm."

"Well, think about it. As John Robert [i.e. John Robert Colombo, the
well known Canadian author] and you both discovered at the same time,
Hochelaga is a word from the Bible. One of the well known variants of
Hochelaga is Hochila, as you and John Robert discussed many times",
she said. " 'And do you not know that David hides among us in a
stronghold on a hill in the land of Hochila?'" she intoned. "Or something
like that. Kings?"

"Samuel I…I think…"

"Whatever. And this so-called Iroquois village of Hochelaga was a
perfectly triangular palisaded town," she went on. "Enfilade fire covering
the entrance from those corners. Neat."

"Palisaded? Okay…"

"By the way, what did the Iroquois call themselves?" she asked in triumph.

"Haudosonee," I answered. "Or something like that. Superior men."

"'Something like that' is right. *Haut de sa née*," replied Joey, grinning. "Of high birth. In Medieval French. Well, close enough."

In *Grail Knights of North America*, I had already suggested that the mostly French ex-Templars at Rosslyn had learned to speak a Scottish-English-Scandinavian dialect that was spoken by everyone around them.

Any historical record of theirs would have been written, I had assumed, in this "public" patois that Smith was able, with a lot of effort, to read.

But, among themselves and their descendants, I had also suggested that a kind of Medieval French would have been preserved. As everyone knows – even the French – the French are a stubborn and chauvinistic people.

Thus, in 1924, the Canadian anthropologist, Jill Crossly-Pratt, allegedly found a Turkish valley high up in the mountains that was still inhabited by descendants of French Crusaders.

They still spoke medieval French. Their traditional clothing made them resemble homespun extras in a film like Charlton Heston's *El Cid*.

Joëlle had quickly suggested back in 1997 that the Grail Refugees might have referred to themselves as *Sanguiniers*, Medieval French for "Bloodline People", more or less, thus giving birth to words like "Seguna," "Saguenay," "Saginaw," and so on.

In fact, the highest chiefs of the Mi'kmaq Indians of Nova Scotia were always called "Saginaws" and this is the supposed origin of these Indian words and place names. And maybe it is – though not in a way that conventional historians would welcome very enthusiastically.

An hour later, as I stood at the streetcar stop with Joëlle, she had a parting comment. "Anybody who doubts that Grail Refugees settled the Niagara Peninsula should take a close look at a map of St. Catharines," she said, grinning. "A strange way to spell 'Catherine' to begin with. St. Catharines keeps the 'Cathar' in Catherine. "Then there's Avalon Place, Armour Drive, Blackfriars Road, Black Knight Road, Friar's Court, Hidden Key Place, Knightwood Drive, Iron Street, Camelot Court, Viking Drive, Maltese Blvd."

"Those are just modern names from when the town was laid out and built," I said.

"Of course they are. But maybe some prominent local Masons, people maybe in charge of naming streets, remembered what had happened."

188

The King Street 504 streetcar was approaching. "And on the Lake Erie side there's Camelot Beach just south of Wainfleet," she called as she disappeared up into the tram.

And, of course, there was Vineland, Ontario through which we had driven half a hundred times. In *Grail Knights of North America*, I had suggested that Lief Eriksson's Vinland wasn't just the simple matter of an accidental landfall.

What are we to make of all these scraps of information and conjecture?

Maybe nothing should be made of them. Maybe they are meaningless.

But perhaps they are memories of a lost North American history. And, if so, we should learn about it because our historical self-conceptions mould our collective national identity. And this influences our social direction and our international policies.

Could Joseph Smith have "translated" the Book of Mormon from information that was readily available to him in 1830? Did he need any "golden plates?"

I am not certain of the answer myself. I suppose it is barely possible that no plates existed and no plates were needed.

Frontier America was then obsessed with "The Moundbuilders", the supposed descendants of the "Lost Tribes of Israel."

The Newport Tower was even in colonial times a subject of some controversy and speculation in newspapers and magazines.

Then too, historical information about Algonquin (Huron) and Iroquois traditions *was* in publication, including legends of the great fire that had devastated southern Ontario.

The Smith family moved from Vermont to New York State in 1815, the aftermath of "The War of 1812," and so ten-year-old Joseph Smith would have heard of the great struggle between the Americans and the British for the Niagara Frontier. Maps had been published in the newspapers of the day and the battles were topics of excited conversation among men and boys of the region.

The Erie Canal was under construction in 1815 and for ten more years until 1825, all during Smith's teenage years.

It was the huge national project of the time, the canal that made continental America a reality. Bert Wheeler had several old newspaper articles about "brass plates" that had been found by workers digging the long ditch.

Joseph Smith supposedly couldn't read in 1827, but he could look at pictures and maps and he could listen to conversations. I suppose it is just conceivable that he could have put the story of the Book of Mormon together in his head using information from all these sources. But how could he have dreamed up the defensive strategy of "Moroni I," the Nephite general?

The Welland Canal wasn't even begun when he translated the first 116 pages and it wasn't yet opened when the longer elaboration was published as the Book of Mormon in 1830.

Is it likely that Smith could have heard of something so obscure as the Welland Feeder Canal with its associated "doughnut lakes" *before* it was supposedly constructed?

But he may have had another source, his mother. A fair amount is known about Joseph Smith's father and grandfather – who had written a book, by the way. Literary interests and ability seems to have been a family trait.

But almost nothing is known about Lucy Mack's ancestors. They seem to have just "appeared" in the Green Mountains in the late 1600s.

After reading just about everything ever published about Joseph's mother, Lucy Mack Smith, Joëlle came to the conclusion that she may well have been one of those "Melungeons" that we have noted previously.

That is to say, Lucy Mack's ancestors may have been survivors of pre-colonial Europeans who had once inhabited the Green Mountains.

It should also be kept in mind that Joseph Smith was born in Sharon, Vermont in 1805.

His natal farm was within a mile of one of the better-preserved stone-built constructions that were apparently built by the ubiquitous "Ancient Celts" along the Connecticut River Valley.

Nowadays, motorists see just one modern road sign that shares directional information to both "Joseph Smith's Birthplace" and "National Heritage Site".

Lucy Mack Smith was in charge of Joseph's schooling, insofar as he had any, and Joëlle suspects that she may have recounted family tales of the Grail Refugees to her most gifted and favourite son.

So, either through "golden plates" or through his mother, Joseph Smith may have had a direct source for his book.

It is only my own opinion, of course, but to me the Book of Mormon reads like real human history, if one discounts the consciously biblical style and the biblical names.

They were almost obligatory within the frontier culture of the times. I do not think there is much doubt that the history refers to Northeast North America because so many geographical details fit.

And I think there can be even less doubt that reduced Zarahemla after the treaty must be the Niagara Peninsula.

Together with the hard artifacts, the Book of Mormon gives an exaggerated and romanticised, but very human, history of the Grail Knights of North America.

Notes to Chapter 6.

1 Illustrated in *Holy Grail Across the Atlantic*, page 145. Referred to in *Grail Knights of North America*, page 133.

2 Illustrated on page 54 of *Holy Grail Across the Atlantic.*

3 Discussed at length on pages 229-260 of *Grail Knights of North America.*

4 It is obvious, however, that Joseph Smith uses "forty days", "forty years", etc., as something of a canonical figure just as in the Bible. Nonetheless, even so (I believe) we can get the gist of relative distances.

5. Again, see *Grail Knights of North America*, pages 324-335.

Epilogue

It has often occurred to me since the publication of *Grail Knights of North America* in 1998 that "swords at sunset" did not refer only to the last stand of North America's Grail Refugees about AD 1570 in the Green Mountains and Niagara Frontier regions. Swords at sunset may refer just as well to the events of our own time because the conflict in the Middle East can all too easily escalate into a nuclear Armageddon.

The Anglo-American allies and, so rumour has it, Israel, are not the only nuclear powers.[1] France, Russia, Pakistan, India, China and North Korea also have nuclear weapons and all have economic interests in the Middle East. Some of these powers, notably North Korea, may have as much, or even more, interest in remaining independent of Anglo-American-Israeli military, financial and cultural domination. Five of these six nuclear powers have emphasised, within the United Nations and outside it, their determined opposition to Anglo-American Middle East policies, which have been rather obviously goaded by the stated Anglo-American need to protect their joint creation, Israel.

This commitment is basically due to the strength of our biblical conditioning that Judaism is fundamental to the orthodox Judeo-Christian Tradition. We have seen that this biblical motivation was no different in 1922 when Howard Carter was warned to suppress the archaeological facts revealed in Tutankhamun's tomb. Protection of the orthodox Judeo-Christian Tradition invoked the "Curse of the Mummy" in 1923 when it began to silence Lord Carnarvon, Arthur Mace, Richard Bethell, Howard Carter and their close relatives who knew about the Christian content of Tutankhamun's tomb and the papyrus records of a different kind of Exodus.

Between 1998 and 2003, the world was diverted by pseudo-archaeology in an effort to provide some objective historical support for the Judeo-Christian Tradition. Israeli antiquities dealer, Oded Golan, "discovered" the so-called "James ossuary." This was a stone box that, so Golan claimed because of the inscription on it, had contained the bones of James, supposedly the brother of Jesus.

Initially, this artifact was enthusiastically welcomed by fundamentalist Judeo-Christians as "the first and only archaeolo-gical evidence for the historical existence of Jesus." In the summer of 2003, however, fourteen experts of the Israeli Antiquities Commission unanimously declared the James ossuary to be a crude fake.[2]

This pronouncement by Israeli archaeologists had a definite political and financial downside for the Ariel Sharon government and Israel. Aside from North American Jews, North American fundamentalist "New Testament-type" Judeo-Christians are the backbone of Israel's financial viability. Together, North America's Jews and fundamentalist Christians have contributed about $10.4 million *per day* to Israel since 1947 in one way or another. For example, Christian church group tours to the now fairly dangerous "Holy Land" continue to be a major source of foreign currency for Israel. The Israeli government would have much preferred to keep American fundamentalist Christians happy in their ignorance.

But Israeli scholars have often been at odds with the wishes and policies of the Israeli government, as we have seen with the pronouncements of Dr. Ze'ev Herzog of Tel Aviv University.

The expert verdict about the James ossuary did not bode well for Golan's other artifact that was awaiting promotion in his Jerusalem condo. This was a tablet referring to the Temple of Solomon. It was confiscated by police when they searched Golan's apartment for other "artifacts in progress", so the verdict isn't in on this inscription but everyone has more than sufficient reason to be sceptical.[3]

Had these two artifacts been accepted, Golan would have provided archaeological support for two of the main pillars of the Judeo-Christian Tradition – the myth of Solomon's kingdom in biblical Palestine and the historical existence of the New Testament's Jesus. This is the core of the Judeo-Christian Tradition and what Anglo-American-Israeli policy in the Middle East is asserting, but there remains no objective evidence for the historical truth of Judeo-Christian territorial and religious claims. Perhaps it will come as no surprise to learn that Oded Golan, according to Israel's respected *Ha'aretz* newspaper, enjoyed a close relationship with both the Ariel Sharon government and Israel's secret service, the Mossad.

While undertaking our own modest archaeological excavations on the Niagara Escarpment between 1998 and 2003, I did not only think about Helen's jewellery and the Mycenaean death mask uncovered by Heinrich Schliemann. I also mused about Oded Golan, Howard Carter and Tutankhamun. After about 1945, with the recovery of the Nag Hamadi texts and the nearly simultaneous publication of the work of French anthropologists Marcel Griaule and Germaine Dieterlen, it became

193

increasingly clear that an early and simple form of Christianity had come to Ancient Egypt from the West. Judaism is irrelevant to true and ancient Christianity, just as it is central to the New Testament's Judeo-Christian Tradition.

Christianity had apparently originated on the Atlantic Coast of Europe, perhaps today's Brittany, or else had been brought there from islands out in the Atlantic of which only remnants still exist – Lyonesse and "Atlantis" have been names for this Atlantic civilisation and its outposts. It became equally clear that the world-regenerating womb of the Great Goddess had been the original Grail and equally obvious, too, that this Grail had been the conception of the Cro-Magnon people of Atlantic Europe. [4]

They had made the Neolithic-megalithic culture that had once extended from Ireland to western India and which archaeologist Dr. Marija Gimbutas has popularised as the "Civilisation of the Goddess" in over twenty books. *They* had conceived of the Great Goddess and her Good Shepherd consort. What had this "Holy Grail" once been all about? And why had so much conflict among European peoples swirled around this so-called "Holy Grail?"

Back in December 1978, or almost exactly three years before I became aware of the Nova Scotia castle ruin that introduced me to the Holy Grail, my book *The Iceman Inheritance: Prehistoric Sources of Western Man's Aggression, Racism and Sexism* (Dorset Publishing, Toronto) had been published. Dorset's president and founder, Larry Goldstein, was pleased with everything but the artwork for the cover of the book. York University anthropologist, Dr. Judith Posner, had written in her Introduction: "*The Iceman Inheritance* is a worthy model to keep in mind when reviewing the long range of human history, and more especially when looking into the future."

The book was initially very well received and was excerpted by Toronto's *Globe and Mail* in two full pages, by the *Calgary Herald* (one page) and by the old *Ottawa Journal* (one page). About 20 major U.S. newspapers either printed lengthy articles about it or generally favourable reviews of it. There were scores of radio and television interviews. I appeared as a co-guest with Bill Cosby on Tom Snyder's NBC "Tomorrow" show from Los Angeles – supposedly, at least, the final step before appearing on Johnny Carson's famous "Tonight" show out of New York.

The book was featured at the American Anthropological Association's convention held in Los Angeles in 1979. *The Iceman Inheritance* was at first judged as a valuable contribution to understanding the pattern of human history. Warner Books, then arguably the largest paperback publisher in the world, bought mass market rights and put out an edition that sold some 40,000 copies in the first two weeks in the New York City test market alone.

Then a reaction against the work set in, and it quickly became violent.

New York City bookstores then carrying the book were threatened with firebombing if they didn't remove *The Iceman Inheritance* from their shelves. My guest lectures were violently disrupted and I was threatened with death or maiming. A Jewish extremist tried to stab me on the podium of Kennedy-King College in Chicago. Warner Books instantly pulled the book out of its distribution system because of organised threats and pressure applied by the B'nai Brith, the Anti-Defamation League and the Jewish Defence League.

Jews had been mentioned, and blandly, just once in *The Iceman Inheritance*. And, of course, both the original publisher and the anthropologist author of the Introduction were Jewish. I couldn't understand what was going on because I had not then read the works of A.N. Poliak, A.M. Artomavov, J.M. Bury or Arthur Koestler. And *In Search of Noah's Flood* had not yet even been published.

Nonetheless, *The Iceman Inheritance* had generated immense interest. I managed to sell the rights to a New York Afro-American publisher but they could not satisfy the demand. At least four pirate editions, photocopies of the original Canadian hardcover or the Warner paperback, were also being distributed. By 1992, Dr. Ray Winbush of the Bishop Joseph Johnson Black Cultural Center at Vanderbilt University, an institution responsible for analysing Afro-American cultural and reading trends, estimated that at least 400,000 copies of *The Iceman Inheritance* had been sold. By 2004, the total may be a million or so. It remains one of the most influential books among Afro-American and non-Western university professors and students in North America and Europe.[5]

The controversy and violent threats that swirled around *The Iceman Inheritance* upset my wife and contributed somewhat to our marital break up in 1980-1981 and her decision to remain in Nova Scotia with our son, Jason. When I went to Nova Scotia with Deanna Theilmann-Bean in order to help Jason over this difficult time of transition, the controversy and threats resulting from *The Iceman Inheritance* contributed to my depression and despondency.

This mental state of mine was one of the reasons I responded to the delightfully eccentric Englishwoman's letter of late 1981 about the ruined castle in her Nova Scotia backyard. When it became obvious that Henry Sinclair and possibly the "Holy Grail" were involved, I could not imagine anything further removed from the controversies surrounding Neanderthal anthropology. I gratefully immersed myself in this – so I thought at the time – politically innocuous episode of history.

Nonetheless, I must have had a premonition even back then that the Holy Grail would turn out to be at the crux of Western civilisation's most basic conflicts. I see, rather surprisingly, that more than fifteen years ago I concluded the "Author's Forewarning" to *Holy Grail Across the Atlantic* with the following paragraph.[6]

> In 1978 I argued in *The Iceman Inheritance* that Western man has exhibited more aggression than other major groups of humanity. This speculation has subsequently been supported by forensic analysis of Neanderthal-Caucasoid skeletal material (see "Hard Times Among the Neanderthals," *Natural History*, December 1978) and even by a recently-discovered 12-page manuscript of Sigmund Freud (see "Hangups Due to Ice and Id of Byegone Era," *London Observer*, August 6, 1987). If indeed, Western mankind suffers from psychosexual aggression resulting from glacial evolution, then it may be that those of the Holy Grail have had to labour harder among us. We of the West may have proved more difficult to shepherd toward culture and humane civilisation. It may be that we needed the gift of the Holy Grail more acutely than other peoples and it was given more generously to us. For that reason, perhaps, the Holy Grail attained more prominence in our culture.

As I finished *Grail Knights of North America* in 1998 and was drawn toward *Swords at Sunset* as the necessary conclusion of the Holy Grail's North American adventures, something of this unconscious premonition or foreboding became unavoidably obvious. It was while I was in the Languedoc region of southern France on my honeymoon with Joëlle Lauriol in Narbonne in December 1999, that I took the time to look into the Neolithic site of Viols-le-Fort about 100 kilometres north of Narbonne.

The site had been discovered only the previous August (1999) and had just been radiocarbon dated to about 10,000 BC.[7] This date suddenly and surprisingly made Viols-le-Fort the oldest known Neolithic site in the world, and it was on that Garonne River corridor. Viols-le-Fort gave a strong indication that much of Western Civilisation had come from the Atlantic Coast, through southern France, and on out into the Mediterranean. It had eventually reached Ancient Egypt and finally the

Middle East. And it came to me in Narbonne that the ancient conflict between the Neanderthal-Caucasoids of the Middle East and the Cro-Magnons of Atlantic Europe was what the Holy Grail was really all about.

In two books, *The Iceman Inheritance* (1978) and *Chosen People from the Caucasus* (1992), I have argued that there was fundamentally an increasingly genetic component to the immense but elusive cultural difference that marks the boundary between the Mediterranean so-called "Ancient World" and the so-called "Judeo-Christian Era."

The Hebrews invaded Palestine about 2000-1700 BC, or so most scholars think, as part of the Hyksos migration southward from the Caucasus Mountain region. Until as recently as 1997, however, no one (including me) could make any constructive or sensible suggestion as to *why* the Caucasus tribes living around the Black Sea should suddenly have decided to migrate from their presumably original homelands. But migrate they certainly did and they inundated modern Turkey, Iraq, Syria, Lebanon, Israel-Palestine and even part of Ancient Egypt as "Hittites," "Mitanni," "Hurrians," "Hyksos," and "Hebrews."

But in 1997, *In Search of Noah's Flood* by Columbia University oceanographers Walter Pitman and William Ryan was published. Their massive collation of diverse evidence placed beyond any shadow of scientific doubt the fact that the Black Sea Basin had been flooded out in 5600 BC.

During the last "Ice Age", the present Black Sea had been a fairly large freshwater lake about the size of Lake Ontario (roughly 7500 square miles in surface area). But with the end of the "Ice Age" about 11,500 BC, the larger ice caps of the glacial era began to melt and the world's sea level began to rise. After about 6000 years of this glacial melting, or about 5600 BC, the world's sea level had risen by three hundred feet. This was enough for the Mediterranean to break over the present Bosphorus and cascade down into the Black Sea Basin. As we have already seen in the Atlantic, this same 300-foot rise in world sea level flooded several large seamounts that could have collectively been legendary "Atlantis" and also progressively flooded Brittany's group of offshore islands once known as Lyonesse.

Salt water poured down into the Black Sea Basin at the rate of roughly two hundred Niagaras for almost two centuries. The lush steppe-land around the shores of the former lake was flooded at a rate of about half a kilometre per day all around the former lake's shore. In a bit less than two centuries, the present and now-salty Black Sea reached world sea level, its present surface area of about 275,000 square miles and its present average depth of about 1,500 feet or 500 metres above the freshwater boundary.

Underwater archaeology presently in progress by the famous *Titanic*-finding Robert Ballard team, using remote television cameras and also recovering artifacts from the sea bed, has already proved conclusively that the margins of the former lake had been very thickly populated before the flood. The bottom of the Black Sea is dotted with numerous wood-built homes and farmsteads. The former inhabitants around the lake, and skeletal evidence shows that they had marked Neanderthal physical traits, had to flee for their lives as their former grasslands disappeared beneath a gradual but inexorable deluge of Mediterranean salt water. These people were primarily herdsmen of sheep and horses. As we have seen, *Hyksos* means "shepherd kings" and *Hi-bi-ru* apparently signifies minor herdsmen in the Ancient Egyptian language.

These particular shepherds, however, could not have been very gentle and tolerant. The Caucasus Mountains were the last refuge of the Neanderthal genetic strain, or "race", of people because the glacial climate to which the Neanderthals had adapted lingered in the Caucasus region after the last "Ice Age" had ended elsewhere in Europe and Western Asia. This was due the relatively high average altitude above sea level of this mountainous Caucasus region.

The Alpine foothills, the Pyrenees, Italy's mountainous spine, France's Massif Central and the Balkan Mountains were also something of a refuge for specifically European Neanderthals, and they are remembered as the mountain trolls and gnomes of European folklore. So, fairly pure Neanderthals must have lingered in the higher mountains of Europe until relatively recently. Dr. Chris Stringer of the British Museum has maintained that cohesive groups or tribes of nearly pure Neanderthals existed in European highlands only 10,000 years ago, or 8000 BC.[8]

But the Caucasus Mountains and the complex jumble of Taurus, Zagros and Elburz mountains leading from them was the biggest and most recently existing refuge for Neanderthals.

Whether fairly pure Neanderthals still exist or not is a highly controversial matter. As of the 1950s, it was generally accepted by most physical anthropologists that some local populations in the mountainous regions of Europe – Italy's spine, the Massif Central of France, the Balkans, etc. – were very "Neanderthalish" for all practical purposes. Some populations of the Caucasus and other Middle Eastern mountain chains still exhibit more extreme Neanderthal skeletal characteristics than the "type specimen," a French Neanderthal dated to about

50,000 BC. It is now politically incorrect even to suggest such a thing. As early as December 1978, Drs. Eric Trinkhaus (then of Harvard) and T. Dale Stewart of the Smithsonian, undertook a forensic-style study of every Neanderthal bone then known. They found that Neanderthals exhibited about twice the number of violence-caused injuries as any comparable number of other ancient humans. Their joint article, "Hard Times Among the Neanderthals", *Natural History* magazine of the American Museum of Natural History in New York, concluded with the words: "Neanderthals must be considered among the earliest of modern humans, if only because of their propensity for violence."

Neanderthal culture and society had already been shown to be extremely aggressive and xenophobic toward anyone who was different in culture or physical appearance from themselves. There are both theoretical reasons, and also actual cultural and religious evidence, indicating that "strongly Neanderthaloid" people have an anti-feminist mindset and tend to worship male sky gods, not Earth Mothers. The evidence is too complex and too specialised to cover here.

But there is one Neanderthal characteristic that is not shared by any other fossil or living human population. This must be explained at least superficially if we are to understand Western civilisation. And it may also be of crucial importance to an understanding of the Western world's religious history. Although literally dozens of "Ice Age" Neanderthal cave sites and rock shelters have been excavated and investigated, not one Neanderthal cave painting has ever been found.

Although they were larger-brained than many living Europeans today and were presumably extremely "intelligent," their intelligence was not artistic or creative in a visual way. This makes Neanderthal intelligence and mental orientation significantly different from all other ancestral human populations.

There may be an evolutionary reason for this. The *National Geographic* (August 2002) reported that some skeletal remains of a hominid similar or identical to *Homo habilis* had rather surprisingly been discovered in the Caucasus Mountains of the former Soviet Republic of Georgia.

Homo habilis was previously known only from East Africa and dated to about 1-3 million years ago. Some features of these bones, notably the lower jaws, seem to me quite similar in some characteristics to typical Neanderthal jaws. Neanderthals *may* (note the emphasis), therefore, have evolved from this early hominid. *Homo habilis* is thought to have been "human", all right, but not the branch of *Homo* that evolved into most of present and modern humanity.[9]

Although there is presently much controversy about it, Neanderthals were once classed as *Homo sapiens neanderthalis*, that is, a separate "race" or subspecies of modern humanity, *Homo sapiens sapiens*. These days, though, it is not polite to suggest that there are physically identifiable genetic "races" of humanity with different mental and emotional characteristics. Unfortunately for political correctness, however, the *National Geographic* article at least suggests that the older "politically incorrect" perspective is possibly or even probably "factually correct" after all – Neanderthals may have come from another type of "mankind".

Neanderthals may not have been able to draw or paint, but they were, however, obsessed by numbers. Like "the Count" on Sesame Street, they could not help but tally and enumerate things. The first known human evidence of "time-factored living" are Neanderthal records of lunar phases (or menstrual cycles) scratched on bone that date from about 50,000 BC. These notations *predate* the famous Western European cave paintings by at least 20,000 years, according to present knowledge.

Alexander Marshack in his *The Roots of Civilisation* (1971) illustrated many examples of Neanderthal numerical notations and he showed that they were just as important to the development of civilisation as the more "visually artistic" intelligence of Western European cave painters. In fact, as Marshack demonstrated, the Neanderthal penchant for playing with numbers was probably *more* important for the development of mathematics, surveying, physics, science and technology than Western European visual artistic ability.

In terms of easily seen cultural impact on Western Civilisation, this means that it is still possible to draw a line on a map from about the German-Polish border on the Baltic Sea to the Italian-Slovenian border on the Adriatic Sea. You will find that acknowledged world-class visual artists were generally born west of the line, while a disproportionate number of world-famous mathematicians, physicists, musicians and composers lived east of it. Music is, of course, an appreciation of numerical proportions expressed in sound.[10]

This line is also the boundary that separates good chess players from obsessive ones and which also separates the extremely wide EEE men's shoe size, common in Eastern Europe, from the narrower men's feet of the West. EEE shoes are not normally manufactured west of today's Czech Republic. Neanderthals had very wide feet, a wide "plantar index". As Dr. Carlton Coon put it in his National Academy of Sciences-sponsored *The Origin of Races* (1968 edition): "Neanderthals had Russian feet rather than English feet."

This line was "more true" before 1800 than it is today, of course. Two centuries of relatively fast and inexpensive travel have allowed people to intermarry and mix their genes. Nonetheless, even now (October 2003), the line remains at least roughly valid.

I have suggested in various writings, including *The Iceman Inheritance* and *Chosen People from the Caucasus*, that Neanderthals, because of their obsession with numbers, must have been fascinated with the number "One" or 1. It is the sudden difference between nothing and something. "Everything" that exists can be viewed as multiples of "One", but without "One" there is nothing. I have suggested, therefore, that Neanderthal and "highly Neanderthaloid" people had an "inbred" or genetic tendency toward monotheism, the conception of just One God who created "Everything". And, because they apparently could not render anything visually, this "Neanderthal" One God would have been a totally abstract entity.

And further, simply because they could not draw or paint very well and did not value or respect that ability, the Neanderthals and "highly Neanderthaloid" people would have viewed the figurative art, particularly the religious art, of other people as blasphemy and "idolatry".

So, in sum of Neanderthal characteristics, we have a very high numerical and logical intelligence, high aggression, male-dominance, anti-feminism, xenophobia, materialism (if you can count 'em, they're real) and possibly or probably also a proclivity toward monotheism as Neanderthal mental traits.[11]

The Caucasus and directly related mountains constituted the largest and most recent refuge for lingering "Ice Age" Neanderthals and "highly Neanderthalish" people. However, these mountains themselves could support only a limited population. As it happens because of geographic factors, though, vast and fertile steppe-lands extend outward from the foothills of the Caucasus and related mountain ranges.

These steppes therefore absorbed excess Neanderthal population that the mountains themselves could not support. Further, the exceptional agricultural and herding potential of the steppes permitted this excess population to increase explosively, and then to decline rapidly as people migrated outwards until the population achieved a critical concentration once more.[12] The history of the West has been a cyclical one – waves of Caucasus- steppe people inundating the outside world.

The map on the next page, from *The Iceman Inheritance* graphically shows the salient characteristics of Western history.

201

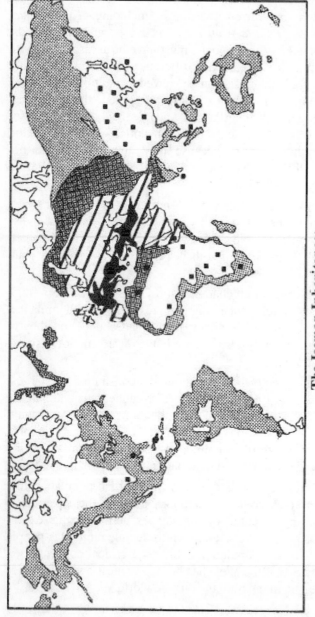

The Iceman Inheritance:

Neanderthal homeland
100,000 - 30,000 BC

Neanderthal-Caucasoid
dramatic "Flood-driven"
expansion 5600 BC - AD 622

Euro-Arabic "Western"
expansion AD 622 - AD 1400

European maritime colonial
expansion AD 1400 - 1850

Western colonial, technological and
cultural expansion, AD 1850 to present

Resistance to modern globalization
based on borrowed Western technological, political and cultural
developments

The Great Black Sea Flood of 5600 BC caused the basin's inhabitants to scrabble over the ever-nearer coastal mountains and out into the wider Western world. Thus, the historical pattern of cyclical Caucasus expansion began *for the very first time in known human history*. These highly Neanderthal Caucasus people genetically inundated the European Old Civilisation of the Goddess. The first fortified towns have been excavated in Thrace, Romania, Bulgaria and Macedonia. They mostly date from about 4500 BC.[13]

Because of the flood-out of the Black Sea Basin, the Western world became increasingly Caucasian – that is, having recognisable Caucasus physical traits – as Cro-Magnons inter-mixed with Neanderthals on a scale never previously witnessed in Europe and Western Asia. Consequently, the Civilisation of the Goddess was transformed, gradually and to a greater or lesser degree, into a civilisation dominated by male-dominant monotheism and materialism.

Hyksos and Hebrews apparently scaled the coastal mountains of modern Turkey and the former Soviet Republic of Georgia and trekked down the Euphrates Valley. This led them, eventually, to Sumeria.

This was not a purposeful migration toward a known destination. The Caucasus and Taurus Mountains had insulated these people from the outside world and it is highly unlikely that they knew anything about the cities of civilised Sumeria. At least, no evidence of cultural contact between the Caucasus and Sumeria before about 3000 BC has so far been discovered.

These cities had been founded by representatives of the Old European Goddess-worshipping civilisation, locally called the Ubaid Culture by archaeologists, sometime around 8000-7000 BC as the "Mediterranean Race" was slowly expanding toward India. The Black Sea refugees simply moved slowly down the Euphrates Valley as available grazing for their herds dictated. They reached the vicinity of Ur in Sumeria by about 3000 BC. By about 2000 BC they crossed Syria into Palestine. By 1700 BC, they had invaded the North-eastern part of Egypt's Nile Delta adjacent to Palestine and called "Goshen" in the Bible.

Archaeologists can roughly trace and date this migration by a trail of domesticated horse bones. These Caucasus people had domesticated the wild "Ice Age" horses (or "tarpans") which lingered on the steppes. The first domesticated horse skeleton so far discovered in Ancient Egypt dates from about 1650 BC[14] in the Nile Delta, giving archaeologists a rough date for the arrival of the Hyksos and associated Hi-bi-ru there.

This quasi-military occupation may be the real reason why the Hebrew tribes resided in Northeast Egypt for a time. The Bible is confused about the length of their residence in "Goshen"...four centuries or four generations?

To complete the story, these Hyksos and Hebrews were expelled from Egypt between 1550 BC and 1350 BC by a counter-offensive launched by the Egyptian princes of Thebes. This counter-offensive was initially led by Amose (or "Amasis") I and its success founded the Eighteenth Dynasty and began the so-called "New Kingdom" of Ancient Egypt. After two hundred years of sporadic fighting, the expulsion from Egypt of the hated Asiatic "shepherds" was finally complete. This final expulsion seems to have been the Exodus of the Bible. We have already covered this as well as the presently available facts permit.[15]

After the Exodus, the Old Testament of the Bible bears ample witness to the Hebrews' aggression toward neighbouring tribes, their absolute certainty of righteousness if they served their God. "He" was the only "true God" in a big world filled with many other peoples and cultures which had their own gods and goddesses.

The Old Testament also records the fact that many early Hebrews retained marked Neanderthal physical traits from their Caucasus Mountains origin. Hairy Esau is known to most Bible readers, but what most of them do not know is that Esau was not alone. Esau-like people were very common among the early Hebrew population. According to the earliest Hebrew commentators, there were enough "Esaus" to contest Jacob's leadership of the Israelite tribes. *Levitecus Rabba*, the oldest exegetical work in Hebrew, calls these people "the destroyers, the sons of Esau" and *Zohar* says that they were "the beast within Israel" that had to be eradicated.

The biblical Hebrews must have come originally from some extremely concentrated source of Neanderthal genetic stock back in their old Caucasus homeland. But unfortunately, not enough is known about early human populations in this area to pinpoint the probable geographic location of Hebrew ancestors. But the many "Esaus" of the Old Testament and commented on in ancient exegetical works indicate this extreme degree of Neanderthal genetic material in the Israelite tribes.

One other characteristic of Hebrew culture also testifies to the same thing. Of all known early peoples or nations of Europe and Western Asia, *only* the biblical Hebrews mounted a concerted effort to establish or perhaps retain a purely male-dominant Godhead in their also-unique monotheism. Although they apparently suffered frequent lapses of at least part of their people cleaving unto idolatry and even worshipping the goddesses of neighbouring nations, the mainstream of Judaism remained faithful to the One God. *He* was first known as *Aten* (in the original Egyptian) and as *Adonai* as Hebrew evolved into a separate language. *He* was known secretly to the priests as the vowel sounds that approximated the name "*Jehovah*" or "Yaweh". That is why vowels are not written in Hebrew and in some other "Semitic" languages.[16]

These physical, intellectual, emotional and "religious" Neanderthal characteristics remained relatively undiluted because of Hebrew cultural and religious taboos against inter-marriage with any other peoples.

Elsewhere, the same Black Sea Caucasus people, driven by the flood and by the desperate jostling of other refugees, began to percolate into the Balkans and Greece in various waves that scholars identify as Mycenaean, Dorian, Thracian and Aeolian so-called "Greeks."

The decipherment of Linear B Mycenaean script by Michael Ventris in 1954 showed that the Mycenaean language was, indeed, basically an early form of the Indo-European dialect of "Greek." It came originally from the "Russian" Caucasus-steppes. But the Mycenaeans were a transitional phase of the Caucasus inundation, a true warrior elite, who imposed themselves upon a much larger population of indigenous people and who at least partly adopted the religious conceptions of the conquered natives.

We know that the Mycenaeans, for example, generally and nominally worshipped a Great Goddess as the supreme deity, although there were also lesser gods and goddesses. But the rapidly subsequent invasions of yet other tribes of "Greek-speaking" steppe barbarians, especially the so-called Dorians, ended the Goddess-worshipping Mycenaean world and inaugurated a rude Dark Age about 1000 BC. It was within this Greek Dark Age, from about 1000 BC to 700 BC, that the poet (or a collection of poets) called Homer wrote about the Trojan War. Homer also wrote about the homeward voyage of Odysseus, and other magnificent seafaring heroes and beautiful heroines of the vanished and glorious Mycenaean Age that had flourished about five hundred years earlier.

Perhaps there were not so many of these Caucasus-steppe "Greeks" as was the case with the main Hyksos/Hurrian/ Hittite/Mitanni/Hebrew horde which seems to have travelled southward along the broad valley of the Euphrates River. Therefore, although they certainly introduced their male sky gods into Greece, at first they not only tolerated but also accommodated to the prevailing Old European Goddess-worshipping major religious orientation. Gradually, however, the ancient goddesses, all of whom had originally represented only some aspects of the Great Goddess, became mere unwilling "wives" of the invaders' sky gods. The stormy relationship between Zeus and Hera in the transition to the Classical Greek pantheon illustrates this process clearly enough.

Roughly the same situation played itself out in Italy. Believers in male sky gods from the "Russian" Caucasus steppes gradually percolated into Europe going across or around the Alps and then migrated southward down into the Italian Peninsula. They also encountered Old European worshippers of the Great Goddess and her Good Shepherd consort-son, but they reached an accommodation by which a pantheon of roughly equal gods and goddesses was achieved. Nonetheless, as in Greece where male Zeus was ruler of all gods and goddesses on Olympus, male Jupiter was Chief of the pantheon in Italy.

At about the same time as the Hyksos and Hebrews arrived in biblical Goshen, say about 1750 BC or so, other close relatives of Indo-European speaking Caucasus-steppe people reached India from Persia. Known as "Aryans", they over-ran the older so-called Indus Cultures represented by the cities of Harappa and Mohenjo-daro, which had been founded by Goddess-worshipping people of the Old Civilisation. There, too, after the Aryan invasions, a great pantheon was established.

Aside from Greece, Italy and India, a similar evolution of religion took place all over Europe and Western Asia. Polytheistic accommodations were negotiated all over Eurasia and initially had strong representation by goddesses. As mentioned before, however, only the Hebrews repudiated polytheism and goddesses completely when the convergence of Hebrew culture with the Old Religion replaced the Great Goddess with the male God.

Only in Ancient Egypt, some geographic enclaves of Northwest Atlantic Europe, southern France and on some Mediterranean islands during Greco-Roman times, did the Old Religion continue to flourish in relatively pure form with Isis as the Great Goddess and the Messiah as her Good Shepherd consort husband-son. This Egyptian Christianity survived and developed to become the official religion of Ptolemaic (Greek-ruled) Egypt about 320 BC.[17]

This version of Messiah worship achieved some popularity in Rome not long before the "Christian Era" because of the emotional impact that Cleopatra had made on the common people of Rome when she, very dramatically, entered that city as Julius Caesar's consort. Roman veneration for Isis and "the Crestus" [i.e. "the *Christos*" in Ptolemaic Greek] continued even after Julius Caesar was assassinated. Only when Julius Caesar's legally appointed successor, Octavian or "Augustus Caesar," defeated Antony and Cleopatra at the Battle of Actium did belief in Isis and "the Crestus" begin to be suppressed in Rome. This suppression started in AD 19, according to the Roman historian Tacitus – but this date is at least a decade before the ministry of New Testament Jesus supposedly began.

Within three centuries after the lifetime of orthodox Christianity's "St. Paul", or only about eleven generations, barbarians began to over-run the Roman Empire. Called Visigoths, Ostrogoths, Lombards and Vandals in our history books, they were distant relatives of biblical Caucasus-steppe people who had fled from the Great Black Sea Flood and who had invaded Palestine and Egypt as Hyksos and Hebrews about two thousand years earlier.

As research into the obscure steppe histories has tediously and slowly progressed, it has become clear that the Visigoths, Ostrogoths, Lombards and Vandals were pushed into desperate migration, in a kind of "domino-effect", by the terrible Huns to the north and east of these other tribes. Greco-Roman writers first heard of the Huns and mentioned them in AD 272, possibly because of stories told by scattered Visigothic refugees trickling into northern Greece. These Huns were located in the vaguely known lands at the northern end of the Caspian Sea.

It is now known, however, that the Huns were a Caucasian steppe tribe that had, during the third century BC, made an earlier onslaught against China.[18] The Ch'in Dynasty of that time built the Great Wall in order to hold the Huns at bay.[19] This apparently worked because the Huns then returned westward to what seems to have been their original homelands north of the Caspian. But Chinese culture, from then onward, tended to be inward looking and not typically expansive. Perhaps the Huns, even though they were stopped, had seriously intimidated the Chinese. In any event, as late as AD 1325, Chinese maritime expansion was halted by Imperial decree for fear of "encountering the hairy barbarians" that were known to exist in the Middle East.

The Visigoths, set into terrified motion by the Huns, made their debut on the stage of European history at the Battle of Adrianople in Greece in AD 378. There, their cavalry thoroughly defeated a Roman army. It soon became apparent that the usual Roman infantry legions were no match for the new Visigothic armoured horse warriors wielding long lances and long swords. The Visigoths, Ostrogoths and Lombards successively over-ran Greece and Italy. The Visigoths sacked Rome itself in AD 410.

However, the Visigoths, Ostrogoths and Lombards, although fierce warriors in their own right, could appreciate civilisation to some degree, at least, and could be assimilated. Many of these barbarians became officers in the Roman army and became Roman citizens. They helped Imperial Rome to develop its own corps of armoured cavalry, called in Latin *clibanarii* (Western Empire) and *cataphracti* (Eastern Empire), with which to oppose the inevitable onslaught of the Huns.

Even the fierce and warlike Visigoths, Ostrogoths and Lombards who settled in conquered Rome doubted that the Huns were fully human, according to reports preserved in the chronicles. The Huns were described as extremely hairy "goblins" with big heads, big noses and short legs. Christianised barbarians described them as "the Scourge of God" because of their ruthless extermination of enemies and the hideous atrocities they visited on their hapless captives.

The long-dreaded onslaught came about two generations after the fall of Rome to the Visigoths when Attila led his Huns through Central Europe between AD 449 and 451, leaving behind a swath of destruction and genocide. In that latter year, AD 451, Attila's horde of predominantly mounted archers was somewhat surprisingly defeated at the very closely fought Battle of Chalons in central France. The victors were a desperate coalition of Romanised Visigoths, Ostrogoths, Lombards, Roman infantry, native Celtic levies and Teutonic forces from east of the Rhine. The Teutons had already experienced the terror of the Huns and the *Rings of the Niebelungen* cycle of epic poetry prominently refers to this conflict.

Readers with wide literary interests will find it thought-provoking that in Year 2000, J.R.R. Tolkien's *The Lord of the Rings* was voted "The Most Important Book of the Century" and "The Most Important Book of the Millennium" by two separate groups of book buyers and readers. One group was British, the other group was American, and both were polled by a major international book retailer, Amazon.com. This may also be of unsuspected social importance.

Tolkien's "Middle Earth" was rather obviously the "Elder Days" of the Old European Neolithic-megalithic Civilisation. Specifically, "The Shire" was meant to be pre-industrial England. The "High Elves" who had come from the West, bringing civilisation to Middle Earth, were our putative "Atlanteans" or Cro-Magnons from the West who brought civilisation to Western Europe.

The Eastern realm of Sauron's "Mordor" represented the Caucasus tendency toward extreme and fanatical monotheism. There was only One Lord in Mordor, the Dark Lord, Sauron. In legal terms, there was no distinction in Mordor between civil law and religious law. Everyone worshipped and obeyed Sauron absolutely. In terms of technology, the land of Mordor in *The Lord of the Rings* was modelled on a mixture of early medieval Hun/ Khazars and modern Western industrialism. The soldiers of Mordor are called "*Orcs*", which is Gaelic Irish (the Goidelic branch of Celtic) for *pigs*. The word "Khazar" itself also means "pig" in the Gothic branch of Germanic that influenced Yiddish. We will soon learn the significance of this.

Tolkien therefore told an allegorical, but nonetheless true, history in his masterpiece. The great and almost hopeless struggle was the West's ancient and continuing battle against genetic domination by ferocious Caucasus-steppe barbarians.

Even the "Civilisation of the Goddess" was reflected in Tolkien's work because of the three rings of power that still had strength to do at least some good in the world, one was wielded by the elfen queen, Galadriel of Lothlorien. Arwen Evenstar of the elfish stronghold of Rivendell was betrothed to Aragorn, the hidden King of the West. Arwen's potential children by Aragorn were the only hope for any future leadership of the West.

It can be no accident, therefore – for a man of Tolkien's erudition – that the Evening Star is the planet Venus and that "Galadriel" is the "Elfish" name for the Morning Star... again, the planet Venus. But you have to read Tolkien's long appendix "On the Language of the Elves" to discover this. The Latin word Venus was given to the planet, but the name is interchangeable with Aphrodite, Ishtar, Cybele and Isis. The planet was named in honour of the Great Goddess because of its beauty.

Our present symbol for the female sex is also the sign for Venus, and both these symbols come from the shape of the "Ancient Egyptian" ankh, the symbol of life itself. But Tolkien, the Oxford scholar of Teutonic and Celtic lore and literature, knew that even this "Ancient Egyptian" symbol for *life*, the ankh, was apparently brought to Egypt along with basic Christianity by Neolithic and megalithic migrants from the Atlantic West.

A very well known German scientist with the unfortunate name of Dr. Otto Muck went further than Tolkien. Muck suggested that the shape of the Celtic cross, the ankh and our symbols for both the planet Venus and the female sex all derived from, and are slight distortions of, the city plan of "Atlantis" as described by Plato. According to Plato, concentric canals surrounded the city to serve its various sections. This system of concentric canals was intersected by four short transverse canals to provide easier access to each "quarter." This urban planning gave the city of Atlantis its distinctive shape.

Here is a dubious map of "Atlantis" promoted by Paul Schliemann in 1912. He claimed that his famous grandfather, Heinrich Schliemann, had found a cruder representation of it scratched on a pottery shard at Troy. There's no record of this in the elder Schliemann's records, but it made a good story in 1912.

The provenance claimed by Paul Schliemann for this map is much

209

more than just questionable, of course, but that's not the point here.

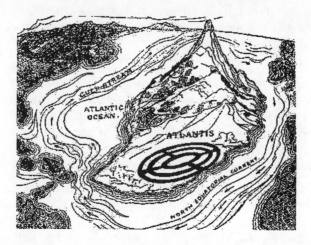

The point is that the city of Atlantis shown on it faithfully reflects Plato's descriptions in the *Timaeus* and *Critias* dialogs. The city of Atlantis as depicted here *is* a Celtic Cross. The small crossbar on the "mirror of Venus" (symbol of both the planet and the female sex) and the crossbar on the ankh may both represent the island's coastline. At the coast, according to Plato, there was a major shipping channel from the sea that connected with the canal system.

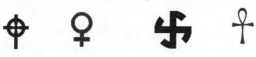

Celtic Cross   Venus/Female   Swastika   Ankh

If so, the crossbars are in slightly different positions on the ankh and the "mirror of Venus", but that's all. Perhaps, over centuries since legendary Atlantis supposedly sank, the length of this ship channel representing the city's distance from the coast had been forgotten. On the other hand, people just like to modify certain motifs as their societies evolve. You can see for yourself that Otto Muck's argument is clever even if it may not be true.[20]

The "Good Shepherds" are also well represented in *The Lord of the Rings*. Gandalf, the Wizard, and "Strider", the disguised King Aragorn of the West, escort the vulnerable hobbits toward Mordor. Perhaps it is not going too far to think of the hobbits as innocent and pretty ignorant sheep. Poor Frodo the Ring bearer carried what seems suspiciously like the orthodox Christian burden of "Original Sin," being Bilbo's heir.

But, to be fair to Tolkien, he disliked and mistrusted allegorical interpretations of his work – which has not prevented many people from indulging in them, including me. However, I have had the great honour and immense advantage of corresponding with the renowned British poet and author, Robert Graves (1895-1985) during his last years on Mallorca. Graves had been a special friend and confidante of Tolkien's and they had often discussed *The Lord of the Rings* because it had so much resonance with Graves's own work in *The White Goddess* (1947).

Robert Graves received one of the first copies of *The Iceman Inheritance* and he wrote, with the help of his wife Beryl because he was too ill, that the "theory" presented in the book was the history that Tolkien had chosen to tell in an allegorical form.[21] Therefore, I'll stick to my interpretation of *The Lord of the Rings*. And, to continue with it, soon, I think, it will become clear why Tolkien very obviously equated Huns and Khazars with rampant Western industrialism.

If anyone is inclined to dispute my interpretation of Tolkien's *The Lord of the Rings*, an appraisal of the character named "Gollum" should help to dispose of any argument.

Gollum was obsessed with the Great Ring that had once belonged to Sauron and was the source of Sauron's power. Gollum's obsession prevented him from developing any normal personality and he became progressively more infantile. In *The Lord of the Rings*, Gollum's dialogue is all baby talk.

As Sigmund Freud observed in *Moses and Monotheism* (1939, pages 118-125), a society dominated by a fearful monotheistic and all-powerful "father figure" cannot achieve a healthy psychosexual balance, or "grow up," and will habitually display a resultant adolescent kind of aggression as a consequence. Freud moved to London in 1938 where he completed *Moses and Monotheism*.

But he had previously met and corresponded with Howard Carter, discoverer of Tutankhamun's tomb and, in fact, Anna Freud was invited to, and attended, the official opening of King Tut's crypt (Sigmund Freud himself could not attend). And while in London in 1938 and 1939, Sigmund Freud also met J.R.R. Tolkien. There are reasons for believing that Sigmund Freud contributed some insight into Gollum's character.

There were several "Golems", or manlike and rather pathetic "monsters", in Eastern European Jewish folklore and literature. The word "Golem" means *embryo* in Hebrew. Tolkien was not wholly ignorant of Jewish literature and he may have heard of the several Golems of Jewish stories.

But Freud could have conveyed the psychological significance of

"Gollum's" name to Tolkien. Only a people that is psychosexually maladjusted toward reproduction would think of casting *embryos* as potential "monsters". And this is precisely what Tolkien did with Gollum. No, Tolkien's message in *The Lord of the Rings* is almost impossible to avoid – unless someone is very determined to avoid it, that is.

What may be considered surprising is the immense and overwhelming popularity of *The Lord of the Rings* by a generation at the apex of our technology. This may indicate a strong subconscious desire to rediscover the West's true history and, at least partly, to return to its originally healthy psychosexual values that included female divinity in its religious orientation.

But now we must return to the Huns and also discuss the Vandals because of their unsuspected importance to the modern Western world and even today's newspaper headlines.

Like the Hebrews themselves back in Palestine about 2000 BC, these later Caucasus-steppe Visigoths, Ostrogoths, Lombards, Vandals and Huns of the third to fifth centuries AD had a male-dominant mindset and worshipped male sky gods. And just like the biblical Hebrews, they tended to reject the idea of any serious reverence for goddesses. Among these invading barbarians, as among the biblical Hebrews previously, ordinary women had little enfranchisement in their societies because there was no strong female representation in their cultural conceptions of divinity.

St. Paul's moulding of the New Testament ensured that emerging Roman Judeo-Christianity in Europe would have a fundamental and hopefully sympathetic relationship with Judaism. This hope was largely fulfilled although orthodox Christians have occasionally indulged in bouts of anti-Semitism. Europe under the Judeo-Christian Tradition also, however, notably reduced the former social status of women and even indulged in massacres of women as "witches."

As the Visigoths, Ostrogoths, Lombards, Vandals and Huns inundated the Mediterranean world, it was natural that belief in Egyptian Isis, the Great Goddess with her Good Shepherd consort-son, was religiously abhorred, emotionally repudiated and historically all but erased. Paul's version of the Christian story shifted the emotional, religious and social focus of the Mediterranean world to Palestine and Rome, making Egypt increasingly irrelevant to the Western world.

Orthodox Judeo-Christianity of the Roman Church grew at phenomenal speed during the first few centuries AD. This was partly because the Emperor Constantine accepted it as an official religion of the Roman Empire in AD 312 and its orthodoxy was codified at Nicea in AD 325. But it was also because the already-encroaching barbarians from the Caucasus steppes were genetically predisposed to accept its male Saviour and male Godhead. It was this demographic and genetic shift in emphasis that divided the Mediterranean "Ancient World" from the orthodox Christian Era's mindset. And this nearly wholesale acceptance of the orthodox Judeo-Christian Tradition started Europe's inexorable evolution toward the modern world.

The barbarians were gradually converted to the orthodox Judeo-Christian Tradition of the Roman Church, and they gradually intermixed with the native European people around them.

Perhaps the nominally Roman participants at the Battle of Chalons were surprised at their bloody victory in AD 451. They were certainly relieved. The Huns trickled back through central Europe to their former homeland near where the Volga River empties into the Caspian Sea. The "Roman" victors at Chalons were not anxious to follow them for a re-match. Attila, High King of the Huns, died in his Volga capital called Kazaran-Itil in AD 453.

It must be said that of all the barbarians that invaded the Roman Empire (aside from the Huns, that is), the Vandals in particular were also destined to play a crucially important role in the development of our modern world. Because of their original location on the western side of the Caucasus Mountains, their route of invasion into the Roman world took them southward down the Eastern Shore of the Mediterranean. They invaded modern Turkey, Lebanon, Syria, Israel-Palestine, Egypt and then continued all across North Africa to the Atlantic coast at Morocco.

A Christian mob led by a half-Visigothic Roman Bishop named Theophilus burned the great Alexandria Library and massacred Egyptian Christians in AD 391. But the Vandal invasion about half a century later – AD 450 to AD 500 – completed the destruction of any vestige of living Ancient Egyptian or Greco-Roman culture in the Middle East and North Africa. Our modern word "vandalism" aptly recalls the wanton destruction wrought by this particularly ferocious tribe of Caucasus-steppe barbarians. There was not much intermixing between the Vandals and indigenous people. Unlike the Visigoths, Ostrogoths and Lombards in Europe, the Vandals (like the Huns) tended to exterminate the native peoples they encountered in the Middle East.[22]

The Vandals were nearly as fiercely aggressive, xenophobic and "anti-feminist" as the Huns themselves. *And it was directly from this*

213

"Vandalised" emotional and cultural outlook that Mohammed drew his inspiration and that Islam took its root. Islam, at least among the original "Vandalised" Middle Eastern people who developed and embraced it, is no less aggressive, anti-feminist and monotheistic than Judaism. This is not surprising since both Judaism and Islam were conceived and developed originally by very closely related Caucasus-steppe people.

In the 287 years separating the retreat of the Huns back to the Volga in AD 453 from the emergence of the Khazars into the light of history in AD 740, the Vandals had destroyed Ancient Egyptian and Greco-Roman culture in the Middle East and all across North Africa. And, by AD 622, Islam had begun its explosive expansion.

By about AD 700, the Moslem "jihad" had conquered Persia and was threatening the Eastern Roman Empire based at Constantinople, which was just starting to revert to its older Greek name of "Byzantium". The Eastern Empire had not fallen along with Rome because the barbarians had gone around it to the west, down through Greece. The Eastern Empire at the western edge of the Turkish peninsula had not succumbed to the Vandals either, because it was far to the west of the Vandals' invasion routes. But by AD 700, the Christian (Greek Orthodox Church) Eastern Empire was being threatened by the Islamic Caliphate in nearby Persia.

A large and dominant steppe tribe called "Khazars" – possibly the more modern word "Cossack" derived from this tribal name – controlled the regional balance of power. Consequently, Constantinople's emissaries tried to convert them to Christianity and Persian emissaries tried to convert them to Islam. Surprisingly, and ironically for Western history, the Khazars rejected both.[23]

The Jewish position in the Western world was to be immeasurably strengthened when, in AD 740, an estimated 1-3 million people from the Russian-Ukrainian steppes, the people called "Khazars" by chroniclers of the day, surprisingly chose to convert to Judaism..[24] Because the Jewish Khazars represented by far the largest population of "Jews" anywhere in the world, the well-known Jewish author, Arthur Koestler, referred to them as *The Thirteenth Tribe* in his 1976 book of that title.

The aggression, chauvinism and militant xenophobia of biblical Judaism apparently appealed to the ferocious Khazar psychology, although there were also geopolitical and economic factors that contributed to their preference for Judaism. They became effectively immune from Christian and Islamic missionaries and thus retained their

214

geopolitical independence. This so-called "Khazar" tribe is known to have been just a later name for Attila's Huns.

After acquiring some greater social cohesion through their shared religion of Judaism, the Khazars carved out a modest true kingdom or empire that ruled the steppes from the Caucasus Mountains in the east to the Carpathians in the west. That is, they ruled the steppes north of the Black Sea. This Khazar realm was noted by chroniclers of the time and by writers of the later medieval period. Modern historians of the Eastern Roman Empire, like J.M. Bury writing in 1912, briefly mentioned the Khazar conversion to Judaism and the resulting Khazar domain. But very little was known about it.

The first book devoted solely to the history of this Khazar kingdom was *Khazaria: The History of a Jewish Kingdom in Europe* (Beliak Mossad, Jerusalem, 1950) by the Tel Aviv University historian Dr. A.N. Poliak. The Khazar capital city of Kazaran-Itil on the Volga was excavated between 1946 and 1960 by the Soviet archaeologist, Dr. A.M. Artomonov (*Khazaria*, Moscow, 1961).

The Khazars were hated and feared by their Slavic neighbours in the Ukraine, Russia and other parts of Eastern Europe because they were raiders and slavers. In fact, Khazars gave the word "slavery" to the world by capturing and selling Slavs in truly staggering numbers. The word "Khazar" means "pig" in Gothic, the now almost extinct Germanic language that was spoken on the southern steppes, the Crimean Peninsula and all the way to the western Black Sea fringe of the Khazar kingdom.

Joseph Jacobs in *Jewish Contributions to Western Civilization* (Jewish Information Service, 1921) described what he called the "wretched business" of Khazar slave raiding, including the violent way that the Khazars "processed" their captives.

After about five centuries of terrifying the Slavs, the brief but intense Mongol invasion of modern Russia and the Ukraine starting in AD 1218 crushed the Khazars as a cohesive Caucasus-steppe power. In company with lesser steppe tribes (Magyars, Bulgars, Alans, etc.), the Khazars were either dispersed within Russia and the Ukraine, or else were pushed into the territories of Eastern Europe.

They lost their warlike cohesion as Khazars, but they retained their Judaism and some steppe customs. Surrounded and hated by their former victims, they congregated in so-called rural "stetls" (small villages sometimes protected by stockades) or in definite sections of the cities that were just starting to develop. These Khazar enclaves became the "Jewish ghettos" of Eastern Europe.

I have placed the word "Jewish" in quotes, and will do so for a few more paragraphs when referring to the Eastern European "Jews," because whether they are really *Jewish* or not is a moot point. The biblical Israelites or Hebrews considered themselves to be a definite and distinct ethnic group – the descendants of biblical Abraham and Sarah. According to Mosaic Law and also the Talmud, *to be a Jew it is necessary that one's mother is or had been Jewish in this ethnic sense.* Quite obviously, this Judaic law cannot apply to religious converts like the Khazars and their descendants.

Medieval Jewish scholars and Rabbis who visited Khazaria, and who were actually descendants of Hebrews from the so-called "Holy Land," referred to these Eastern European "Jews" as *Ashkenazim* or, sometimes, "Ashkenazi Jews" in order to distinguish them from "real" Jews who could trace their descent from Abraham.

Because they were outnumbered and surrounded by their former victims who hated them, the Ashkenazim had to give up overt Khazar-style armed aggression.

And in any case, their neighbours often took steps to prevent these Eastern European "Jews" from riding horses because they remembered the raids of mounted Khazar slavers all too well.

According to the Jewish linguist Moishe Miesnes (*Die Yiddishe Sprache*, 1924), the original language of the Khazars was Gothic, an early branch of the Indo-European Germanic proto-language that was spoken on the steppes north of the Black Sea. But the language that developed among these stetl and ghetto "Jews" was a mixed dialect of Gothic, Slavic and basic Hebrew called *Yiddish* (from "Yid Deutsch" or "Jew German").[25]

Therefore, as far as the history of the world is concerned, we are faced with a significant and terrifying genetic fact:

Just one group of very aggressive Caucasus-steppe barbarians has played an inordinately large role in moulding the general pattern of world history.

As Caucasus-steppe tribes once known as "Hyksos," "Mitanni," "Hebrews," "Hurrians" and "Hittites" they invaded the Middle East from the flooded out Black Sea Basin sometime between about 5600 and 2000 BC.

They established monotheism, known best as biblical "Judaism," by about 1300 BC in parts of the Middle East, notably in Ancient Egypt, in Yemen and around the immediate vicinity of Jerusalem in Palestine.

The Huns from that same Caucasus area between the Black Sea and the Caspian Sea attacked China in the third century BC, but they were thwarted by the Ch'in Dynasty's Great Wall. However, in memory of these "hairy barbarians" from the Middle East, Chinese civilisation remained psychologically inhibited and relatively (relative to the West, that is) non-expansive territorially.

Then, these same Huns returned to their Caucasus-steppes, terrorised their neighbours and brought about the Fall of Rome.

A related tribe, called the "White Huns" invaded India at about the same time that Attila invaded Europe, bringing about the end of the brilliant and artistic "Gupta Period" of India's history and leaving India prostrate for the soon-to-follow Islamic onslaught.

The European Huns brought about the European "Dark Ages" following the barbarian invasions of the Roman Empire. These invasions coincided with the establishment of "Judeo-Christianity" in Europe and parts of the Middle East.

Then, pushing the Vandals to over-run the Middle East, these Huns inspired the monotheistic religion of Islam (or, more correctly "Judeo-Islam," since Islam is also firmly based on the Judaic tradition) in AD 622. This resulted in the Moslem "jihad" – or "Holy War" – that conquered the Middle East from the Mediterranean to India and also conquered East Africa and North Africa.

In a new guise – the Huns as "Khazars" converted to Judaism in AD 740 – and they were to mould the modern Western World's technological, financial, military and cultural expansion – and also the Western World's major conflicts.

For example, although most people have been too polarised by propaganda to realise it, modern Communism and modern Capitalism were both developed by mainly Ashkenazi economic theorists, activists, lawyers and entrepreneurs.

Both Communism and Capitalism served their purpose of Neanderthalish domination in different ways that were tailored to different societies.

Cro-Magnons and Neanderthals had occasionally intermixed ever since the Cro-Magnons had arrived in Europe during the warmer interlude of the last Ice Age called the Gottweig Interstadial. This "relatively" warm respite from the last Ice Age lasted from about 38,000 BC to about 28,000 BC. The hybrid "Lapedo Child" skeleton discovered in Portugal caused something of a media stir in 1998, for example. It was found up in the foothills where pure Neanderthals and pure Cro-Magnons were most likely to have encountered each other from time to time. The child's bones have been dated to about 23,000 BC. Another Neanderthal-and-Cro-Magnon hybrid was reported from the highlands of the Czech Republic in 1999 and it dated from a little earlier, about 32,000 BC.

An entire cave-full of pure Neanderthals ranging or "evolving" into "modern" hybrids with Cro-Magnons was found at Mount Carmel in modern Israel between 1934 and 1964. This collection of bones, including several very interesting and diagnostic skulls, is usually called the "Skuhl Series" by physical anthropologists.

The pure Neanderthal bones range in date from about 40,000 BC, while hybrids begin to appear about 30,000 BC and then start to become fully "modern" humans by about 25,000 BC.

This very early date for the appearance of "modern man" in the Holy Land can, of course, be explained by the cherished belief that God created humanity there. But then one wonders how and why equally modern humanity of the Far Eastern variety appeared about 50,000 years earlier around Beijing.

More likely is the mundane explanation that the Eastern Mediterranean was at the very southerly limits of "Ice Age" Neanderthal distribution, while the local climate was mild enough to tempt Atlantic Cro-Magnons to migrate eastwards along the coast of North Africa even before the Gottweig Interstadial began. Therefore, the two groups simply met and mixed in Palestine first due to climatic factors rather than to Divine intervention.[26]

All native Europeans and Western Asians today, from Ireland to Western India, are hybrids of Neanderthals and Cro-Magnons in various proportions. The time frame of the most active mixing between these two groups must have been just after, *and because of,* the Great Black Sea Flood in 5600 BC, during the period about 4500 BC to about 1500 BC.

Because of the Flood, Neanderthals had to migrate out of their mountain-girt Black Sea Basin and they swarmed out into the Cro-Magnon world of Old Europe that Marija Gimbutas has called the Civilisation of the Goddess.

This time frame is not really in the dim and distant past, although many people would naturally like to push the Neanderthal and Cro-Magnon hybridization as far back as possible into the very dimmest past. This time frame for massive inter-mixing is truly just on the cusp of human memory where legend and folklore meet history.

Our modern year AD 2004 is, for example, the year 5764 in the

Jewish calendar and, although Jewish years are not precisely the same as Gregorian years, this takes us back to about 3700 BC when some continuity of this particular tribal group began to be chronicled. Sumerian (Ubaid Culture) king lists go back just as far or a little further.

About 4500 BC is the very earliest cultural horizon of our present cycle of civilization. Some of our most ancient holy books and some of our oldest epics, like the *Epic of Gilgamesh*, contain clear references to this era. By the way, Gilgamesh's friend, the "wild man" Enkidu, is quite obviously a highly Neanderthalish character. The story of Cain and Abel in the Bible also seems to be a memory of this epoch.

Just how mixing between Neanderthals and Cro-Magnons was accomplished, it is hard to say. I have my own ideas about it, but they are simply my own conjectures and should not carry any great weight with readers.

Given the known aggression, and my own arguments about psychosexual aggression among Neanderthals, I think that there must have been widespread extermination of Cro-Magnon men wherever Cro-Magnons and Neanderthals encountered each other – along with the simultaneous widespread rape of Cro-Magnon women. The habits of the *Nephilim* of the Bible probably refer to this Neanderthal conquest. At least, I would prefer to think that the biblical phrase "those from on high" (Jerusalem text) referred to Neanderthals from the uplands rather than to Von Daniken's notions of outer space aliens coming to earth.

I have covered this in very great detail, with *correct* translations of the earliest known Hebrew texts of the Bible by Rabbi Yonah ibn Ahron of New York City. I chose ibn Ahron's translations for use in *Chosen People from the Caucasus* because he is a United Nations-accredited linguist as well as a Rabbi. Ibn Ahron was selected to work on some of the very earliest biblical fragments for modern Israel's famed "The Shrine of the Book."

He must also be one of the few linguists or Rabbis to have some anthropological training. He studied zoology and anthropology under Ivan T. Sanderson of Cambridge. Ibn Ahron's translations of Genesis, especially the story of Cain and Abel and the story of Jacob's deception of Isaac to acquire Esau's birthright, are highly supportive of this construct.

Ibn Ahron himself mentioned that Esau seemed to be a very "Neanderthalish" character. In fact, ibn Ahron's translations partly inspired *Chosen People from the Caucasus*. And, of course, no one could accuse me of referring to a questionably "expert" opinion.

219

Given this sexual activity between Neanderthals and Cro-Magnons, which anthropologists like to call euphemistically "peripheral gene flow", it is obvious that pure Neanderthal characteristics would have become diluted within a very few generations. Cro-Magnon genetic characteristics would have been roughly equal with Neanderthal ones in the very numerous first generation offspring of rapes.

But when these many children of rapes mostly bred with one another as they became sexually mature, Cro-Magnon genes would have become preponderant within the composite population and Neanderthal ones would quickly have become less represented on a demographic basis. Within a few generations, pure Neanderthals would have virtually "died out."

And this is what anthropologists see from the bones of what is called the "early modern population" of Europe and Western Asia. Nonetheless, it remains true that Neanderthal physical characteristics were so distinctive that, in a very diluted and vestigial form, they are still *the* diagnostic traits that separate "Caucasians" from other "major genetic groups" of humanity. The very word *Caucasian* means "from the Caucasus region."

Neanderthals could only have remained relatively pure, or "more pure," among tribes that valued their genetic identity. The obvious way of ensuring genetic purity or at least slowing inevitable genetic dilution, was to acknowledge children as being members of the tribe only if their *mothers* were Neanderthal or were acceptably Neanderthalish – no matter how many non-Neanderthal women the husband and father had managed to rape.

This tribal value would also imply strict injunctions against intermarriage with potential sexual partners outside the tribe. The children of hapless and raped Cro-Magnon women would be outcasts from the tribe and would be of no value to the tribe, except possibly as slaves and sexual toys. This attitude is reflected very well in the biblical story of Abraham and Hagar and their son Ishmael, as opposed to Abraham and Sarah and their son Isaac.

Counting twenty years to a generation, modern Europeans and Western Asians – that is "Western humanity" or "Caucasians" – are the product of 350-400 generations of mixing and re-mixing since the Great Black Sea Flood of 5600 BC. We are so well mixed and re-mixed that we have difficulty recognizing that our "racial" characteristics represent a nearly infinite combination of Neanderthal and Cro-Magnon physical traits. By contrast, ancient hybrids of the two relatively pure and distinct groups, when their bones are sometimes found, are fairly easy to recognise.

Nonetheless, as I observed previously, even now it is still possible to draw a line of demarcation between "more Cro-Magnonish" people and "more Neanderthalish" ones. The line goes from the German-Polish border on the Baltic Sea to the Italian-Slovenian border of the Adriatic Sea. Where there are exceptions, you will find Neanderthalish people reside in the highlands or *came from the highlands* in historical times, and Cro-Magnonish people are concentrated along the river valleys and seacoasts.

It is also interesting that anyone can plot the locations of modern Western conflict and you will almost invariably find that chronic trouble spots, from the Pyrenees to the Pamirs, consist of remnant highly Neanderthalish people. And you will find that mountain-steppe people who were isolated by geographical factors or who adopted cultural and "religious" prohibitions against intermarriage with other peoples, are the most consistently aggressive examples of Western humanity.

A second diagnostic indication of highly Neanderthal genetic content would be the coincidence of anti-feminine cultural or religious injunctions along with obvious sheer aggressive behaviour. And, if my notions have any validity at all, a third diagnostic indication of highly Neanderthal genetic expression would be fanatical monotheism.

No one who reads newspapers or watches televised news needs to be told that conflict between two such groups, the Israelis (supported by the vast majority of North American Jews) and the fundamentalist Moslems, threatens world survival with a nuclear Armageddon in the Middle East.

There have been many recent attempts, as most newspaper readers will know, to deny any Neanderthal physical traits or other "racial" proclivities in modern humanity. Most of this research has been undertaken since *The Iceman Inheritance* was published in 1978 and since *Chosen People from the Caucasus* was released in 1992. These politically correct studies have, of course, been highly promoted, and especially on North American television and in North American newspapers and magazines. Typically, they involve complicated statistical analysis of DNA and Y-chromosome genetic comparisons.

Whether these studies are science or "pseudo-science" is a matter of highly controversial opinion. Most of the public cannot grasp the difficulties of making DNA comparisons between living people and ancient human populations.

Then, too, statistics are so easy to manipulate and distort that they can usually be made to "prove" whatever the researcher wants to prove. As someone once put it, and as we have quoted previously, "first come lies, then damned lies and then statistics." [27]

221

However, it seems to me that these studies purporting to disprove the existence of Neanderthal racial characteristics in modern humanity are themselves vain and even ridiculous exercises in psychological denial.

If we take yet *another* area of conflict aside from religion, the socio-economic conflict between so-called "Capitalism" and so-called "Communisim" in the very modern era of the twentieth century, we can see a pattern similar to the one on the map of "The Iceman Inheritance" earlier in this epilogue. The authoritarian subjugation of the Soviet people, and one based on a "single political party system", is too much like religious monotheism to be ignored by any intelligent observer. It is an example of monotheistic racial proclivities transplanted into the realm of supposedly atheistic economic and political dialectics. It is an economic version of Judaic or Islamic monotheism.

It can be no accident at all that three of the five major formulators of modern Soviet Communism – Karl Marx, Friedrich Engels and Leon Trotsky – were all three Russian Jews from the modern Ukrainian and Russian steppes. Of the remaining two formulators of modern Communism, Vladimir Lenin was born on the Volga near the old Hun and Khazar capital of Kazaran-Itil while Joseph Stalin was born in Gori, Georgia in the shadow of the Caucasus Mountains.

Quite obviously, modern "Communism" was moulded primarily by genetic influences, and not by objectively theoretical economic ones, although Communism was exported as a cultural commodity and found favour among some non-Western peoples who were being oppressed by modern Colonialism and Capitalism. The Chinese are an example of a non-Western population that adopted Western "Communism" as a defense against Western "Capitalism" and Colonialism. So-called "Communism" does not have to be authoritarian.

The Egyptian "Therapeutae," a sect of early Christians (before Jesus) were "Communists" in terms of the economic organisation of their communities, but they were anything but authoritarian.

The Western world has very seldom been involved in purely religious conflict or in purely socio-economic conflict. Behind almost all the cultural disguises of confrontation, and the excuses for it, there has usually been an element of *genetic* competition.

I think that something else must be at least mentioned here, even at the risk of over-taxing an already complicated epilogue. "The Conquest" of the New World and the subsequent transatlantic slave trade in Black Africans had a definite genetic component, although the rationalisation for both was always primarily "religious" at the time.

Both "The Conquest" and the transatlantic slave trade were basically manifestations of barely concealed and purposeful genocide. Our "mainstream" and sanitised history books nowadays mostly indict the "Spanish" and "Portuguese" Conquistadors as being the major perpetrators of these crimes. But this is only because Spain and Portugal have little intellectual influence in today's world and they therefore cannot contest effectively a very real miscarriage of historical justice.

Both Iberian and Jewish historical sources make it very clear that from fifty to seventy-five percent of the sixteenth century Iberian "Conquistadors" were actually Jews. All Jews were expel-led from Spain on August 3, 1492 – the very same day, by the way, that Columbus set sail on his epic voyage of discovery.

There are many unsettling surprises in store for people who are curious enough to look beyond the bland pages of school history books. It is interesting, for example, to comb the records of Australian and South African colonisation in order to learn how and why Australia's aborigines and South Africa's *Saan* people were virtually exterminated. It is even more fascinating to view World Wars I and II from the enemy's perspective and not from the bias of our propaganda alone. Napoleon once characterised conventional history as "the lie commonly agreed upon." But Henry Ford said it more succinctly: "History is bunk."

We may recall the true origin of Christianity's "Madonna and Child" artistic motif from Chapter 3.

Mother Isis and Horus as the original "Christian" Madonna and Child.

The present world could rather obviously use a revival of Neolithic "true Christianity."

Only some sincere reverence for the ancient Great Fertility Goddess and her Good Shepherd consort-messiah can save us lost lambs that have gone astray.

We have turned our over-exploited world into a life-threatening geopolitical, religious and environmental mess.

We have believed that male-dominant monotheism represents the apex of compassionate spirituality, while polytheistic paganism reflects the depths of moral and materialist depravity.

But the present state of the world's political security and environmental purity vehemently argues otherwise.

The only truly *demonstrable* "salvation" is, of course, the continual regeneration and maintenance of a vital environment.

That was always the message symbolised by the original Madonna and Child. It still is, but nowadays the symbolism has been distorted in a wry, ironic and tragic way.

Some anti-pollution and environmental groups have adopted as a symbol the photograph of a woman's nurturing breast.

But, because of environmental pollution, the photo bears the ironic and bitter caption: *Unfit for human consumption.*

This message about salvation through a continually regenerated and healthy biological environment, represented and symbolised by the union of the Great Goddess and the Good Shepherd, is in direct opposition to the lifeless Judeo-Christian and Koranic promises of sterile and eternal "salvation" in some sexless – or definitely non-reproductive – monotheistic heaven.

This realistic and alternative message is the 10,000-year-old biological truth of what the "Holy Grail" basically stands for.

The "Holy Grail" was originally the womb of the regenerating Great Goddess who was endlessly fertilised by her dying-and-reborn husband-son, the Good Shepherd.

This frankly biological view of human life and wellbeing has always both threatened and offended Neanderthalish tendencies toward anti-feminist "spiritual" sensibilities caused by psychosexual ambivalence and confusion.

It is obvious, however, and it must be freely admitted, that although the deepest meaning of the Grail was never completely lost, at least by some people, the tradition of the Holy Grail was itself obscured and distorted by many people who nominally believed in it.

This was because of the virtually complete dominance of the orthodox Judeo-Christian Tradition and the Church of Rome in the European world.

The medieval version of the Holy Grail legend accepted Jesus and Mary Magdalene of the New Testament as real historical characters of first century Palestine.

This primary misapprehension, the direct result of all-pervasive Judeo-Christian propaganda of the New Testament, inspired the First Crusade (AD 1096-1099) as a misguided military effort to capture the "Holy Land" from the Moslems.

This Holy Land was "Holy" to Judeo-Christians and Judeo-Islamics only because of mythic Old Testament so-called "history."

This arid territory had, and has, no relevance whatsoever to true Christianity or to the Grail that has always symbolised it.

This European occupation of the misnamed "Holy Land" led directly to the completely justified and inevitable Moslem counter-offensive of AD 1187.

And this, in turn, led to the terrible Albigensian Crusade that very nearly caused the extermination of Grail Believers.

The Anglo-American allies are presently replaying the same mistake of the First Crusade a millennium later. As the cliché goes: "Those who cannot learn from history are doomed to repeat it."

And when Baudoin formed his "Poor Knights of the Temple of Solomon" he was betraying an ignorant and conditioned subservience to the Judeo-Christian Tradition.

The structure pointed out as the original "Temple of Solomon" – the remains of the so-called "Wailing Wall" today in Jerusalem – was actually in existence as early as 1468 BC because it is mentioned in the annals of Tothmosis III. This pharaoh either built it or repaired it.

But Solomon traditionally reigned about 1000 BC to 950 BC, or about five hundred years after the Temple attributed to him.

Besides, all the objective evidence argues that David and Solomon were never in Palestine and even the modern Israeli archaeologist Dr. Ze'ev Herzog agrees that their kingdom in Palestine is a biblical myth.

Therefore, Cathars, Templars, Freemasons, Rosicrucians, Illuminati and many other esoteric groups have laboured to discover and reveal the truth about Western history and religion while being encumbered with the orthodox Judeo-Christian burden of purposefully distorted history.

The teachings of these esoteric groups could have freed many more people from the bonds of organised Middle Eastern monotheistic religions – except that their own beliefs were garbled and incoherent, crippled by the weight of their burden.

In 1988, I concluded *Holy Grail Across the Atlantic* with the following thoughts:

> Although we were three thousand miles from Camelot, it was easy to imagine the jingling of chain mail, armour and horse-trappings as the dying Arthur was borne up the hill under the defiant, snapping dragon-banner of Wales. The banner, like the name of his father, were clues to the real nature of the Holy Grail.
>
> Human will. Animated by love. Tempered with compassion. *Guided by knowledge*, the dragon, that much-maligned "Serpent" in the Garden of Eden. Human will animated by love, tempered with compassion, and guided by knowledge finds itself obligated to take action that people recognise as "courageous." Armed with love, compassion and knowledge, one can cast off the cumbersome and crippling armour of religious dogma or political and economic dialectics to carve out, with supple and determined strokes, more appropriate social structures and a more rewarding human environment, using equally sharp edges of intellect and heart. That is what knights and heroines of the Grail have always done. That has been their job. It is still, and anyone with a properly moulded Will can join the elite company of the Grail because the battles, and the ramparts, are all around us.

Ten years later, in 1998, I concluded *Grail Knights of North America* with the following view of American democracy:

> From the heights of Iotigolo's tomb overlooking the Susquehanna, it is not so difficult for the eye of imagination to follow the river's course down to Philadelphia where the Declaration of Independence was signed. Where the Liberty Bell rang out its defiance and hope. Spectres of grizzled knights hovered behind those signatories. Their armour had been dented and their swords had been notched in the clangour of a thousand battles in defence of the Holy Grail. Their battles had been fought from brave ramparts of Albigensian fortresses to crude palisades in the Appalachians. It was this metallic cacophony of many struggles for human freedom that American rebels in Philadelphia heard as the carillon of one cracked bell.

In the year AD 2004, many of our protective palisades have fallen. Some of our ramparts have crumbled, eroded because of our infatuation with lifestyle, comfort, trivia and the distractions of entertainment.

We have lost our focus on the true foundations of our culture, *just as we were both encouraged and intended to do.*

North American media's ever increasing emphasis on trivialized, make-believe sex-and-violence entertainment reflects ancient Ice Age Neanderthal proclivities toward psychosexual aggression.

The media's presentation of "headline news" and "key word" current affairs without any in-depth perspective is purposeful "information overload."

And fundamental issues are glossed over with dissonant punctuations of SFX, driving music and a garnish of meaningless Hollywood glitz.

Financial news, including stock market reports, has become a regular feature along with the traditional coverage of news, weather and sports.

There are two fundamental issues that North American media seeks to obscure at all costs.

The first is the true history of Israel and the "Holy Land."

The second is the fact that the values of the great *Western* Democracies were founded on the ancient ideals of *Western* European "Cro-Magnon" ancestors.

These democratic values do not derive from the Judaic "Ten Commandments."

In fact, these commandments were originally eight in number and were incorporated into Pharaoh Akenaten's famous "Hymn to Aten." Nor do Western democratic values owe anything to the Judeo-Christian New Testament.

As North American and Western European civil rights leaders and advocates have been emphasising for years, the values and Constitutions of modern Western democracies owe *absolutely nothing* to the Judeo-Christian tradition – *or to any other Middle Eastern religious perspective.*

In fact, rather the reverse. The first and most crucial victory of modern Western democracies was the firm separation of Church and State.

And it is only because of one of the most incredible ironies of history that the foe thought to have been defeated so long ago at the Battle of Chalons in AD 451 has been welcomed into the fold of most modern Western societies.

Has this Caucasus-steppe influence gradually undermined our traditional Western European social, cultural, entertainment, religious, political, legal and financial perspectives? Has this ironic circumstance confused and aggravated the West's response to the 1.3 billion-strong Islamic world?

Had this Ashkenazi influence not infiltrated the very heart of the West, would the West have viewed the Islamic world as a serious cultural, financial and religious *competitor*, perhaps (and with good reason), but not necessarily as the *enemy*?

Could a more humane accommodation between the West and the Islamic world possibly have been reached through peaceful negotiation?

Yet now there is a religious and genetic war in the Middle East.

And it may soon, with the recent revelation of Israel's nuclear weapons, destroy the world as we have known it. This happened previously at the end of the last Ice Age and the end of "Atlantis."

But even Armageddon will supposedly devastate only the so-called "Holy Land."

And the destruction of this "Holy Land" could perhaps be the very best thing that could ever happen for most of humanity.

There will yet be battles aplenty to fight for liberty, equality and fraternity wherever courageous men and women remain inspired by the knowledge of living a good life on earth rather than dreaming visions of sterile eternity in heaven.

The hearts and minds of Western European people are still with "Mary" and the Good Shepherd.

Their souls yet remain in Atlantis and Lyonesse. And their knights and heroines have always rallied to their oldest and most cherished symbol, the Holy Grail.

Notes to the Epilogue.

1   As *Swords at Sunset* neared completion, Toronto's *24 Hours* and *Metro* early morning newspapers carried the story of Israeli "whistleblower," Mordecai Vanunu ("Israeli Whistleblower Freed, Defiant: 'Happy to do what I did'", photo feature, April 22, 2004, *24 Hours* page 12). The *Metro* had a smaller sidebar story on page 3. Vanunu, who was freed on April 21 after spending the past eighteen years in Israel's Shimka Prison, had been employed as a low-level technician at Israel's Dimona reactor.

In 1986, Vanunu leaked documents and photos of the nuclear facility to *The Sunday Times* of London. From this information, British and American intelligence experts were able to estimate that Israel had *at that time* the world's sixth largest stockpile of nuclear weapons, an arsenal presently estimated at from 200 to 300 nuclear warheads (but which may be even larger). Nonetheless, to this day, Israel has consistently denied that it possesses any nuclear (or other) weapons of mass destruction.

If Vanunu's information was correct, and if British and American intelligence estimates based on it were accurate, than President George Bush knew very well that the biggest stockpile of "weapons of mass destruction" in the Middle East was in Israel, not in Iraq.

On April 20, 2004, Spain announced the immediate withdrawal of its 1400 troops from Iraq. The next day (April 21), Honduras announced that it would recall its 370 soldiers from Iraq and on April 22 in the wake of Vanunu's release and repeated accusations, Poland announced that it was considering the withdrawal of its 10,000 of soldiers from Iraq. Spain, Honduras and Poland have all charged that they were mis-led about Iraq's alleged possession of "weapons of mass destruction" as a reason for joining the U.S.-led invasion of Iraq in March 2003.

An anonymous strategic analyst at Britain's Royal Military College at Sandhurst said (*The Times*, April 22, 2004, page 2) that Vanunu's revelations explained the seemingly "desperate nature" of U.S. policy in the Middle East with the invasions of Afghanistan in early 2002 and the invasion of Iraq a year later. "Clearly, the Americans were under some pressure to smash Israel's enemies conventionally under some secret knowledge or threat that, otherwise, Israel could unleash nuclear war on the entire region."

2   Mitch Potter, "Coffin linked to Jesus is a fraud, experts rule", *Toronto Star*, Thursday, June 19, 2003, page A3.

3   Ibid.

4   There is no satisfying answer presently about who the so-called "Cro-Magnons" actually were in a "racial" sense. The name simply comes from a French site where the first thirty-odd Cro-Magnon skeletons were found. They have been satisfactorily dated to about 33,000 BC.

It is very evident, however, that the Cro-Magnons were a highly artistic people in a visual way. Their cave paintings from the Dordogne region of France (and extending into Spain and North Africa) are considered masterpieces of human artistic creativity. But it is also a fact that their paintings show a great deal of affinity with *Saan* ("Bushman") art that was still being created in Africa in historical and colonial times.

Either the Cro-Magnons were simply *Saan* who had migrated north from Africa or else they were a completely unknown "race" that had inhabited the larger Atlantic islands and seamounts when these land masses were still above sea level during the last "Ice Age". There is evidence that the Cro-Magnons were, indeed, a separate Atlantic race of which the now extinct "Guanches" of the Canary Islands were the last surviving remnants. But, if so, they had thoroughly intermixed with the *Saan* on the Atlantic islands off the coast of Africa before reaching the European coasts, or continued intermixture after both peoples arrived in Europe.

The origin of the Cro-Magnons and the Guanches represent fascinating mysteries of human evolution. The late Thor Heyerdahl came to believe in later life that the Guanches held the key to the start of Western civilization.

But we have to understand that the Cro-Magnons were not "Caucasians" or "whites" as we would use that term today. Rather, they were a café-au-lait coloured race that has often been called the "Mediterranean Race".

5 In May and September 2003, the London-based *Afrikan Business and Culture* magazine published two separate articles on *The Iceman Inheritance*. *Afrikan Business and Culture* is not a large circulation magazine, but it does reach many non-white educators, Third World business and economic leaders and most diplomats of the United Nations.

6 *Holy Grail Across the Atlantic*, page 14.

7 *L'Almanach du Languedoc*, November 1999, page 21.

8 "Neanderthals mated with modern humans", BBC Online News, April 21, 1999.

9 Some authorities are of the opinion that *"Homo habilis"* was not actually human at all – that is, belonging to the genus *Homo*, but a later evolutionary development of the *Australopithecines*.

10 Alexander Marshack had suspected, as early as 1971, that some inscriptions on Neanderthal cave walls might have been attempts to express musical notation. But he had no proof. However, in April 1998, a cave bear's femur was found in a Slovenian Neanderthal cave (in the Balkan mountains) and it was neatly perforated with four holes. It has been tentatively dated to about 42,000 years old, although testing since 2001 has indicated that the bone may be only 28,000 years old.

American musicologist, Bob Fink, has hailed the discovery of this "Neanderthal flute" as the first known human musical instrument because it plays notes on the do, re, mi scale when the holes are covered and uncovered. Dr. Ivan Turk of the Slovenian Academy of Sciences accepts the artifact as being a flute. However, Drs. April Newell and Philip G. Chase of the

University of Pennsylvania believe that the bear's femur was chewed by a wolf and this accounts for the perforations that are only "coincidentally" in the correct positions to produce the notes. Needless to say, the controversy continues, and will continue until another musical instrument is discovered.

However, *if* this artifact is a purposeful musical instrument, it is interesting that the distinctively Western "do, re, mi" of eight notes in an octave seems to have been established among the Neanderthals at least 28,000 years ago. It is also interesting that this artifact comes from just east of the line that separates highly "Cro-Magnonish" people from "highly Neanderthalish" people.

11 There can be little doubt that the Neanderthals also supplied the "white" skin that is supposedly characteristic of the Caucasians or the "White Race." But actually, extreme hairiness is *the* diagnostic physical characteristic of Caucasians, along with certain skeletal features (such as the wide diameter of female "pelvic rims"). This extreme Neanderthal hairiness acted as a "sunscreen" to bleach out the pigment of the skin beneath the pelt. This, combined with the fact that the "Ice Age" sun wasn't very strong anyway contributed to the lack of pigment in "Caucasian" skin. But skin colour is a dangerous criterion for distinguishing "races" although it is such an obvious one that it has been widely used, but mostly by "Whites".

In actual fact, however, Caucasian skin ranges in colour from almost albino white through "olive" to café-au-lait that verges on brown. Norwegians, Pakistanis, Germans, Spaniards, Sicilians and Maltese are all "White", or representatives of the highly variable "Caucasian" so-called "race" or "major genetic group".

12 The exceptional fertility of the Russian and Ukrainian steppes is explained by the massive deposition of a certain kind of soil, actually a rich volcanic ash, called *loess*. Loess was deposited from the Hungarian plains to China and it even occurs on the Canadian prairies, showing that it was originally spread as a thick cloud of airborne dust that, in smaller quantities, was even carried across the North Pacific ocean. The millions of tons of loess also must have been deposited in the relatively recent past because this soft and fertile soil has not eroded away.

Dr. Otto Muck, who (in my view) has written the most scientific work on the former existence of "Atlantis", considered that the recent deposition of loess was due to the volcanic debris from the Atlantis destruction being thrown into the atmosphere and then carried downwind across Asia by the prevailing Westerly winds. Given that there is no known other volcanic eruption that could account for the huge amount of loess, except an eruption of the Mid-Atlantic Ridge where "Atlantis" was traditionally located, Muck's view is hard to refute. Loess must be evidence of a tectonic catastrophe that was truly massive and which occurred in the Atlantic less than 20,000 years ago.

13 See Marija Gimbutas *Civilization of the Goddess* (1991) where she emphasizes these dates in several places.

14 See Ahmed Osman's *Out of Egypt* for a discussion of horse-skeleton dates in the Nile Delta.

15 The success of this Egyptian counter-offensive was due to the rapid Egyptian adoption of Hyksos methods of warfare. The horse-drawn chariot and the composite (laminated) bow were both adopted at the start of the Eighteenth Dynasty.

16 Although our modern vowels (in the Roman alphabet) are now placed in the order AEIOU, this was not always the case. Robert Graves in *The White Goddess* shows that the earliest known vowel order was IAOUE – which approximates the sound "Yaweh" or "Eee-aah-ow-oo-eh".

17 At this time, the Greco-Egyptian saviour, considered to be Horus (son of Osiris and Isis) was generally known as "Serapis", a healer. "Serapis" and "Jesus" were often confused – especially by Roman commentators – because their attributes were identical and visual representations of them were often identical as well. Then, to confuse things even more, priests of Serapis were often also Christian priests and vice versa. Ahmed Osman has shown that there was no real distinction between the two.

18 *The Columbia Viking Desk Encyclopedia* (1968 edition) notes this under the entry "Huns" on page 494. See also the entry for "Khazars" on page 565.

19 Ibid. Same entries. But be advised that by the 1976 edition of *The Columbia Viking Desk Encyclopedia*, all references to "Huns" and "Khazars" in relation to Ashkenazi Jews had been dropped. This was the same year, 1976, in which Arthur Koestler's *The Thirteenth Tribe* was published amid strident cries of "anti-Semitism"

20 It is interesting that Otto Muck included the Swastika in this collection of Atlantis-derived symbols as a sort of Celtic cross with gaps representing the walls of Atlantis in a ruined or "breached" condition. Depending on the culture, some peoples chose to remember Atlantis in its heyday before its destruction, while others commemorated its loss. But, if Muck's ideas have any validity, this makes the Swastika an Atlantean or "Cro-Magnon" symbol, not an "Aryan" one. It is not surprising that the Swastika would occur among some Amerindian tribes, and there are several excellent examples from the Mi'kmaq culture of Nova Scotia. Refugees from Atlantis, according to both Otto Muck and simple logic, fled to or were already established on both sides of the Atlantic Ocean when the cataclysm occurred.

However, if Muck is correct, the Swastika should also occur among the Indus Cultures of Harappa and Mohenjo-daro. These cultures were established by Cro-Magnons or the "Mediterranean Race" as they migrated by sea and coastal lowlands all the way to modern Pakistan and western India by 7000 BC if not earlier. And, in fact, the Swastika does appear in these Indus Cultures which were most definitely "pre-Aryan" and which are thought, ironically, to have been destroyed by the Aryan invasions of about 1500 BC. A search on the Internet under "Swastika, Mohenjo-daro" should yield much information and many illustrations.

Therefore, this supposedly "Aryan" symbol is not Aryan at all.

In fact, in addition to the "Holy Grail" (a concept which is difficult to convey visually and evocatively), the Swastika *should* be the most graphic and evocative symbol of those Cro-Magnon peoples whose cultural, religious and psychosexual outlook is so different those of the Caucasus-steppes.

This is an exceedingly esoteric matter – and one that also skirts the very utmost "political incorrectness" – and would itself be worth a few books.

Suffice it to state here that Otto Muck, Otto Rahn, Hitler and Alfred Rosenberg, among prominent philosophers of Nazi ideology, knew very well that the Swastika was an "Atlantean" symbol and chose it on purpose for that very reason in their opposition to their perception of danger from the Caucasus-steppes. Hitler claimed the symbol as "Aryan" merely to sell a simplified concept and distinct symbol to a polarised German public, most of which did not know the esoteric lore behind Nazism. The German public was subjected to propaganda, too, but whether more or less than the "Western Allies" is a very moot point.

The present *name* of the symbol, "Swastika", is however, truly "Aryan" and it is from the Sanskrit. It was probably a translation or transliteration of its meaning among the non-Aryan conquered people of Harappa and Mohenjo-daro. It consists of the syllable-word *Su* ("You", second person familiar) *vasti* ("are") and the suffix *ku*, which, as I have already explained at length in *Chosen People from the Caucasus* means "where?" in all Indo-European languages (in various forms from the Latin "Quo?" to the Goidelic "Cw?"). Thus, roughly: "Where are you [now], Atlantis?"

21 Personal correspondences with Robert and Beryl Graves, 1984-1985.

22 It is well known that Geiseric, High King of the Vandals, crossed the frozen Rhine into Gaul on the night of December 31-January 1 at the turn of the year AD 406-407 and entered North Africa about AD 412 from Spain. Ultimately, this western group of Vandals was defeated by the Byzantine general Belisarius about AD 450. This is all that our western history books have to say about the Vandals.

However, recent linguistic studies show that the peoples of the Middle East and the eastern part of North Africa were also influenced or "inundated" by a Vandal linguistic dialect that came through some part of modern Turkey from the western side of the Caucasus. The most likely explanation is that the original Vandal horde had already been split into two parts by the Huns who were directly behind them. This must have happened even before the Vandals entered Poland and Germania to cross the frozen Rhine in AD 406-407. The general history of the western group, under Geiseric, is known to western historians. But the history of the eastern contingent of Vandals is completely obscure.

23 The Khazar adoption of Judaism has been documented by J.M. Bury's *A History of the Eastern Roman Empire* (1912), Joseph Jacobs' *Jewish Contributions to Western Civilization* (1921) and most completely by A.N. Poliak's *Khazaria: The History of a Jewish Empire in Europe* (1950, in Hebrew). The well-known Jewish author, Arthur Koestler, supplied an English-language version of this obscure research in *The Thirteenth Tribe* (1976). As early as 1924, the Jewish linguist Moishe Miesnes had shown that

233

the Germanic element in Yiddish was actually a South Gothic dialect spoken by the Khazars (*Die Yiddishe Sprache*).

24 This estimate of "1-3 million Khazars" derives ultimately from the figures given by Bury, Jacobs, Poliak and Koestler about the size of Khazar armies that are *reliably* described in medieval chronicles. When multiplied by the accepted demographic ratios of combatants to non-combatants routinely used by historians for nomadic populations (i.e. about 1:15), this gives a total of *at least* 1.5 million Khazars who were immediately converted to Judaism in AD 740.

25 See Moishe Miesnes' *Die Yiddishe Sprache*, page 3.

26 From a purely anthropological perspective, the Mount Carmel "Skuhl Series" is interesting because it may shed some light on Neanderthal origins, a matter that has always been controversial.

If it is true that Neanderthals evolved from *Homo habilis* of East Africa, then *Homo habilis* must have reached the Caucasus area somehow. The obvious route would be through modern Palestine. It would be interesting if the oldest Neanderthal skulls of the "Skuhl Series" show a greater affinity with *Homo habilis* jaws than the three specimens of *Homo habilis* mandibles described in the *National Geographic's* August 2002 issue. But, to my knowledge, no such re-examination of the "Skuhl Series" has so far been undertaken or announced. Diagnostic would be the ascending ramus of the coracoid process and the degree of overlap with regard to the molars.

For, while Mount Carmel may represent the most southerly limit of Ice Age Neanderthals, it may also represent the northerly point of entry for *Homo habilis* into the Middle East sometime between 1-3 million years ago before the last "Ice Age" began about 80,000 BC.

A re-examination of the early Mount Carmel Neanderthals might clench the matter of whether *habilis* was truly *Homo* or a species of Australopithecus. Of particular interest would be the incidence of the "Y-5" (human) or "Square-4" (Australopithecus) molar cusp pattern.

27 After a lot of searching, I have finally discovered that something like this was supposedly said by the British statesman Benjamin Disraeli (1804-1881), or at least attributed to him by Mark Twain. "There are three kinds of lies: lies, damned lies and statistics."

Afterword

The book you've just read very nearly died an early death - prior to ever being published.

Narrow-minded interest groups lobbied against its publication and the author's views were subjected to an extraordinary degree of criticism and ridicule long before his the book ever saw the light of day in any bookstore.

Author Michael Bradley was subjected to hate-mail and hate-phone calls from those who disagreed with his views – but felt they couldn't stop there – and made a point of disrupting his life and harming his health (the stress is believed to have contributed to the author's heart condition).

And you, dear reader, were very nearly denied the opportunity to read Bradley's fascinating account of Grail knights meeting their demise in Niagara, Canada and in the U.S. state of Vermont. Influential individuals and groups very nearly had their way in dictating what is acceptable for you and me to read.

It's that underlying assumption – that we need to be protected from the truth or someone's belief of what's true – that got my back up as a publisher and caused me to seriously consider publishing Swords at Sunset. This is very much an issue of freedom of speech and expression.

On reading the manuscript I came to the inescapable conclusion that author Michael Bradley presents intelligent, well considered arguments that should be pondered.

His is a voice that deserves to be heard.

Indeed, Michael Bradley is one of the most talented, thought-provoking writers I've ever met - and I've met quite a few.

Bradley is the author of literally dozens of critically acclaimed books, including several bestsellers on the Holy Grail.

He approached my publishing house, Manor House Publishing Inc., after his former publisher, Dundurn Press dropped Swords at Sunset despite a signed contract, on grounds the book was too controversial and wasn't the book they'd thought it was when the papers were signed.

Among other things, Bradley's non-fiction book contends that Jesus had children who carried on his bloodline through generations, via a living Holy Grail - an assertion that runs counter to the teachings of major organized religions.

You'll find similar contentions in Dan Brown's fictional Da Vinci Code, which has sold more than 25 million copies (Bradley was employed as a researcher/consultant for Ron Howard's film production of the Da Vinci Code).

It was, for me, difficult at first to understand why Bradley's book aroused such animosity.

Then it hit me: Brown's work is fiction and pretends to be nothing more than that.

Those who fear religious scrutiny can simply dismiss Brown's book as a creative endeavour that has no basis in reality. It's no more of a threat than Star Wars

Bradley, on the other hand, has produced a first-rate work of non-fiction that draws on numerous sources of evidence, including ancient artefacts to support his theory that Holy Grail knights came across the Atlantic, travelled North America and died in clashes with local tribes in Niagara.

Instead of presenting a story intended purely for entertainment value, Bradley has presented a well-researched, well-investigated thesis that compels us to think well outside the accepted boundaries of organized religions.

He asks us to think in new ways, to set aside conventional knowledge and consider new and intriguing evidence that there is far more to the stories of Jesus and the origins of Man than we were ever taught in school.

Bradley, in fact, seems to take delight in shaking established religions to their core. He challenges us to think outside the box - way outside the box. He presents intriguing possibilities – you don't have to buy them all.

Some in our society aren't ready for the free-thinking Bradley advocates. Whole nations and political structures are based on certain "truths" that if found questionable could undermine the basis of society.

I invite such fearful critics to read Bradley's book and allow themselves the luxury of free thought.

To these critics I say: Give the book a chance, and if, in the end, you reject the author's arguments, so be it.

But why not consider an alternative viewpoint.

What are you so afraid of?

Michael B Davie, publisher, *Swords at Sunset,*
author, *Inside the Witches' Coven, Why Everybody Hates Toronto,* and
Poetry for the Insane: The Full Mental

Bibliography

Andrews, Richard and Schellenberger, Paul, *The Tomb of God*, Little Brown, London, 1996.

Ashe, Geoffrey (Ed.), *The Quest For Arthur's Britain,* Granada Publishing Limited, London, 1968.

Baigent, Michael; Leigh, Richard and Lincoln, Henry, *The Holy Blood and the Holy Grail*, Jonathan Cape, London, 1982.

Baigent, Michael, *The Temple and the Lodge*, Jonathan Cape, 1989.

Barber, Malcolm, *The Trial of the Templars*, Cambridge University Press, 1993, c1978.

Blake, Peter and Blezard, Paul S., *The Arcadian Cipher*, Sidgwick & Jackson, London, 2000

Bogin, Magda, *The Women Troubadours*, W.W. Norton, New York, 1976.

Bradley, Michael, *Chosen People from the Caucasus*, Third World Press, Chicago, 1992.

Bradley, Michael, *Grail Knights of North America*, Dundurn Press, Toronto, 1998.

Bradley, Michael, *Holy Grail Across the Atlantic*, Hounslow Press, Toronto, 1988.

Bradley, Michael, *The Columbus Conspiracy*, Hounslow Press, Toronto, 1991.

Bradley, Michael, *The Iceman Inheritance, "prehistoric sources of Western Man's racism, sexism and aggression,"* Dorset Publishing Inc., Toronto, 1978; reprinted in the United States by Warner Books, New York (1979) and by Lushena Books, New York (1992).

Carter, Howard, *The Tomb of Tutankhamun* (3 Vols.), Cassel, London, Vol. I 1923, Vol. II 1927, Vol. III 1933.

Chambrun-Ruspoli, Marthe de, *L'épervier divin*, Éditions du Mont-Blanc, Genève, Suisse, 1969.

Collins, Andrew and Ogilvie-
Herald, Chris, *Tutankhamun: The Exodus Conspiracy*, Virgin
Books, London, 2002.

Coon, Carlton, *The Origin of Races*, Alfred A. Knopf, N.Y., 1968.

Cooper, James Fenimore, *The Last of the Mohicans*, Dodd Mead, 1984.

Cooper, James Fenimore, *The Deerslayer: or the first war-path*,
C. Scribner's, 1925.

Davies, Norman, *The Isles: A History,* Oxford University Press, 1999.

Dewar, Elaine, *Bones: Discovering the first Americans*, Random House
Canada, 2001.

Eschenbach, Wolfram von, *Parzival*, trans. Helen M. Mustard and
Charles E. Passage, Vintage, New York, 1961

Esty, Katherine, *Gypsies, Wanderers in Time*, Victore Gollancz, London
1962

Fisher, Douglas Alan, *Steel, from the Iron Age to the Space Age*, Harper,
1967.

Forster, E.M., *The Hill at Devi: and other Indian writngs*, 1927, Edward
Arnold, 1983

Freud, Sigmund, *Moses and Monotheism*, Knopf, 1939

Gardner, (Sir) Laurence, *Bloodline of the Holy Grail*, Element Books,
Shaftesbury, 1996.

Geoffrey de Monmouth, *History of the Kings of Britain*, ed. and trans.
Lewis Thorpe, Penguin, Harmondsworth and Baltimore, 1966.

Gibb, Sir Hamilton Alexander Rosskeen, *Islamic society and the West; a
study of the impact of Western civilization on Moslem culture in the
Near East*, 2 vol. Oxford University Press, 1962-1963.

Gimbutas, Marija, *The Civilization of the Goddess: the world of Old
Europe,* Harper San Francisco, 1991

Goodrich, Norma Lorre, *King Arthur*, Franklin Watts, Danbury, 1986.

Graves, Robert, *The White Goddess*, Faber and Faber, London, 1961

Griaule, Marcel and Dieterlen, Germaine, *Le renard pâle,* Institut
d'ethnologie, 1965.

Hapgood, Charles, *Maps Of the Ancient Sea Kings*, Chilton Book
Company, Randor, 1968

Hesiod, *The words and days; Theogony; The shields of Herakles*,
translated by Richmond Alexander Lattimore, University of
Michigan Press, 1959.

Hoffman, Bernard G., *Cabot to Cartier: sources for a historical
ethnography of northeastern North America, 1497-1550*, University
of Toronto Press, 1961

Jacobs, Joseph, *Jewish Contributions to Western Civilization*, Jewish Information Service, 1921.

Koestler, Arthur, *The Thirteenth Tribe: the Khazar Empire and its Heritage*, Random House, 1976.

Lincoln, Henry, *The Holy Place*, Little, Brown and Company, New York, 1991.

Lomas, Robert and Knight, Christopher, *The Hiram Key*, Harper Collins, UK, 1998,

Maccoby, Hyam, *The Mythmaker: Paul and the Invention of Christianity*, Weidenfeld & Nicolson, 1986.

Mann, William F., *The Labyrinth of the Grail,* Laughing Owl Publishing Inc., 1999.

Marshack, Alexander, *The Roots of Civilization*, McGraw-Hill, New York, N.Y., 1971.

Martin, Tony, *The Jewish Onslaught:* Despatches from the Wellesley Battlefront, The Majority Press, Canton, MA, 1993.

Mowat, Farley, *The Farfarers*, Key Porter Books, 1998.

Osman, Ahmed, *Strangers in the Valley of the Kings,* Harper & Row, 1987.

Osman, Ahmed, *Out of Egypt: the roots of Christianity revealed* , Century, 1998.

Picknett, Lynn and Prince, Clive, *The Templar Revelation,* Touchstone Books, Simon and Shuster, London, 1997

Pindera, Loreen and York, Geoffrey, *The People of the Pines*, Little, Brown, New York, 1991.

Pitman, Walter and Ryan, William, *In Search of Noah's Flood: the new scientific discoveries about the event that changed history*, Simon & Schuster, 1997.

Plowden, Sir Edmund, *The Commodities of the Island of Manati or Long Isle within the Continent of Virginia*, The Plowden Company, 1632

Pohl, Frederick, *Prince Henry Sinclair*, Clarkson N. Potter, New York, 1974

Pohl, Frederick, *The Lost Discovery*, W.W. Norton, New York, 1952

Poliak, Dr. A.N., *Khazaria: The History of a Jewish Kingdom in Europe*, Beliak Mossad, Jerusalem, 1950.

Polo, Marco, *The travels of Marco Polo, greatly amended and enlarged*, Oliver & Boyd, 1844.

Rolt, L.T.C., *Narrow Boat* , Eyre Methuen, 1978.

Rolt, L.T.C. *The Inland Waterways of Britain*, George Allen & Unwin, 1950.

Salibi, Kamal, *The Bible Came from Arabia*, Jonathan Cape, 1985.

Sinclair, Andrew, *The Sword and the Grail*, Crown Publishers, New York, 1992.

Silverberg, Robert, *The Moundbuilders*, New York Geographic Society, Greenwich (Conn.), 1968.

Starbird, Margaret, *The Woman with the Alabaster Jar*, Bear & Company Publishing, Santa Fe (New Mexico), 1993.

Tolkien, J.R.R., *The Lord of the Rings*, Ballantine Books, New York, N.Y., 1986.

Trento, Michael Salvatore, *The Search for Lost America: The Mysteries of the Stone Ruins,* Contemporary Publishing, 1978.

Trinkaus, Dr. Eric and Stewart, Dr. T. Dale, "Hard Times Among the Neanderthals", *Natural History*, American Museum of Natural History, New York, December 1978.

Trinkaus, Dr. Eric, *The Neandertals: of skeletons, scientists, and scandals*, Vintage Books, 1994.

Williamson, Ronald F., *Legacy of Stone: ancient life on the Niagara frontier*, Eastendbooks, 1998.

Wiesenthal, Simon, *Sails of Hope: The Secret Mission of Christopher Columbus*, Macmillan, 1973.

Manor House Publishing Inc.

452 Cottingham Crescent, Ancaster, Ontario, L9G 3V6

905-648-2193 www.manor-house.biz